THE $10 BOOK
THAT CAN
MAKE YOU RICH

THE $10 BOOK THAT CAN MAKE YOU RICH

by Joe Bart

Lyle Stuart, Inc. / Secaucus, N. J.

First printing

Copyright © 1976 by Joe Bart
All rights reserved, including the right to reproduce
this book or any portion thereof in any form anywhere
in the world.

Published by Lyle Stuart, Inc.
120 Enterprise Ave., Secaucus, N.J. 07094
Published simultaneously in Canada by
George J. McLeod Limited, 73 Bathurst St., Toronto, Ont.

Address queries regarding rights and permissions
to Lyle Stuart, Inc.

Manufactured in the United States of America

ISBN 0-8184-0232-6

CONTENTS

THE $10 BOOK
THAT CAN
MAKE YOU RICH

INTRODUCTION

I SINCERELY BELIEVE this can be the most valuable book you have ever owned. I believe if you read it carefully, with an open mind, it can help to set you on the path to riches, perhaps beyond anything you have ever dreamed possible.

Why am I so confident?

Because the information and advice it contains, and the principles it enumerates, are authentic—not the work of an author who earns a living grinding out how-to-do-it books, but practical, usable information by a man who knows firsthand what it is to start from scratch and make it big, fast; who has done it not once but several times; and who is willing to show you how he did it as frankly and honestly as he can!

That's right! No matter what you think, no matter how remote the possibility may seem, becoming rich is not an impossible dream or even overwhelmingly difficult.

You don't have to be a genius to make money. You don't have to be a superintellect to be rich. You do, however, have to have the drive and the desire. You must *want* to be rich. You must have a passion for it. You must want wealth more than anything else, and you must move toward it with great single-mindedness. You must set your goal and head for it with energy and determination, and keep on heading for it until you arrive.

Then you must supplement your desire with know-how! Now, this book can't put drive and determination into your head, but it can help to strengthen what is already there, and it can give you the know-how!

It puts you in the right ballpark. It gives you a keen insight into the kind of thinking it takes to make money, and it gives it to you frankly, honestly, with nothing held back. Most of all, it gives you what I sincerely believe are revelations of great value—precise, practical, step-by-step instructions on how to put together the type of hard-sell promotional effort that sold you on this book and sold millions of others on other products and services.

Introduction

I hope you are canny enough to recognize their value, for these are the principles of hard sell that have made fortunes for the relatively few who are aware of them—and they can do the same for you.

Read this book. Think deeply about the information and advice it contains. Weigh carefully the principles it advocates. Then put them to work for you—not next week or next month, but right now!

YOU HAVE to REALLY WANT to BE RICH

L ET'S BEGIN at the beginning. I don't know who you are or what you do for a living. I don't know whether you're young or old, happy or sad, or anything else about you, except for one detail. You bought this book, and from that it doesn't take much deduction to conclude that you are ambitious, that you want to better yourself, and that you are wise enough to know that the one sure way to do just that is to get rich!

Mister, you're on the right track!

Being rich can make an incredible change in the quality of your life. It can make your life easier. It can make it more comfortable. It can make it more exciting. It can introduce you to new people, take you to new places, open up new worlds you never knew existed. And it can do wonders for you psychologically, too! It can increase your self-confidence, enhance your self-respect, and help make you the complete, happy person you have every right to be!

Now, that doesn't mean being rich can solve all your problems. But it can eliminate a lot of the small ones, such as not being able to pay bills, or worrying about what you would do if the car broke down or if the oil burner went, or how you are going to manage to get the kids through college, or what happens if economic conditions get worse or prices keep rising.

When you're rich, you won't worry about those annoying details. You won't have to cope with all the petty hassles of life. You won't drive an automobile that may not make it through the winter, or suffer the inconvenience of crowded clinics when you need medical attention, or stand on a long ticket line at the ballpark, or eat hamburgers when you'd rather eat steak!

And you won't work at a job you hate, either!

Being rich may not be everything, but it's a lot closer to it than being poor.

Fifty or a hundred years ago it was different. Life was easier then.

This is a cold, hard world. We live in the shadow of nuclear power, of instant destruction, of lying and cheating and vicious exploitation on every level. In the old days you didn't have to fight for breathing space in the subway or jam onto a crowded bus or race the guy next door for the last space in the parking lot.

If you made a decent salary then, you could afford to live a decent life. If you were a policeman or a machinist or a milkman you could afford to buy a house and a small car and raise your family in a fairly decent way. You could live in a neighborhood where you could walk your dog late at night without getting hit over the head, and you could leave for work in the morning content in the knowledge that your wife would still be intact and your possessions would still be there when you got home at night.

But that was long ago. Those days are long since gone. Today, most of us live in a tough, rough, competitive world. The standards we were brought up to live by no longer hold true. Somewhere along the line they have kicked the props out from under most of the things we once held dear.

True, in a materialistic sense things are better now. Our supermarket shelves are bulging with foodstuffs, and our department stores are loaded with every conceivable kind of gadget. We eat fast, we live fast, we drive fast. Sometimes we even die fast.

Once upon a time we did everything by hand. If we had to drill a hole, we did it with a brace and bit and a little elbow grease. Now the only effort we expend is remembering where we put the electric drill. In the old days we got along pretty well with the basic necessities of life. Nowadays no home is complete without two TVs, a washing machine, a drier, a power mower, an air conditioner, and a camper in the backyard.

Why am I going into this now? Because I think you have to be able to see the world you live and compete in clearly. You have to see it for what it really is. You have to understand how and why it functions the way it does. You have to be able to recognize the world's shortcomings and advantages, and you have to decide what you want out of it and how much you are willing to pay to get it.

You see, despite all its faults and complexities, and even though in many ways it is a hard, cruel, inhospitable place, some people have managed to get a lot out of it. Some men and women are leading incredible lives. They live luxuriously and well in a world of fine homes, gourmet restaurants, fast cars, travel and vacations, and all the other good things of life.

You can do the same thing! The rewards are out there waiting to be gathered up. You don't have to be a genius to get them. You don't have to have an enormous intellect or possess great skills to be rich. The main requirement is inside you right now. It is called *desire!*

To Get Rich You Must Really Want to Be Rich!

You have to honestly, truly, sincerely, from the bottom of your heart, want to be rich! You have to want it with every fiber of your being. You have to want it more than anything else in life. It has to be your desire, your aim, your goal, your hobby; and everything else, but everything, must be subordinated to it! That doesn't mean you have to stop loving your wife or ignore your kids or give up fishing or golf or football games on TV, but it does mean that they can no longer dominate your existence.

If you plan to get rich, that has to be the dominant thought in your mind at all times. The people who succeed at any endeavor are the people who are single-minded, who know what they want and are prepared to make any sacrifice necessary to get it. Bobby Fischer wouldn't be the greatest chess player in the world today if he hadn't started out when he was a little kid and pursued his goal with relentless fury every waking hour of his life.

Jack Nicklaus wouldn't be the golfer he is today if he hadn't lived and breathed and dreamed golf to the exclusion of all else from the time he was nine years old. And you can be sure J. Paul Getty wouldn't be the richest man in the world if he hadn't kept energetically amassing more and more wealth ever since he was a young man.

There are few people who excel in any field who don't pursue their goals with vigor and determination every minute of their day. That happens to be a simple fact of life. Check out almost anyone you can think of who has achieved great success in his chosen field, and you'll find he has worked at it with great drive and determination, because that's what it takes to succeed.

Okay, I know what you're thinking. You have other things to worry about. You can't give up everything you are and everything you do at this stage of your life. Of course not. Nobody expects you to. You're not eleven years old. You can't turn back the clock and start all over again, and I'm not suggesting that you do. All I am saying is that you have to have the desire. Getting rich is winning, and you know that you can't win if you don't really try.

Now, I know that a lot of us who were brought up in modest circumstances have been led to believe that poor is good and rich is bad. I've heard people say, "I'd never want to be rich," or "It's a lot of trouble being rich," or "You'd always be worried about your money." Baloney! The simple fact is that being poor is a lot more difficult than being rich. And believe me, poor people worry a lot more about not having money than rich people worry about having it.

Having money doesn't make you a superman, but it doesn't make you a bum, either. It's nice to have money in your pockets. It's nice to drive a car that you know is going to get you there and back. It's nice to be able to take the family out for dinner and not worry about whether you're going to have enough left over to tip the waitress. It's nice to be able to send your kids to college and afford good vacations and all the rest, so don't delude yourself to the contrary. If you harbor prejudices against money or people who have it, better lose them right away, because it just isn't so. And don't you forget it!

10

LEARNING to THINK
LIKE a RICH MAN

OKAY, YOU DO HAVE the desire. You do want to be rich, no ifs, ands, or buts. You want to make money and lots of it, and you are prepared to make whatever sacrifices are necessary to do it. You are prepared to think hard, to work hard, and to be hard!

What's your next step?

You have to think like a rich man!

Now, when I say "rich man" in this book, I don't mean a long-established individual who has built a successful business bit by bit over a lifetime or who inherited a family business or a family fortune or who has a rich wife or a rich uncle. I mean the man who started from scratch and made his money on his own in a relatively brief period of time, a man who is adept at promoting the products or services he sells or the business he operates, a man who is constantly looking for money-making opportunities and who has found enough of them to have become rich and stayed rich.

What is he like? What makes him tick? What makes him successful? What has he got that you haven't got, and what does he know that you don't know?

If you have been—or are—confined to a job or a series of jobs in which your only contact with money is picking up your paycheck on Friday night and spending it for groceries on Saturday morning, then at this point you probably don't have much in common with the rich man we are talking about. Why? Because your world isn't money-oriented. Money isn't part of your daily life, and therefore, you aren't accustomed to thinking about it—and how to get more of it—as the rich man is.

For the most part, money is made by people who are exposed to dollars. Nobody ever got rich working a nine-to-five factory job. Comfortable? Yes. But rich? It rarely happens. You just don't amass wealth working for an hourly wage—even a very good one—and you generally don't amass wealth working for somebody else.

13

You may have a good job, earn a good income, and be reasonably sure that your job is going to be there for as long as you want it and that it's going to provide you with a fair income when you retire. That's fine, and I'm not knocking it. All I am saying is that it's not the way to get rich.

You get rich when you are involved in an area in which a substantial flow of money takes place and the nature of your involvement is such that part of that money ends up in your possession.

The more money that passes through your hands and the greater the percentage of it that you keep, the more you make. That holds true on every level. If you do not work around money—if you work in a large factory, for example—you don't have much opportunity to see money changing hands. You don't get a strong feeling for how money is made, and the whole process probably seems a great deal more mysterious than it really is.

Suppose, for example, that you work in a gasoline station. Now, that's about as far from high finance as you can get, but at least money passes through your hands. People pay you for a product, and you are aware that part of that money is profit, which your boss keeps. If you observe carefully, you notice that when a customer steps out of his car, for a Coke or a trip to the restroom, the customer has an opportunity to see items for sale—tires, chains, wipers, tourist guides, etc. There is a greater chance that he will buy some of those items than the guy who pulls in for gasoline, fills up, and goes on his way.

If you are alert and ambitious you may start to get ideas. Maybe your boss should be putting in more items. Maybe he should be installing coffee, candy, and sandwich machines, because they obviously induce people to get out of their cars, and that increases the sale of other items, many of which throw off more profit than gasoline.

On the other hand, perhaps your boss isn't progressive enough to care and you should save the idea for yourself and run your own gasoline station.

Do you see what I am saying?

You have far less to stimulate your thinking about moneymaking when you are operating a lathe than when you are in contact with or involved in the exchange of dollars.

Wherever you work, whatever you do, get in the habit of thinking about the moneymaking process. Analyze the operations involved and think especially of why customers buy a product and what factors, if any, would induce them to buy more. Salesmen are in a particularly advantageous position in this regard. A good salesman understands the nature of the business he is involved in. He understands costs and overhead and markups, and he is keenly aware of how the business makes money for his boss. He is aware, for example, that he is frequently a key man in the process by which the sale of goods or services produces profits for the man who owns the operation.

This is particularly true in relatively small businesses where more intimate relationships exist. In these instances the step from star salesman to partner is not great. Indeed, many businesses are run by two partners, the inside man, who runs the technical aspects, and the outside man, who spends his time on the outside selling.

True, in some instances the salesman's function is not vital. A man may be a great car salesman, for example, without being vital to the success of the business. He doesn't design or build the car or control the customers who buy it. He sells, and that's important, but if he didn't, someone else on the floor would.

Some salesmen play a more vital role. They don't sit in a showroom waiting for customers to come to them. They are out in the field searching out buyers, and in certain instances they service that buyer so well that they become very important to him.

This is particularly true when production problems are handled by the salesman, as is often the case in the printing industry. In many instances the printing salesman is so intimately involved in the operation that his customer comes to depend upon him, and should the salesman change jobs, the customer frequently comes right along with him.

Some printing salesmen end up as brokers. They don't work for any one firm, but take each printing order to whatever concern they feel can best do that particular job. Instead of working on a commission, they add what they consider a fair markup as their profit. They may operate out of a tiny office, or even out of their hat, but at the end of a good year they can chalk up enormous earnings.

It's not hard to see why a lot of successful salesmen ultimately make the transition to boss of their own operation. Certainly it is a lot easier and more natural to make that change than to jump from factory hand to head of the business.

In any event, the point is that *your proximity to money helps to stimulate your interest in it.* So, to a great extent, does the company you keep. Everything is relative. If everybody you know is broke, it doesn't matter as much whether you are too. The desire to get money isn't as urgent when you associate with poor men as when you associate with wealthy men.

Park in front of the local gin mill in a beat-up car and it doesn't matter particularly because there are plenty of other old heaps to keep it company. But pull up to the local country club in an old rattletrap, and you know it's going to be an embarrassing experience.

If you are going to be rich, raise your sights, and do it right now! *To be big, you have to look big and think big.*

Loser is an ugly word. Some people would rather lose than win. They would rather be sad than happy. They would rather complain and bemoan their fate than be successful. Why? Because they have some psychological hangup.

I think it is destructive to be like that, to think like that, and to associate with people like that. It's a bad habit from every point of view. Don't do it. Give yourself a break. You are going to be successful. Starting now, do your damnedest to associate with successful people. Observe the way they live, the way they dress, the cars they drive, the houses they live in, the things they own, and the things they do.

Be envious, too. Why not? If they have more than you do, it's only natural to be envious. You wouldn't be human if you weren't, and besides, the envy you feel can spur you on to bigger and better things. You can't make yourself taller or younger, but you can make yourself richer. And if it takes a little bit of envy to help you do it, what's wrong with that? Rich people do that all the time, if not on a conscious level, then certainly unconsciously.

Successful people reject the close company of men and women who don't measure up to their standards. They don't want to associate with people beneath them. They want to associate with people who are above them in terms of wealth and accomplishment. It's somewhat akin to playing tennis. Tennis buffs aren't eager to play with inferior players. They want to play with better players, because that's where the challenge and excitement are, and that's how they improve their game.

Remember, too, that people tend to discuss the things that interest them. Football players talk about football, golfers talk about golf, and money-makers talk about making money. They talk about deals, investments, tax shelters, business conditions, business trends and business opportunities—and that's how you learn!

I have spent time with men who are so rich and successful that it is difficult to imagine their being even vaguely impressed with anyone else, and yet they are. They know what it is to make money, and they admire and respect—and often envy—other men who make it big.

I have a good friend who is a brilliant and extremely successful publisher. He makes—and spends—fortunes with careless abandon. I have seen this man close up his office on a whim, cart his whole staff, from lowliest shipping clerk to the presidents of his various subsidiaries, off to Europe or Vegas or wherever his fancy dictated, spend more money on those trips than the average man makes in a lifetime, and never blink twice!

I was with him not long ago, and what did he talk about? About a friend of his who had just bought a fabulous new custom-made Rolls-Royce. About a guy he knows who is in the process of building a restaurant empire. About a mutual friend of ours who, on the basis of a five-minute explanation, bought a piece of a deal for $150,000 and paid for it on the spot without written contracts or formal agreements.

Money isn't the be-all and end-all with this man. He has other inter-

17

ests, other hobbies, and other concerns. But he is aware that the acquisition of money is often a creative, interesting, and rewarding pursuit. He is happy when friends of his make it, and open enough to admit his happiness. Indeed, in several instances, he has helped casual acquaintances of his to make sums of money far in excess of anything they would have made without his help. You know that if you could associate with a man like that, you would have to come out ahead.

I have another friend who is worth four or five million dollars, and do you know what impresses him more than anything else? Men who are worth six or seven million dollars. He loves to tell stories about business coups friends of his have pulled off. He gloats over their skills and successes, and despite his own wealth and success, he's jealous as hell. Successful men are like a carrot on a stick for him. They spur him on, inspire him, help keep him running—and he's not the least bit unusual.

Spend a little time at the bar of an expensive country club, and you'll see exactly what I mean. The spirit of competition exists within us all. Being around men of drive, wealth, and accomplishment helps to stimulate you toward such success. Successful people love to associate with even more successful people. It's a perfectly natural, perfectly understandable phenomenon, and you should make every effort to do the same, if you can. If you don't have wealthy contacts or friends who are involved in the pursuit of wealth and with whom you can kick around ideas and aspirations, you are handicapped, but not overwhelmingly. You can still learn a great deal about the men who acquire money by reading about them. There are books and magazines devoted to acquiring money. These publications are constantly recapping the careers and experiences of successful businessmen. The more you read about them, the more you will understand how they think, and the more of that thinking will rub off on you!

CASE HISTORIES of MEN WHO HAVE MADE IT

W HAT ARE SUCCESSFUL men really like? What makes them tick? What special characteristics make them money-makers?

Like any group of men anywhere, they vary widely. They are short, tall, fat, thin, attractive, unattractive, neat, sloppy, and so on. Some of them are bright, some of them are superbright, and a few don't appear to be very bright at all. All of them, however, seem to share certain common traits. Obviously they are all ambitious. No one makes it in any field unless he has a desire to get ahead, and that's what ambition is all about.

Sometimes an individual is blessed with such outstanding attributes that he makes it without that superdrive. He makes it because he is so naturally bright and personable and attractive or has such innate qualities of leadership that advancement is thrust upon him. However, individuals like that are rare, and even they have to strive to maintain their position.

I think one of the single most important traits common to virtually all successful men is their ability to get things done. They are accomplishers. They don't procrastinate. They don't put things off. When something has to be done, they do it rapidly, they do it thoroughly, and they do it well.

One tycoon type I know is compulsive about doing it *now* and getting it done with. He calls subordinates up at three o'clock in the morning to convey a thought relative to his business. He jumps up in the middle of dinner, at home, in a restaurant, or anywhere, to make a call if it will help him to get something done. He stays at the office until the wee hours to be sure a project gets finished, and whoever is working on that project with him stays right alongside! This man *finishes* things with a venegance, and his bulging bank account proves it!

One successful man I know practically lives with a notebook in his hand. He's always jotting things down—things he has to do, things he

21

has to remember, ideas he gets, and so on. But more than merely jotting down notes, *he follows up!* He does the things he has to do. He makes the calls he is supposed to make. He remembers to perform the little services for people that he promised. He is a rock of dependability, thanks to that little notebook. If you are scatterbrained or forgetful, as most of us are, get yourself a notebook and use it! . . . It's a good habit to acquire.

Perhaps the single trait most characteristic of successful men is their doggedness. They have the ability to stick to a project and see it through to the bitter end. They are not discouraged, they are not dismayed, and they are not put off by misfortune. If bad luck does strike, they shake it off and persist nevertheless. I think this trait is probably more important than any other.

I know one man—a former mail-order operator—who was fantastically successful and was one of the few who managed to hang on to his fortune and retire with it. He had an overwhelming singlemindedness of purpose that I think was the primary reason for his great success. He wasn't very creative or even especially bright, but he was incredibly persistent. He worked on one thing at a time, and only one, but how he followed through! Nothing dismayed him, nothing distracted him, nothing put him off. Talk about concentration!

I wrote copy for him many, many years ago, and I still shudder when I remember those long, painful sessions we used to have in his office long after everyone else had left. I remember going over and over and over the same words, the same sentences, the same ideas, night after night. I am sure he was aware that people considered him difficult and ornery, but it didn't bother him one bit. He didn't mind asking the same questions over and over. He didn't mind ranting on and on about the same minute details. He was concerned with every aspect of every deal he was involved with, and since it was his money on the line, he had every right to be. His doggedness and determination paid off, because that man had one hit after another for a long, long time.

I have never known a real money-maker who was lazy. They all had a lot of energy and drive, and they didn't mind using them. A good officer leads his men into battle, and in a way that is true for any leader. If you expect to make money you have to spend time and energy to do it. There's plenty of time for playing around after the money has rolled in.

Most successful men like to live well. They enjoy fine homes, big cars, good clothes, beautiful women. These are some of the incentives that drive successful men on. Of course, there are exceptions. Some rich men lead miserly lives, but they are few and far between. All the really successful men I know spend well and live well.

Most money-makers are fairly aggressive. They know what they want and how to go out and get it, and if they have to step on a few toes in the process, they are not loath to do so. Now this doesn't mean that you have to be a hard-nosed, loud-mouthed clod. On the contrary. You do, however, have to forge ahead aggressively. You have to set your sights on your objective and head for it unswervingly.

Perhaps the best way to get a firmer conception of what rich and successful men are all about is to learn a bit more about them. Now, I don't claim to be on intimate terms with captains of American industry. I know one or two tycoons who are pompous bores, haughty and autocratic and very self-impressed. They are strong, intelligent men, shrewd and calculating and aware of their own importance and not about to let their guard down for a minute. On the other hand, I know a few who are pretty decent guys. They make a point of being regular, humble, democratic, and so on. But irrespective of their personal characteristics, men on that level are a world apart. They are fawned upon, catered to, and treated with great reverence and respect by their subordinates.

How do men like that achieve their lofty positions? The ways are many and varied. I have one friend, for example, who is not only a very important executive in one of the world's largest communications corporations, but one of their two or three top stockholders as well, and he made it through the back door in a manner of speaking.

He is an extremely intelligent man with a very solid academic background. He came from a very poor family, was a brilliant student, studied market research and associated areas, and went on to teach those subjects on a college level. At the same time, he undertook several market-research studies for various firms and, still in his mid-twenties, established a very lucrative business in that field. I think that is somewhat of a tipoff to the kind of man he is. He could very easily have concentrated his efforts in purely academic pursuits. He was being well paid to teach, and a teacher he could have remained, but he chose to go further. He had enough drive and enough ambition and, perhaps because he was born poor, enough desire for all the better things of life to want to go further, and he did.

One confidential market study commissioned by the chairman of the board of a very large firm with many retail outlets changed the course of his entire life. He had submitted a justifiably negative report, in which he pointed out that in view of changing consumer preferences it was vital that the firm make immediate changes in merchandising policies or face dire consequences. He pointed out that the president of the firm had consistently embarked upon programs in direct contradiction to the very obvious market trends that were then occurring.

As a direct consequence of the excellence of his report, he was offered the presidency of the firm. His intimate awareness of the basic instability of the company, however, quite logically convinced him to decline the offer.

As frequently happens in cases like that, his reluctance to accept the position made him more valuable in the eyes of the chairman, and during the following months the offers became so attractive—huge salary, very favorable stock options, and so forth—that my friend eventually felt that he had no alternative but to accept.

The new policies he instituted proved fruitful, the firm prospered under his guidance, and long before he reached his thirtieth birthday, he was well established as the successful president of a successful firm.

Several years later he was offered a commensurately important position with a large, aggressive, and rapidly growing advertising agency. Aware of the solidity of the firm, impressed by the vision and ambition of the principal officer, who was offering him the position, and eager to take on new challenges, he accepted. As he anticipated, the firm continued to grow until it dominated the field and ultimately went public. At that point he acquired a substantial block of stock, to which he continued to add.

He holds a key position with the firm and enjoys a very, very substantial salary and a great many peripheral benefits besides. He travels a great deal, lives extremely well, and enjoys the unique distinction of advising a number of the world's most important executives on matters of business policy.

Okay, that was a somewhat unusual case. That man was a scholar to begin with, and his initial success in business really depended upon that fact. But scholarship is not a prerequisite for success. Some of the most successful men I know are barely aware of what the inside of a school looks like. You don't need a diploma to run deals or make money.

My friend R. is a great example of a consistent money-maker and he has never had more than a year or so of high school. He was one of the best and the most successful promoters I know and he reached his pinnacle through a completely different route.

R. left home in his very early teens, kicked around New York City's Greenwich Village, and then hitchhiked back and forth across the country doing odd jobs. After several years of varied and not particularly successful adventures, he became a pitchman, working in carnivals, at country fairs, on street corners, in open-front stores in large cities, or anywhere else a crowd could be attracted. He demonstrated and sold a diverse line of products—old time cure-alls, knife sharpeners and glass cutters that work like magic, silver polish that requires no rubbing or scrubbing, kitchen gadgets that slice and dice at the flick of a wrist, various devices alleged to decrease the fuel consumption of automobiles and make them run better, faster, and more economically, and anything else he was clever enough to dream up. Of course, a pitchman's products rarely live up to the exaggerated claims made for them, and sales are far more dependent upon the skill of the pitchman than upon quality.

R. became one of the top pitchmen in the country. He developed keen insights into what it takes to sell merchandise successfully. He was ambitious and hardworking and enjoyed the luxuries of life, and he was always capable of making a good living wherever he happened to be.

In the early 1950s, after having established himself as one of the top-earning pitchmen around—he was then thirty-nine or forty years old —he reasoned that if he could sell to live audiences, why not to a television audience? Accordingly, he modified a vitamin pitch he had used very successfully, performed it live on a TV station in a small city on the East Coast, and was deluged with orders far beyond anything he ever expected. On the basis of his overwhelming hit, he made a deal with a wealthy backer-partner, set up an organization, and within months was heading up an incredible coast-to-coast mail-order operation the likes of which has never been seen before or since. If you were old enough to turn a radio or TV knob back in the early fifties, chances are you saw or heard those remarkable pitches, several of which appear in this book.

After about a year and a half of incredible profits, he and his partner sold out to a large national drug company for several million dollars. R. drifted about for a bit, ran several more very successful mail-order deals, and ultimately went to Europe, where he became a very successful movie producer.

What were his most important attributes? R. is a bright, resourceful, energetic person with a great talent for selling. Years of working in contact with live audiences all over the United States have given him an uncanny feel for what people want and a unique ability to dream up the items that will satisfy those wants. He's never been afraid to go the full route! When he gets involved in a deal, he gives it everything he's got—time, effort, cash—and in most instances that I know of, his efforts have paid off.

I think energetic, resourceful, and ambitious men like R. can make it anywhere in any profession. A good friend of mine, M., bears this out. Although his training is academic and his occupation—landscape architect—rates him as a professional man, he has the innate qualities that would make him a success in any line of endeavor.

M. was born to parents of very modest means and spent most of his early years in very small towns and rural areas. He worked hard as a kid, helped to supplement the family's income, and put himself through college. Before age forty he was considered the top landscape architect in the entire country. He runs the largest landscape-architecture company in the United States. He is its founder, guiding light, top salesman, and chief designer. In addition to running this large company, he is a full professor and head of the landscape-architecture department of a large Eastern university at a very substantial salary; is the designer of various types of playground equipment, for which he receives very substantial royalties; and just to keep himself amused, dabbles in real estate and makes a lot of money from it.

What is the secret of his success? There is no single answer. M. is a talented man with a number of outstanding attributes. He is, first of all, a hard worker. Even as a boy, he was always involved in some kind of venture—raising chickens, running his own small nursery, doing landscaping for neighbors, and so on. As a successful adult, he still manages to keep gainfully occupied virtually all the time.

He is very quick and very bright, with tremendous drive and energy and an uncanny ability to get things done. This man probably accomplishes more in a day than most men do in a month, partly because he sees issues with great clarity. He knows that the shortest distance between two points is a straight line, and that's the way he operates! He gets from A to B without meandering or stopping along the way.

He is well organized. When he gets an idea he doesn't dawdle or procrastinate or analyze it to death. He recognizes his goals and seems to know precisely what to do to bring them to fruition, and he follows through, allowing nothing, including his family, to stand in his way. Although he is a good family man, a fine father and a devoted husband, his work comes first.

Like many successfull executives he has a number of highly competent helpers, whom he can depend upon thoroughly. He has a very good secretary, a first-rate design assistant in whom he has complete confidence and trust, a model maker who knows how to translate M.'s concepts into the necessary three dimensions, and a great many other helpers he can depend upon. Most important, he doesn't mind passing responsibility along to them. That's important. *Successful men know how to use other people.* I don't mean that in a derogatory sense. There is just so much time in a day, and unless you can get help in performing many of the less important functions, there simply isn't enough time to get everything done. Better to pay a helper to do routine tasks than to spend your own valuable time.

Another friend, N., is a millionaire many times over. He is a very clever, very knowledgeable man. He expresses himself well, presents himself well, and can be very persuasive and charming when he wants to. He is very ambitious, but despite his success and wealth, and even though he could have retired to his palatial Florida home, he is still active and eager, still loves to make deals, and still relishes the idea of making money from them.

What distinguishes this man from other men who are equally bright and equally ambitious and energetic who haven't made it on his level? I really can't tell you for sure, but one thing I do know. This man is an ardent believer in success. There is nothing negative about him. Ask him how he feels, and he doesn't say, pretty good, or fine. He says, *great!* and he means it. Ask him how he is doing, and he tells you the good things that are happening to him and the successes he contemplates. Sure, he has his failures occasionally, but when he does, he doesn't bemoan his fate. He analyzes them and learns from them and uses them in a positive way.

That doesn't mean that he is naïve enough to think that deals can't sour or that business conditions can't reverse. It simply means that with himself at the helm, controlling his own destiny insofar as humanly possible, he is confident that things are going to go right, and you can be sure he is going to do his damnedest to see that they do.

How did N. make it in the first place? He started as a publicity man. He had a feeling for show business, represented a number of acts, and eventually expanded his list of clients to include industrial accounts. The techniques by which products were developed and introduced to the public began to intrigue him, and soon he ventured into product promotion on his own. His first choice was good. He was aware that many Europeans were accustomed to "taking the baths." They visited health spas, where they bathed in natural hot springs rich in various chemicals. His product was a mix of chemicals that, when stirred into hot water, closely simulated the hot springs, and his market was the people who visited the spas.

The product and the promotions he dreamed up to merchandise it were successful, and N. was hooked. His interest in public relations was replaced by a keen desire to develop a substantial drug-product business, and that he did. He dug in with confidence and zeal, and soon he was developing some products, buying others, setting up companies, floating stock issues, and making fortunes. And he's still at it, still enjoying it, still doing it successfully!

PROMOTION IS WHAT IT'S ALL ABOUT

Unless they have made it in a highly specialized way, most rich men know and understand the importance of selling and promoting and are good at it. I don't mean that they are necessarily supersalesmen or superpromoters in the traditional sense, although most of them are. Most of them have an innate promotional sense. They have an instinctive grasp of what it takes to interest other people in the goods or services they have to offer, and this ability is perhaps the most important one you must acquire. You have to think in promotional terms. You have to become acutely aware that in this rough, tough, competitive world, how you sell is just as important as what you sell.

It would be nice if it were otherwise. It would be nice if all you had to do was build a better mousetrap, but that just isn't enough. People aren't going to beat a path to your door unless you sell them an idea first, and you do that by promoting.

Promotional efforts vary widely, depending on the nature of the business. In some instances that effort may consist of nothing more than creating a proper image. A doctor I know has an immaculate office. When he sees patients, he wears a clean, white, very medical-looking jacket. He's crisp and confident and businesslike, and it all adds up to a hell of an image.

Another doctor down the street has a drab, dingy, sloppy office. His furniture is old and beat up, his clothes are rumpled, and the whole effect is somewhat seedy and unimpressive.

I haven't the vaguest idea which of these men is the better physician, but I know that the first man does about three times the business of the second, and the reasons are obvious. Doctor number 1 is putting his best foot forward. He has a great "bedside manner," and that's a form of promotion. Doctor number 2 couldn't care less, and his lack of interest is reflected in his relative lack of patients.

Any situation in which you create an image or an atmosphere that

33

engenders interest and confidence has to accrue to your advantage. There are examples of this everywhere we look. There are two delicatessens in my town. One has a large sign in the window that says, WE MAKE DELICIOUS SANDWICHES. The other, about a block away, makes sandwiches too, but they are too dumb or too lazy or too indifferent to bother with a sign. They do about a quarter of the business that the first deli does. The quality of the sandwiches has little to do with it. The difference in the volume is substantially in the sign. The first guy is looking for sandwich business, and he promotes in order to get it. The second guy is probably just as eager to make money as his competitor, but he doesn't promote, and therein lies the difference. *You have to be the guy who does!*

The examples of this type of promotion are numerous and varied, and they are applicable in almost every field. A friend of mine has a very successful art gallery on Madison Avenue in New York, where a great many galleries are clustered. He is constantly rearranging exhibits, switching furniture, altering lighting, and so on. Why? As he explains it, when his customers see the changes in the store's appearance, they get the impression that he has changed merchandise as well. They look more, and as a consequence they buy more.

Promotion exists on numerous levels. You see examples of it all the time. A restaurant gives a free glass of wine with dinner. Another gives free limousine service to the theater district. A huge pharmaceutical firm mails out millions of sample tubes of toothpaste. A cigarette company distributes free samples of a new brand they are introducing. Banks give gifts to new depositers, food companies offer money-saving coupons, supermarkets mail out weekly circulars, and some department stores are constantly running sales. All these devices are promotions designed to sell more goods and services.

Several flourishing organizations do nothing but dream up sales promotions for large corporations. They come up with a concept for a "treasure hunt," for example, and they supply all of the bits and pieces necessary—window signs, the "treasure chest," directions, prizes, and so on. Then they sell the whole package to a large corporation that uses the treasure hunt to lure people to dealer showrooms, where lurking salesmen can pounce and push TV sets, automobiles, washing machines, and so on.

Now, you know that big, tough, aggressive companies are not about to waste dollars on promotions of this type unless they know for sure that they produce results. Having a better product may be part of the game, but unless that product is backed up with a powerhouse promotion, the public may never know it exists. No matter what you have to offer, the overwhelming odds are that you will sell more—and make more—if you promote it properly.

You have to make your thing—whatever it is—known to potential customers, and you have to do it in obvious and unmistakable terms. If you are going to do it, do it! If you are not, forget it. Halfway measures are ridiculous. Either you make the commitment or you don't, and if you do, and you hope to be successful at it, you have to go the full route.

A sign on a fence not far from where I live says very modestly and quietly, BUNNIES FOR SALE, in letters so faded you barely notice them when you are walking by and can't even begin to see them from a moving car. I can only believe that the folks responsible have mixed feelings. They probably want the money or they wouldn't be announcing the availability of their "bunnies," but at the same time, they are perhaps a bit embarrassed or sheepish about it, and so they compromise. Instead of speaking out in a clear-cut, forthright manner, they put up a wispy little sign that can barely be seen, and chances are they make very few sales.

If you are timid about standing out in a crowd, if you are not accustomed or willing to accept the responsibility of winning, you are in for a difficult time. If you have rabbits or anything else to sell, and you really want to sell them, you not only have to know what to say and how to say it to promote those items successfully, but you have to be willing to make the commitment in the first place. You can't compromise with success or the techniques required to be successful. If you are willing to accept that, you are ready to get into the guts of promotion— which is *advertising*.

THE PRINCIPLES of GREAT ADVERTISING

ADVERTISING IS JUST one form of promotion, one means of bringing a product or service to the attention of prospective customers and helping to sell it to them. There is nothing strange or mysterious about it. It's a simple, logical process, and whether you do or you don't plan to use advertising, you certainly owe it to yourself to have a firm grasp of the principles involved. They are basic and straightforward, the same principles I have used to write some of the most successful copy in the history of mail order, the same principles other mail-order copywriters have used with equal success. They are the principles upon which any good hard-sell sales pitch is based, whether that pitch is delivered in a face-to-face confrontation with a prospect or through the written word.

Read them once, twice, a dozen times! Try to absorb them, because they can be the key to incredible success.

These principles have made me rich. They have made people I know rich. Properly utilized, they can make you rich too!

Note, incidentally, that although they are essentially meant to convey information and instruction on the art of putting together advertising, they are no more than the basic principles of selling. Therefore, you can —and should—use them to sell anything.

Now, let's start at the beginning and find out what it's all about. First, forget your preconceived notions of what is and is not good advertising. Ideally, go one step further and forget everything you have ever seen and heard about advertising before today.

If you are a businessman, you spend the major portion of your existence in the pursuit of dollars, which you acquire in exchange for your products, goods, or services. The essential rewards of your business are achieved through selling in one form or another. On its most primitive level, you are like the huckster who sets up his wares in the marketplace and waits for interested parties to buy. As long as they do, all he has to do is sit back and make sales, but when, for one reason or another, customers don't come within range, he must shout out,

"Apples, bananas!" or whatever he is selling. In effect, he has become an advertiser.

Why did he do it? Because he had to make the availability of his product known in order to sell it. He didn't shout because everyone else was shouting. He didn't shout to show the competition how loudly he could yell or to impress the local populace with his dulcet tones. He shouted (or advertised) only to sell his apples, and for no other reason, because no other reason was necessary.

That is the function of advertising. Pared down to its essentials, advertising is selling, period! That is lesson number 1, and it is vitally important that you know and understand it. *The function of advertising is to sell goods* (and that goes for *all* advertising, including institutional, industrial, or whatever).

Okay, if advertising is selling, then *an advertisement is a sales message in print.* No more and no less. That is lesson number 2. Never forget it. Think of every advertisement you see as no more than a sales message in print, and you will never have trouble evaluating advertising again!

Suppose, for example, that you had to hire a salesman. What do you base your choice on? Obviously you pick a man you think will be able to consummate sales. Sure, you want him to be neat and pleasant, a worthy representative of your organization. But essentially he has to be able to do whatever is necessary to sell your product or service. That is the basis upon which you hire him, and that is the basis on which he proves his worth.

What difference, in the final analysis, if he is smooth, suave, and debonair or a funny-looking little guy with a raspy voice, so long as he sells merchandise and keeps your customers happy? Think of advertisements in the same terms, and it will be a lot easier to evaluate their ultimate worth.

Actually there is no mystery about advertising, and it follows, therefore, that there is no mystery about the elements that comprise advertising. There is a tendency on the part of most people to render a kind of mystical reverence to advertising, as though producing an ad was some strange and remarkable phenomenon. In reality, nothing could be further from the truth, and the following pages bear that out. I have put them together as frankly and as openly as I can, and I sincerely believe they can be the key to great personal success in advertising, in selling, in any aspect of money making, and indeed, in all your relationships with others. Do yourself a favor and learn them well.

THE IMPORTANCE OF ADVERTISING COPY

Copy is to advertising what the engine is to the car, what the wings are to the airplane, what the heart is to the body. Without it, advertising is a lifeless, meaningless shell. Copy is everything, and layout, art, typography—all the embellishments—exist only to set it off. This is my opinion; it is the opinion of the relatively few people who really know what advertising is all about; and for your sake, it had better become your opinion too!

Don't ever sell copy short. Don't ever underestimate its power. Don't ever delude yourself into thinking you can substitute pretty pictures or handsome layouts for good, solid, hard-hitting advertising copy. It can't happen. Copy is the be-all and the end-all of advertising, and the reasons are quite obvious.

The function of advertising is to sell; selling takes persuasion, and persuasion requires words! It is just as uncomplicated as that!

As a businessman you know and understand selling. You know that there is nothing mysterious about it. If you have enough judgment to tell the difference between a good salesman and a bad one, you have enough judgment to tell good copy from bad copy. Merely translate what you know about selling into advertising, and you are on your way to a sound and thorough understanding of advertising basics. If ever you are confused about the potential effectiveness of an ad, judge it in terms of nothing more lofty than a salespitch. Here, by way of illustration, is the acid test. It is quick, easy, straightforward.

Simply imagine yourself confronted by a potential customer for your product. Picture yourself right in front of him, face to face. Can you sell him with the appeals presented in the ad you are evaluating? Are they

41

strong enough, persuasive enough? That is the question. If the answer is no, your ad is obviously not capable of functioning the way it should.

Nine Keys to Successful Copy

In the next pages you will read what I believe are the keys to really good copy. By that I mean copy that works, copy that persuades people —and many of them—to buy your product or service. In the final analysis, that is the only criterion for copy. Never mind how many awards it wins or how cute everybody in the office thinks it is. Never mind what the yes-men tell you or how your secretary coos. If it pays off, it is good copy. If it doesn't, it's not, and no amount of rationalizing will change it.

Note, incidentally, that the following elements are not presented in order of importance. They are *all* important, *all* vital to the success of your ad, *all* essential ingredients of successful advertising.

1. Promise

The basis for all advertising is promise. How do you induce people to do something for you? How do you motivate them? Essentially you offer them something in return for their efforts. They do something for you, so you do something for them. No human activity on behalf of another is ever made without the expectation of reward. Even the most seemingly altruistic of humans—the sacrificing mother, the selfless doctor, the dedicated charity worker, and so on—all derive an ultimate reward, if not in material things, then in terms of self-satisfaction on one level or another.

Certainly this applies to the technique of inducing people to buy. Consumers don't buy to make you happy. They buy because the object of their purchase is going to do something for them—and therein lies the key to all! *What will your product do for them?* Will it make them happier, healthier, richer, more attractive? Will it make their work easier, their life more pleasant? Will it relieve them of anxiety, enhance their prestige, elevate their status, turn them into more contented human beings? What will it do for them?

42

Of course, this theme has been done to death in advertising texts of all shapes and hues. It is elemental, obvious, too apparent to even bear repeating, and yet, incredibly enough, it is ignored to a ridiculous degree. Be sure *you* don't ignore it. Here it is once more.

To induce people to buy your product, you must tell them what that product will do for them! Remember that. It is the essence of advertising, and it is summed up in one magic word—*PROMISE!*

What does it mean in practical terms? It means that your audience couldn't care less about you, your product, or how you suffer to make it. Their only concern with your product is how it will help them. You want to run your picture in your ad? Go ahead, but don't delude yourself into thinking it is helping your advertising effort. You want to brag about how hard it is to make your product? Okay. Enjoy yourself. But unless you tell your readers precisely how your efforts will benefit *them*, you are wasting your time.

Remember that old bit about "sell the sizzle, not the steak"? It is substantially true. If you must get involved in a discussion of the cow the steak came from, do it in terms of how it enhances the enjoyment of the sizzle, not merely because you want to discuss cows. In short, don't let your ego get in the way. Forget that you are the world's largest purveyor of whatsits and that everybody at the club is impressed when you walk in. That little old lady out in Podunk couldn't care less. She is concerned only with how that whatsit will help her.

The following example was taken from a successful mail-order ad for a how-to gambling book. The headline and copy are good examples of the use of strong promise.

How to Vastly Increase Your Chances to
WIN A FORTUNE
AT LAS VEGAS
Or *You Pay Nothing!*

Right now, how would you like to walk into any casino in Las Vegas or anywhere else absolutely certain that you will walk away from those tables with a fortune in your pockets? Incredible? Of course. No one can make that guarantee, but—and this is a positive fact—you can greatly increase your chances of winning, and you can do it consistently!

It is possible! You can get rich in Las Vegas. . . .

2. Sell to Prospects and Never Mind the Rest

This admonition—sell to your prosects and stop wasting time and money on others—is probably the crux of all good advertising and sales efforts of any type. Pay attention to it. It can mean the difference between so-so advertising and ads that really work!

Unless your product truly has universal appeal, *address your ads only to the people who are interested in what you have to sell, and forget about the rest!* Don't waste time, effort, and expensive space flagging down people who have no need or desire for your product! This is a basic error most advertisers—and their agencies—consistently make! Use a general approach to sell a specific product, and inevitably you end up with a watered-down ad utterly lacking in sell.

Some years ago, I was involved in an extremely successful reducing company. We were selling pills specifically for reducing weight, using space and direct mail. Our newspaper ads ran a full page in tabloid-size papers and 1,200 lines in standard papers, and were virtually all straight type! There wasn't an illustration in the entire ad, and as a matter of fact, hardly a stick of type over six points in the body copy. It was just one big, grim-looking smear of gray. We ran on Sundays—generally the best mail-order day—and frequently spent ten, twenty, and thirty thousand dollars or more, depending on the availability of space. On Monday mornings, sure as clockwork, my phone would ring and some advertising account executive would say, "Saw your ad yesterday. I'd like to show you how to improve it." I'd ask what he suggested, and then it would come, the old story in a very confidential tone: "Well, first thing, too much copy. Nobody will read all of that. And besides, type's too small. Like to come up and discuss it with you. Couple of illustrations, chop out a lot of that copy, crisp layout, little white space —I'm sure we can show you how to put together a better ad."

And while the voice droned on, I'd look over at the huge table to my right. There were three slots cut into the middle of that table, and under those slots were large wooden boxes. All day long, from nine to five, five days a week, eight people sat around that table opening envelopes and stuffing three-, five-, and seven-dollar checks and money orders down the slots and into the boxes. And there I'd sit, my feet up on the desk and my eyes on the table, while the account executive's voice droned on.

That was mail order, but when we went into department stores, we ran the same straight-copy ad, enlivened only by one relatively small picture whose prime function was to mollify the store buyers. When, on occasion, a store would take exception to our ad and request permission to change it, we would say, "No. It runs the way it is, or it doesn't run at all." And whenever it ran, it pulled and pulled and pulled.

Except for the headline and a couple of subheads, that ad was virtually an unbroken expanse of six-point type, long and somewhat of an effort to read. I'm sure everyone passed it by. Everyone, that is, except the fat people who were our prospects and perhaps a few appalled account executives.

Now, what is the moral? Simply this, *If they—your audience—have a particular need, a particular problem, or a particular desire, and you offer them a solution, they will be only too glad to read what you have to say.* You have merely to attract their attention to your offer and to let them know how it will fill their need or desire or solve their problem. On the other hand, if they have no interest in what you are selling, all the inducements in the world are of no consequence.

Suppose, for example, I had used a curiosity headline, an attractive picture, or perhaps both in that reducing ad. And suppose further that the headline and the picture were good enough to stop just about everybody who happened to be passing by. What would have happened? All the thin people, who had no real interest in that offer, would have stopped for a moment, taken a quick look, and proceeded on their merry way. Those fat people with an interest in what we had to say would have lingered, read, and if convinced, acted.

45

"Fine," you say. "You would have accomplished your purpose anyway. The skinnies who would have stopped off for a while would not have hurt the ad by looking at it, and the overweights, whom you wanted to read it, would have done so anyway."

That sounds perfectly logical, but it glosses over one important point. The picture and the curiosity headline would have occupied space that cost money and produced nothing. On the other hand, the straight-type ad came right to the point. It flagged down only people we wanted to contact. Valuable space that might have been wasted on innocuous pictures was devoted to persuading overweights that our product was the answer to their problems.

The drug companies know and understand this need to pinpoint an audience, and they accomplish it beautifully. Their technique, perfected through long years of practice, was born of necessity. Only people with a cough are prospects for a cough medicine. Only people with a backache are interested in backache remedies. Obviously it would be extremely wasteful—in fact, economically impossible—to run a large ad designed to snare everybody who passed by and then hope to filter out of that large mass the few who happen to be prospects for cough medicine, backache pills, or whatever. Since the market for these medications is relatively limited, it makes good sense to run small ads geared to attract a specific audience and to run them with some frequency.

That this technique works is amply attested to by the existing evidence. Down through the years a great many products, virtually all of humble origins, have entrenched themselves as staple items, and despite the advent of TV advertising, many new products are still using this technique to establish themselves.

Following are a few examples of the sell-only-to-prospects technique.

SKINNY?
Amazing new, easy way puts on pounds of
Firm, Solid Flesh . . .

46

B U N I O N S
Enlarged Tender Joints
Fast Relief

STOP ATHLETE'S FOOT
Penetrates deep. Stops fungus
that causes athlete's foot.

Actually, of course, there is no reason to confine the use of this technique to small space or to drug advertising. As a matter of fact, there is no need to confine it at all!

Reflect on this for a moment: Unless your product has a broad general appeal, people who are specifically interested in what you have to offer are your best prospects. Your chance of selling your motorcycles to old ladies is remote; your chance of selling them to young people is better; but your chance of selling them to people already interested in motorcycles is best of all. That's why you aim your ads at a specific audience to the greatest degree possible. This has always been the essence of media selection. Your ads do best where the most prospects are. Carry it one step further by *aiming your advertising specifically to those prospects*, and it becomes more effective still.

3. Why Reason-Why

In my estimation, the only worthwhile kind of copy or sales pitch is that which is known as Reason-Why—that is, copy that gives the prospect sound reasons *why* he should buy the product or service. The greater the number of sound, logical reasons why it would be advantageous for the prospect to become a buyer, the more effective that copy will be. That is axiomatic. There are no ifs, ands or buts about it! It works that way in selling, and it works that way in advertising. We can only attribute the extreme neglect of reason-why copy to apparent ignorance on the part of many ad men. Obviously, a lot of advertising men have forgotten the basics, have forgotten that the sole function of advertising is to sell goods. No other reason is sufficient. You are not

47

trying to impress customers with how clever your company is. You are not trying to have them chuckle appreciatively over what nice guys you are while they reach for a competitive product. What you are trying to do, or certainly should be trying to do, is to sell merchandise. Never mind whether your audience thinks you are a nice guy or the girl in the ad is pretty. Just see that they walk home with your product under their arms!

Suppose, for example, that you sell automobiles. Your name is Henry Ford, and for some years now you have been making and selling cars. Now, I happen to be reasonably interested in cars. I live in the suburbs, I drive a car, and I couldn't be without one. Although I trade in only every couple of years or so, I am always a prospect—hot sometimes, lukewarm others, but always interested. When I stop to read your ad, it is tantamount to walking into your showroom.

When that happens, what do you do? Do you grab me by the lapels and say, "Look here, buddy, the only thing you will ever have to change in this car is the ashtray?" A few years ago Ford based an entire campaign on that very promise!

What do I care about your ashtrays? I couldn't care less. I only want to know about your car. Why should I buy it? What do you have over a Chevy or a Plymouth? Now stop and think a minute. Here I am—I want to be told, and I want to be sold. I want to believe you have something special for me. I want to believe your car is new, different, better than all the rest. I want to believe, and I want to buy. Just tell me, just show me, just convince me why. But don't expect to do it with pretty girls. Don't try to tout me on to the mechanical virtues of your car via your ashtrays. Give me the facts. Give me reasons why and back them with proof! That's all I ask.

This isn't a $1.98 purchase. I'm not buying a pack of cigarettes. This is the most important purchase I make. I need good reasons why and plenty of them! If your brake drum is a sixteenth of an inch larger than a Dusenberry's and that sixteenth makes for better brakes, tell me and I'll believe it. If your fenders are stamped out of steel that's only a thousandth of an inch thicker than a Whosit's, but that extra thousandth makes your car a little bit stronger and a little bit heavier, and that added weight makes it hold the road just a little bit better, tell me, and I'll believe it because it sounds logical. It's a plus, and I need pluses to convince me to buy your Ford as opposed to his Chevy. These are the things I want to know. Tell them to me. Don't play games. Give me hard, cold, logical facts and lots of them!

The fact is that people want to be persuaded. They want you to give them a sound rationale for buying. For the sale's sake, accommodate them. Let them know that when they buy your product, they're not being spendthrifts. They're not depriving their families, themselves, or anyone else of anything. They are making an investment in their health, wealth, and happiness, their future satisfaction and well-being. And that holds whether you are selling them a washing machine, a new toothbrush, or a pair of spats! Tell them about all the benefits and back them up with good, solid reasons why!

4. Compare

Everything in life is relative. Nearly all judgments depend on comparisons for their basis. There is no big without a small, no good without a bad, and although we never stop to think about it particularly, this is the basis for all selling. We compare.

You walk into a store and say, "Let me see a typewriter," and the clerk shows you half a dozen competing models, three of which happen to fit your needs and your pocketbook. How do you make your selection? Naturally, on the basis of comparison. Maybe one typewriter looks better or feels better than the others, and you make your selection on that basis. Perhaps you ask the clerk, who presumably knows more about typewriters than you do, "What are the advantages of each?" or "Which do you recommend and why?" But one way or another, your ultimate choice is made on the basis of comparison.

Actually, all selling is done on that basis. The salesman says, "Our widgets cost less than theirs do," or "Testing proves that we give you better mileage than they do," or "Ours are made by patient old-world craftsmen," the inference being that the competing product is made by impatient new-world craftsmen, and so on.

In most instances, the more direct the comparison, the more powerful the pitch. If, for instance, your product genuinely does cost less than the competition's, obviously you have a strong selling point and should use it. But what if your product costs more? You have a strong point too. No cheap product, yours, but the very best available, and no wonder! Look how much more it costs!

If your product is made better, designed better, works better, these points should be stressed, and the best way to do that is to compare them to competitive products. You may have noted that on rare occasions the automobile companies do this by name. What a windfall waiting for the first company with enough car and enough guts to make direct comparisons with competitors in their price range and do it consistently!

Since selling depends to a great degree on comparison, and since advertising is no more than selling in print, then advertising must depend to a great extent on comparison. But this blatantly obvious fact is shamefully overlooked in many of today's ads.

If you have something to brag about, do it! If you really believe the baked beans you make are great, say so! Don't say, "We make great baked beans." Say, "We make the *greatest* baked beans!" Your superlative is, in effect, a comparison. If your baked beans are made with barbecue sauce and everyone else's are made with ordinary tomato sauce, say so! Don't just say, "Our beans are made with delicious barbecue sauce." Say, "Other beans are made with ordinary tomato sauce, but not *ours*! Our beans are made with delicious barbecue sauce, and that's just one of the amazing differences! See, taste, compare, etc.!" In short, don't just know it or think it. Say it, and say it emphatically by making comparisons! This is important! Don't underestimate it!

One of the masters of this technique is the copywriter who puts together a well-known midwestern sports catalog. He writes reason-why copy that just won't quit, and the basis for much of it is comparison. This man understands the absolute need to compare, and he does it with great frequency and with obviously good results. When he writes about boots, he doesn't merely tell you that his boots are well made, or that the quality of his leather is first rate, or that they are a great bargain that will last for years and years. That's not nearly enough. He goes into details the likes of which you can't even begin to believe. And it's all fascinating reading if you are even vaguely interested in what he has to sell.

He tells you how close the stitches in his boots are, and then he points out that the closer the stitches are, the better the quality. He tells you how the leather is processed, and where, and why that method is better than anyone else's.

When he talks about his camping shirts, he tells you that they aren't for drugstore campers like competitors' shirts are. He tells you how many buttons they have and how large each button is, and where it is located, and why! I am not exaggerating! For example, he gives you everything but a chemical analysis of the cloth and thread. He tells you about the pockets and what you can keep in each one . . . matches here, extra fishhooks and a snakebite kit there (in case you become lost in the woods), and on and on and on. Before he's through you are not only an expert on shirts and shirtmaking, but you are practically an authority on survival techniques as well. And most important, you are convinced that his boots and shirts and fishing lures and revolvers are the most incredible creations man can make or money can buy. And, for all I know, perhaps they are.

That is what you call "reason why" copy. They make good products, they are proud of them, and they are not embarrassed about telling you why!

5. The Straightforward Approach

Don't be smart, tricky, or cute. If you have something to say, say it and say it in a straightforward manner. Maybe beating around the bush pays off when you are involved in a business deal, but it rarely does in advertising or selling. Come to the point and get there by the most direct route possible.

Good copy begins at the beginning, ends at the end, and doesn't

51

digress in the middle. Resist the temptation to go off on a tangent. That's how you lose readers. Your goal is to urge the reader to action, and you want to reach the point where you can do so as directly as possible.

Don't overestimate the intellectual capabilities of your audience. Not that your readers are stupid, but remember that the audience for most consumer products is comprised of people from various social and economic strata, and it is your job to reach them. You don't succeed in this by writing over their heads or by appealing to the sophisticated few.

There is always the danger that material that appears perfectly obvious to you and everyone you show it to simply doesn't come across to large segments of the public. It is frequently obscure when it should be obvious, confusing when it should be simple, obtuse when it should be right to the point. Keep your copy and your ideas simple and direct. Vocabulary is another important consideration. Write in plain language so that everyone interested in your product can read and understand it. Don't lose a single reader for the sake of a fancy approach or a big word. Sometimes it is difficult to sacrifice a smooth sentence or a good phrase, but if there is even the remotest possibility that it won't be understood, forget it!

This is advertising copy, and certainly in this area, *what* you say is a lot more important than *how* you say it. If your audience is sufficiently interested in your message, they will disregard the lack of embellishments in your ad. So again, leave the tricky, smart-alecky stuff for your competitors. You get in there with a hard-hitting, straightforward sales message, and you have it made!

It is far more effective to present a good sales pitch crudely than to say nothing eloquently.

Here is a pretty fair example of what, in my estimation, is an utterly weak and ineffectual ad. It occupied a full magazine page, the upper two-thirds of which consisted of a good, clear photograph of the motion-picture projector being advertised. The bottom third of the ad consisted of the following copy, in two neat, easy-to-read columns, and nothing else.

IMPROVE YOUR GOLF SWING $200.00*

You don't play golf? Improve your bowling score $200.00. You don't bowl? Improve your traverse $200.00. You don't ski? Improve your lob $200.00. You don't play tennis? Improve your sailing technique $200.00. You don't play golf or bowl or ski or play tennis or sail? Watch travel movies $200.00. You don't travel either? Collect movie projectors—starter kit $200.00. Anything you can do with a movie project, you can do better with our ———. Have some movies of your golf swing? Run them in slow motion and analyze away. You have some old film you like to look at? Fine. This projector will make them look practically new. (You can even run them in slow motion. But if your 16-year-old objects to his baby pictures being in slow motion, don't say we didn't warn you.) You don't have to shout to make yourself heard, either. This projector is very quiet. (We hate noise ourselves.) It's self-threading too. But it's not so automatic that you can't push some buttons and click some levers, if you want something special to happen. After all, the projectionist needs something to do once in a while.

If ever there was obtuse, obscure, hard-to-understand copy, this is it. It's hard to believe that such a clean, crisp, attractive ad could be so ineffectual. I can conceive of this ad's ever having been written only on the theory that lapses occur in every profession, and surely advertising is no exception. But what induces a client or his ad manager to accept an ad like this?

What kind of magic do they think they wield that is powerful enough to induce readers to stop and try to figure this one out? And what makes them think that after it has been figured out it is going to sell projectors?

Contrast the previous ad with the following. This is a far cry from a good ad. It doesn't begin to sell nearly as hard as it should. There is a distinct lack of facts and figures, but at least there is no beating around the bush here. This company produces a movie camera. They show you what it looks like. They tell you why they think it's good, and although the information they give you is terribly sketchy and lacking virtually

* (Give or take a few dollars)

all the elements good copy should contain, at least it is honest and straightforward. When you are finished reading it, you have an idea of some of the features of the camera. Weak though it may be, compared with the projector ad, it's a little gem.

Three small photos appear across the top of the ad. The first shows the film being loaded. The caption reads, "Film cassette loads in seconds."

The second picture shows a profile of the camera. The caption reads, "Battery drive . . . no winding."

The third picture shows a closeup of the camera in use and reads, "Zoom for close-ups."

A very large silhouetted photo of the camera occupies most of the balance of the page, and the following copy appears across the bottom of the ad:

Electric 8
Zoom
Camera
loads in
seconds. . . .

. . . and takes outstandingly sharp, brilliant 8mm movies! The film cassette eliminates conventional threading—and re-threading, too. (When you're ready to expose the second side of the film, just flip the cassette over. It's that simple.) In the _____ Electric 8 Zoom Camera a small, efficient electric motor winds the film for you. You're always ready to catch the action. Zoom smoothly with just a touch of your finger. The electric eye automatically adjusts the exposure. _____ Electric 8 Zoom Camera, less than $160. Advanced with 8-to-1 zoom lens (6.5-52mm), less than $296. Single-lens model, less than $80. See all three at your _____ dealer's.

Here's another ad by the same company that brought you the dismal "Improve Your Golf Swing" projector advertisement. The format is essentially the same, and the copy is just as vacuous.

This, too, is a neat, clean, lots-of-white-space, full-page magazine ad. The copy occupies the top 30 percent of the page. A large, silhouetted photograph of the camera being used, hammerlike, to drive a large nail, fills the remaining two-thirds of the ad.

The copy reads:

WORLD'S MOST EXPENSIVE HAMMER

A _____ movie camera makes a dandy hammer. (Our nail-banging was to show the sturdiness of our electric-eye system. It also makes a nice point about our camera bodies, doesn't it?) If your idea of a status symbol is close to one hundred and fifty dollars worth of hammer, though, make sure it's a _____. Actually, we didn't plan on making a hammer. But when _____ makes something, we make it strong.

In case you're interested in taking movies, we'd like to point out the handy one-handed-zooming affair. Right there under the lens, see? You tuck your index finger in there and zoom smooth as you please. And the electric eye and reflex viewing. And the folding, built-in pistol grip. Naturally, you load this camera with a cartridge. There now, if you have any further questions, ask your _____ dealer. Nice fellow.

Although this ad doesn't reach the depths of confusion plumbed by the first example, it, too, is a rather roundabout attempt at selling.

Undoubtedly this ad will attract attention and a certain amount of readership. It may even evoke some amusement. But—and this is the point—does it evoke that amusement from a specific audience that is a prospect for a movie camera or is it content to garner amused readership from anyone who happens to pass by, and if so, what has that got to do with selling cameras?

Look at it this way. If you as a consumer are *not* in the market for a movie camera, you will find *this ad* more amusing than the previously considered camera ad; however, you will find the former more instructive and more helpful. But in either case, it makes no difference since you are not about to buy a camera.

If you are in the market for a movie camera, the same situation prevails. You will still find the hammer ad more amusing and the former ad more instructive and helpful, but in this instance instruction and help are desired.

As an advertiser, which would you prefer—a prospect in whom you had aroused detached amusement or one who had, at least to some extent, been presold on your product? Which would make a more likely customer, and what is the function of your advertising—to make customers or to titillate passersby?

6. Prove Your Claims

We live in an age of skepticism. TV, radio, and national magazines have made their presence known throughout the length and breadth of the land. As a consequence, naïveté is no longer part of the rural American scene, as it once was. Our vast population, subject to the constant blandishments of ads, has become far more skeptical than ever. Where once there was a tendency to believe almost everything in print, now advertisers must back up every claim with solid proof.

If you make a point, prove it. Don't merely say, "The rubber in our thing outlasts the rubber in our competitor's product two to one." On the contrary, show the tests that prove your claim. Every time you make a statement that you feel may be greeted with even the least amount of skepticism, make every effort you can to prove it. Don't expect your audience to believe it just because you say it. You may be a highly honorable, impeccably honest human being, but how does your audience know? Proof is important. It is one of the ingredients your audience craves. They want to believe, and proof helps make it easier for them.

If concrete evidence to support your claims isn't available, you'll have to rely on the power of your copy to do the job for you. There are ways . . .

No wonder so many people buy _____! No wonder so many of them recommend it to their friends. Surely that's proof of the incredible effectiveness of _____. Naturally _____ wouldn't outsell its nearest competitor two to one (or whatever) if it weren't proved better in so many ways! . . .

It is interesting that the sporting-goods catalog mentioned earlier presents an overwhelming collection of facts to prove their contentions. Just how factual these "facts" are, I am in no position to say. But there is such an imposing array of them, I, for one, can't help but be impressed. These facts are his proof. They are what help to make his ads so persuasive.

7. *Guarantee*

What is better proof that you have faith in your product than to guarantee it? Mail-order ads have long depended on the guarantee to convince readers that they could safely send for a product.

> Send now. Then try _____ in your own hme entirely at our risk. If after 10 days you are not completely satisfied in every way, don't keep it! Simply return at once for a complete refund, no questions asked! You must be convinced that _____ is the best _____ you have ever used in your life or you pay nothing! Now surely we wouldn't dare to make a guarantee like that if we weren't convinced that this product is everything we say and more. So you see, you really have nothing to lose. Why not send now?

What could be stronger or more emphatic than that? What better way to convince the mail-order buyer that he is taking little or no risk by sending for your merchandise? For that matter, what better way to convince *any* buyer that it is perfectly safe to buy your merchandise? Or again, take that sports-catalog approach. They have another way of putting it, and they frequently do so right in the headline. They say, "Order out a pair. If in your judgment they are not the finest _____ you have ever seen or used, return within one month for a full refund including transportation charges." Then, as if those frequent refund offers aren't enough, right across the bottom of *each* page in their huge catalog, they run two lines of bold-face copy that read,

_____ ARE NOT UNDERSOLD. WITHIN 3 MONTHS COMPARE PRICES IN YOUR AREA. IF IN YOUR JUDGMENT _____ PRICES ARE NOT LESS THAN WHOLESALE AND

DISCOUNT PRICES, RETURN ITEM FOR FULL REFUND PLUS TRANSPORTATION CHARGES.

Why restrict guarantees to mail-order merchandise? Why not extend them to all merchandise? Not long ago, the automobile manufacturers began to make a big thing of guaranteeing certain parts for a specified length of time or number of miles. That was probably one of the few smart advertising moves they have made in years, and even at that, they really haven't derived a fraction of the potential they might have by continued reference to it. But at least they tried. What about other industries?

You do stand behind your merchandise, don't you? If one of the items you manufacture slips past the inspectors without its whatsit firmly fastened in place and some irate customer gripes, you are going to make good, aren't you? Then why not say so? Why keep it a deep, dark secret, when letting readers know that you stand behind your merchandise will undoubtedly help sell it?

The same goes for smaller retailers. (The return privileges of the large department stores are well-known.) Of course, you don't want to be plagued with returns, but if you accept them anyway, and surely most retailers do if the returns are justified, why not say so? You don't have to make any unequivocal guarantees, but how can it hurt to say that all merchandise must be in first-class working order or money back? That's what you are doing anyway. Take advantage of it.

Some businessmen fear that if they offer a guarantee, they will be inundated with returns. The facts belie this assumption. Actually, experience indicates that guarantees increase sales well in excess of the increase in refund requests, and in light of these findings it makes good sense to include a positive money-back guarantee in all ads where its use is applicable. Test it and see.

8. Be Specific

This is a cardinal rule. Don't be vague or wishy-washy. Be precise; be specific; paint an accurate, crystal-clear image. It's not only easier to envision a specific than a generality, but a specific carries a greater ring of authenticity and authority.

Say, "Hundreds of people did," and you create an amorphous, "maybe yes, maybe no, maybe it's an exaggeration" kind of impression. You leave your statement open to speculation. On the other hand, say, "176 people did," and that's it, period! There is no room for speculation, no room for conjecture.

Again, in the previously mentioned sporting-goods catalog they do it very well. Everything they write reeks of authenticity, authority, and believability because everything is backed up with *specifics*. One particular example among the thousands in the catalog stands out with great clarity. In talking about a pair of boots, they go so far as to mention the number of stitches to the inch! How can you read details like that without being thoroughly convinced that the writer is an expert on the subject?

As a simple test, take any ad that happens to contain somewhat amorphous statements, change those statements to specifics, and you can see the difference. Offhand, I can't think of a single instance in which a general statement is better than a specific one unless a deliberate attempt is being made to hide something.

9. Urge Action

Just as a sales talk is brought to fruition when the contract is signed, so an advertisement fulfills its function when the prospect becomes an actual buyer. That is the reason for an ad's existence. It has to close; it has to make sales; it has to urge the prospect to get down to the store and make that cash register jingle. It accomplishes that by saying so in plain, unmistakable language.

Don't let your copy dangle. Don't make your pitch and then walk off without making a strong closing. Tell him where to buy it. Tell him how to buy it. Tell him when to buy it. And unless it is entirely impracticable, tell him how much it costs and furnish whatever other details you feel are necessary to make it easy for him.

In short, not only do your best to motivate him to buy with plenty of good, solid reasons why, but do so as strongly as you can!

Okay, you have just read what we have called the nine keys to successful copy, and you have read the reasons why their inclusion in any piece of copy is important. Don't minimize them. Don't make the mistake of thinking they are not applicable in your case!

Whatever your product, whatever your service, your copy—or your sales pitch—will be improved immeasurably if you adhere to these principles. So let's go over them again. They bear repeating, because their inclusion can make an incredible difference in the efficacy of your advertising, and mister, good advertising is money in the bank! Read slowly, read carefully, and absorb.

PROMISE   Absolutely vital to every conceivable type of ad or sales talk for every conceivable type of product, bar none! And remember this—in virtually every instance, the stronger the promise you can legitimately make, the more effective the ad!

SELL TO PROSPECTS AND NEVER MIND THE REST!
        An invaluable premise that will unquestionably make any ad (or salesman) far more efficient, far more effective than otherwise. It is always applicable. Even broad general products such as bread or toothpaste will be enhanced by directing the ad toward a specific prospect—the housewife who does the purchasing, or perhaps the kids who do the influencing.

REASON–WHY   Desperately important! Don't just bark out commands. Tell your readers *why* they should buy your product and give them as many valid reasons as possible! The more you present, the more likely you are to succeed.

COMPARE   Comparisons aren't vital; an ad can exist without them. But don't expect it to do as well when they are not included! Comparisons are persuasive, and persuasion turns prospects into customers! No matter how seemingly innocuous your merchandise, if it has merit, it will benefit from comparison!

STRAIGHTFORWARD APPROACH
        Undoubtedly some cute, facetious ads have succeeded

(perhaps in spite of themselves), but how much better might they have done had they relied on a straightforward approach? Why take chances being cute when you can be honest and straightforward and be sure!

PROOF   Certainly proof will strengthen your ad. It overcomes skepticism and makes for belief and acceptance, which are important in any sales effort. If you can prove it, do so.

GUARANTEE   If you have an honest product, why not? Your ad can get along without it, but this is a plus that can help make the difference!

SPECIFIC   Always! If you have something to say, don't be vague or wishy-washy. Say it precisely. Specifics are more authentic than general statements, and certainly that holds as true on an advertising page as it does in a drawing-room argument!

URGE ACTION   Always! You are not running ads to make media rich. You are looking for results. Don't leave your prospects dangling. Tell them what to do and how to do it so you can achieve the results you are looking for.

HOW to FLAG
PROSPECTS

You flag down a prospect by attracting his attention, and you make him a listener—or a reader—by indicating that you have interesting information for him. In an advertisement, as in a printed article, this is done with the headline. In a live sales presentation, the technique you use to gain a prospect's attention and interest him in what you have to offer is sometimes known as a *hook*. In essence, the same principles apply to headlines, window streamers, posters, and other merchandising devices used to attract and convey a message to a specific audience.

Even if you are never involved in putting advertising together, these sound, basic principles have to broaden your conception of promotional techniques. They are certainly worth the time and effort to read and absorb them.

THE FUNCTION OF THE HEADLINE

A headline has two vital functions and no others. It is not up there for decorative purposes, and it is not up there because of the dictates of custom. It is up there to

1. *catch the attention of all the prospects for your product who happen to be passing by.*
2. *induce those prospects to stop and read your copy.*

It accomplishes the first by shouting, "Hey, you!" to the specific prospect. Then it promises that prospect a reward or dangles an enticement to encourage him to read on. The enticement is a solution to a problem, an offer of help, or the promise of information or advice that will benefit him. And that's it!

If you understand these few simple facts you understand the principles of good headline writing. There is nothing complex or mysterious about it. Just remember what you are trying to accomplish, and go to it by flagging down your prospects and giving them a good reason for reading your ad.

This is important. You flatter yourself and your product if you think a reader should stop and read your ad just because it happens to be there or because you have used some tricky little device to arouse his curiosity. Sure, he may, but then again, he may not. Why gamble? If you want to be sure your ad is read, you need a headline that promises a reward for doing so. And let's face it, the reward system works. It gets puppies to sit, it get's kids to behave, it catches criminals, and it will get your ad read!

THE SUB HEADLINE

A subhead is a device for emphasizing secondary but important points for which no room exists in the headline.

If you are certain you have a powerful and completely self-sufficient headline—that is, if your headline effectively stops your prospects and offers them a sound reason to read your copy, and you have no other important points to emphasize—then no subhead is necessary. On the other hand, if you encounter difficulty in squeezing all the important selling points into your headline, or if you are not sure you are using the strongest possible appeal and you want some insurance, use a subhead.

On occasion, it is practical to use an introductory line preceding the headline. It may be used with or in lieu of a sub-head. Here is an example of all three in use:

New! For the first time in medical history . . .

DRINK YOUR FAT AWAY!

Reduce up to 2 ounces per drink with each
fabulous new NO DIET Reducing Cocktail you have!

Note that we still depend on the headline to stop our reader. It must therefore be capable of functioning without the help of the preceding line or the subhead, both of which may be regarded as adjuncts helpful but not vital to the success of the ad.

In the subhead *new* is a good word. It informs the reader that he has never seen this ad before, which in itself might be a reason to read the ad. *For the first time in medical history* is a more specific way of saying *new*. *Medical history* has a strong connotation—the hallowed halls of medicine, medical researchers, the great discoveries of medicine, and so on. It implies solidity and importance. In essence, then, it qualifies *Drink your fat away* to some degree.

The subhead is a further qualification, but on a more detailed level. The promise is strong, specific, and sufficiently provocative to induce people who are reducing conscious to read on.

THE IMPORTANCE OF BREVITY

Brevity is an asset in a headline. Note that I said asset, not requirement. If unavoidable—that is, if it is the only possible way to get your point across—you may use a long headline. But generally speaking, the fewer words you use, the larger they can be set (within practical limits), the more easily they can be seen, and the more readily their message will be grasped. Very often you can achieve brevity without sacrificing content or impact.

Here is a practical example of how judicious cutting can improve a headline. The following appeared in a local paper in the form you see below. It is a good, strong headline, but because of its length, it doesn't begin to come across with all the impact it is capable of.

IF YOU DON'T CUT
YOUR OIL OR GAS
BILL NEXT WINTER . . . 25%

———

WILL PAY THE DIFFERENCE

Now see the difference eliminating superfluous words can make. Following is the same basic headline but shorter and, as a consequence, much stronger and harder hitting. (Incidentally, the company name is superfluous in this instance. There is plenty of room for it at the bottom of the ad, where it belongs.)

CUT YOUR OIL OR GAS BILL
25% NEXT WINTER . . .
OR WE PAY THE DIFFERENCE!

Note that the words *oil or gas bill* pinpoint the audience quite effectively; the promise *cut your oil or gas bill 25%* is strong; *next winter* ties down the promise and makes it specific; and *or we pay the difference* is a powerful guarantee that lends credibility to everything before it.

This third version, still shorter, isn't quite as good in my estimation, essentially because it isn't as specific. But it still tells the story well, and it is much more convenient from a layout point of view. Although layout is not of prime importance, anything you can do to facilitate making a good layout—provided you don't have to sacrifice copy to do so—certainly is a step in the right direction.

CUT FUEL BILLS 25%
OR WE PAY DIFFERENCE!

In this instance the ideal situation would include the use of a subheadline to amplify the headline. The headline stops the prospect, the subhead helps to convince him to read on, and the copy does the persuading.

CUT FUEL BILL 25%
OR WE PAY DIFFERENCE!
Amazing New Device Guarantees to Cut
Next Winter's Oil or Gas Bill 25%!

BE SPECIFIC

This is a cardinal rule in copy, and it applies in headlines as well. Don't write hazy, fuzzy, general-statement headlines when you can be specific. The more precisely you pinpoint your audience and the more specifically you address them, the more effectively you will get your message across.

Review every phrase you use in your headline, and wherever possible, substitute a specific for a generalization. Note how, in the following section on good headlines, each head is as specific as possible, and note, conversely, that in the section on bad headlines, each is quite general.

EXAMPLES OF GOOD HEADLINES

Following are a number of good headlines. Note that they contain the essential ingredients. In each case they make reference to the specific audience at which they are aimed and give that audience a good reason for reading. When a product has broad appeal, the headline has a correspondingly broad appeal, and when the appeal is limited, the headline is more specific.

HOW TO LIVE TO BE A HUNDRED

This is a superb headline for a book of the same name. It tops a good ad written by one of the few really good copywriters around. It is short, readable, eye catching, provocative, and in a sense, even controversial. Most important, however, it makes a powerful promise of universal appeal.

Note the importance of the words *how to*. The mere statement *live to be a hundred* is no more than a statement. The *how to*, however, promises information and hence furnishes a powerful reason for reading the ad.

REDUCE UP TO 7 POUNDS
THE FIRST 7 DAYS
OR PAY NOTHING!

A number of years ago this headline appeared on a modestly success-ful one-thousand-line mail-order ad. It was a good headline. It flagged reducing prospects, made a strong and unequivocal promise to them, and as an extra, backed up that promise with a firm, money-back guar-antee. When the same headline was altered in this manner, however . . .

REDUCE UP TO SEVEN POUNDS
BY MARCH 15th
OR PAY NOTHING!

a dramatic change occurred! The identical ad now pulled some 30 percent better than it formerly had! The change from *the first 7 days* to *by March 15th* made the startling difference because the date was infinitely more specific. The date was of course changed in each suc-ceeding ad, the theory being that one could reduce seven pounds within seven days after the product arrived. This concept was widely and successfully imitated for a number of products of various types.

DRINK YOUR FAT AWAY

This was another successful reducing headline that worked beauti-fully in mail order and equally well for department stores. The headline is short and to the point. The very concept was so unique (the product was a liquid reducing preparation that was taken with juice, water, etc.) that it was felt, quite rightly, that it would pique the interest of the audience sufficiently to compel them to read on. Hence the words *how to* were deemed dispensable in this instance.

Note, incidentally, the use of the word *fat* instead of a more subtle substitute. Reducing ads seem to be more impelling when the word *fat* is used as opposed to *heavy, overweight,* etc. I say "seem," because there is no positive proof of this. Apparently, however, when you call a spade a spade or a fatty a fatty, you get better results.

SHRINKS HEMORRHOIDS
NEW WAY WITHOUT SURGERY

A good headline because it is pared down. It contains no nonessentials and tells the whole story directly and without equivocating. Obviously this headline would have no appeal to those not so afflicted, and there is no reason why it should, since whether they read the ad or not is of no consequence.

HOW TO LAND A HUSBAND

Another very successful how-to headline for a book. It is short and sweet, comes right to the point, and makes a very strong promise to a specific audience. The ad worked extremely well in book sections and other media devoted to book readers; it did not do so well when it was tested R.O.P.* in the *Boston Advertiser* or the country edition of the *New York Sunday News*, where it obviously reached a non-book-reading audience.

BOOK TITLES

Good book titles have much in common with good headlines. They both have much the same function—to stop browsers and induce them to peek inside. Here are a few of the more outstanding examples of recent years.

How I Made Two Million Dollars in the Stock Market

The appeal here is obvious. The book is aimed specifically at people interested in the stock market, and what such person wouldn't like to earn two million dollars, or at least find out how it was done?

A secondary appeal, partially responsible for the outstanding success of the book, was that these huge earnings were made by a man who

*Run of the paper.

was not a Wall Street pro, but rather a professional dancer. The implication was that if a dancer could do it, certainly a smart guy like you can too.

That secondary but powerful appeal was utilized as a subhead in the ads, on the front of the book jacket, and in the jacket copy as well.

●

How I Turned a Thousand Dollars into a Million Dollars in Real Estate in My Spare Time

Here, again, is the same basic story, but this time real estate instead of Wall Street provides the intrigue, and as an added attraction, we are informed that this million was made in the author's spare time . . . again implying that if he could do it in his spare time, why not you?

●

How To Make A Fortune Today Starting from Scratch

This is another book by the author of *How I Turned a Thousand Dollars into a Million.* . . . Although still a pretty good title, it doesn't begin to generate the power its predecessor did. *How to Make a Fortune* . . . must of course strike a responsive chord among its readers. *Today* qualifies the promise and gives it a sense of immediacy. It also serves a more subtle function. It is natural to believe that whereas fortunes were easily come by in the "good old days," making them now is another story. The word *today* tends to meet this objection by telling you it can be done right now. *Starting from scratch* is designed to assure you that despite what you think, you don't need a million dollars to make more.

Actually, however, the overall effort leaves something to be desired. In my estimation this title is somewhat unbelievable. I am sure that most people doubt their capacity to simply "make a fortune, today" or any other time. Make that headline more specific, however, and it's another story. Add the words *REAL ESTATE*, for example, so that the title looks like this,

How to Flag Prospects

*How to Make a Fortune in Real
Estate Starting from Scratch*

and it now becomes a great deal more believable. Instead of an amorphous *make a fortune*, the specific area in which that fortune can be made now becomes apparent, and because we know others have done it, it becomes conceivable that we, too, may be able to turn the trick. Believability is just as vital in a headline as in any other part of an ad. Don't make wild statements. *Everything you write has to be logical, sensible, and provable!*

•

*How I Started Earning
$50,000 in Sales at the Age of 26*

A good how-to title following in the already proven *How I Made Two Million Dollars . . .* tradition. It is possible that *at the age of 26* may bring out some hidden resentment on the part of older and less successful salesmen, but I doubt whether that objection is sufficiently strong to militate against its use.

•

How to Get an Executive Job after 40

Superficially this meets our requirements for a good title (or headline). *How to* holds forth the promise of information, *executive job* presumably has appeal, and *after 40*, which is the crux of the title, pinpoints our specific audience. I must say, however, that in general I do not like the whole concept for reasons that go something like this:

If a man is an executive, presumably he will continue to be one after age forty, so no one who has reached executive capacity is a likely prospect for this book. Obviously, then, the book must confine its appeal to those who have not reached the executive level by age forty, but are these men avid book readers? Do they still hope to make it, and will enough of them believe that a book can tell them how? My impression is that this market is more limited than it would seem at first glance.

How to Flag Prospects

Calories Don't Count

This is an extremely provocative statement to any overweight person, particularly since for years they have been led to believe that calories do indeed count. Of course, the word *calories* is sufficient to pinpoint the audience and make it perk up and take notice.

•

How to Live to Be a Hundred

A provocative statement that promises to supply the answer to an often-asked question, this title makes no effort to pinpoint a specific group simply because the concept appeals to virtually everyone.

BAD HEADLINES AND HOW TO WRITE THEM

For every good headline there are probably twenty that are pathetically ineffective. They say nothing, promise nothing, do nothing to motivate a browser and make him a reader. In many instances their only excuse for being seems to be tradition. People are accustomed to seeing a phrase at the top of an ad, so the ad man obliges by throwing one in. Here's a superb example of what I mean. It is not horrible enough to serve as a blatant example of what not to do, but it is unfortunately typical of much of the innoccuous nonsense that masquerades as advertising. This one appeared on a two-hundred-line ad for a well-known local men's clothier.

THE SUIT OUR OWN
EXECUTIVES DESIGNED

This is a lousy headline in every sense of the word. It panders to the egos of the store executives, ignores the audience for whom it should be intended, and is, in sum, a bland and unprovocative statement. Most important, it doesn't begin to function the way a headline should. Who cares whether executives designed this suit? Besides, what do they know about designing anyway, and how will their extracurricular dabbling make the end result more attractive to you or me? Indeed, what is there about this headline that could possibly tempt anyone to read on?

The body copy explains that the suit is comfortable for commuting and that it won't wrinkle after a long meeting or get hot under the collar because it is made of lightweight Dacron polyester and worsted. Now surely *comfortable commuting, wrinkle-free meetings, cool under the collar*, and *Dacron polyester and worsted* are all good selling points. They are reasons to buy a suit. In the aggregate they are too long and too unwieldly for a headline, but they could be reduced to something like this:

COOL, WRINKLE-FREE COMMUTING
WITH DACRON POLYESTER WORSTED

Does this headline function in the two ways a headline is supposed to? To some degree we are relieved of the necessity to flag down our prospects because a large picture of the suit appears underneath the headline. This makes it immediately obvious for whom the ad is intended. Then, too, the word *commuter* in the headline helps to qualify this.

To induce our prospects to read further, we rely on the promise of *wrinkle-free commuting*. If that sounds inviting enough, it will encourage prospects to go on. We have eliminated the reference to meetings because that would lengthen the headline unnecessarily and contribute little.

The ad said this suit wouldn't "get hot under the collar," but that's too long also. *Cool* says it in more positive language. We mention *Dacron polyester worsted* because that is our reason why. It sounds scientific and gives substance to our *cool, wrinkle-free commuting* claim.

Now the headline is very much better than it was, but it still doesn't have any real excitement. I have the feeling, too, that by placing the word *cool* where it is, we are somewhat diminishing the impact of *wrinkle free*, which is a strong promise. Suppose we try it like this:

NOW! WRINKLE-FREE COMMUTING WITH
COOL DACRON POLYESTER WORSTED!

Now is a strong headline word with many powerful connotations. It implies new, at last, finally here, and hurry, and I think its inclusion perks up the headline. If Dacron polyester worsted was a new fabric we could really inject interest and excitement by saying,

AT LAST! WRINKLE-FREE COMMUTING
WITH AMAZING NEW FABRIC DISCOVERY!

That's stronger and more exciting, and it gives the prospect more reason to read.

DO-NOTHING HEADLINES

For some strange reason a great many advertising men seem to think, and a great many clients naïvely believe, that if a headline attracts a bit of attention, it has fulfilled its mission. As a consequence of this utterly ludicrous thinking, the so-called curiosity headlines just about dominate today's crop of ads. And no wonder! They may be lousy advertising, but they are a lot easier to come up with than sound, solid, meaningful headlines. The copy guys write it, the account execs push it, and the clients, innocent souls, accept it. And through repeated acceptance, it becomes fashionable and hence is mistakenly believed to be effective.

Here are some curiosity and other do-nothing headlines culled from magazines. In each instance they do little or nothing to impel one to read the copy, and because of this, they fail dismally.

WHO MADE THE ORANGE MORE TEMPTING
THAN THE APPLE?

•

SEE?

•

I FORGET THE TOWN BUT IT SOUNDED LIKE "TURKEY"

HOW A SWINGING TRIO BECAME A QUARTET

•

THEY DON'T MAKE ONE BIG ENOUGH

•

GET WITH IT

•

IT MAKES THE COMMERCIAL SMALLER

As an offshoot of the curiosity headline, new and far more blatant inanities have sprung up. These include the insipid-copy approach, replete with brittle, contrived, phony language; the nasty approach; the effete, pseudo-sophisticated approach; and the negative approach, which, instead of coming right out and saying it, chooses instead not to say it, like this:

IF IT'S SOMETHING COLD AND WET YOU WANT, DRINK WATER

•

IF YOU THINK ALL BEER TASTES THE SAME, BUY ROOT BEER, IT'S CHEAPER

•

IF YOU CAN FIND A SMARTER GROUP OF DIAMOND SOLITAIRES ANYWHERE... PLEASE TELL US!

Then there are the cute headlines. For a while a series of small ads for a foreign airline—120 lines or so—appeared with some regularity in the financial section of the *New York Times*. They were headlined by such inanities as:

SHIP A YO YO TO TOKYO

SHIP A HORSE ON SAS TO A NORSE

Look at it objectively for a moment. What induces an allegedly knowledgeable advertising man to write headlines like that for readers of the financial pages of the *New York Times*? And even worse, what induces a client to accept them?

During the same period another airline ran a series of ads about two-thirds as large but a great deal better.

CARGO TO SWITZERLAND—FRANKFURT
LEAVES *EVERY DAY*
ARRIVES THE NEXT DAY
VIA———

HOW TO WRITE POWERFUL HEADLINES

If you are about to write a headline or any short piece of copy that has to stop people, try this: Think of your product as out-and-out magic! Assume, for the moment, that it is blessed with the most fantastic capabilities. In light of that assumption, think of the most fabulous feats your magic product is capable of performing for a buyer. Jot down the wildest promise you can think of. If that promise could be anything, absolutely anything, what would it be?

Amazing new shoe soles last forever?
Wake up as thin as you like tomorrow morning?
Fabulous new flat-proof tires never wear out?
New gasoline gives you 1,000 miles per gallon?
New dandruff remover works instantly, permanently?

The object is to find the most powerful appeal for your product. Once this has been accomplished, that is, once you have established a valid direction, you proceed to bring your promises back into perspective by making them compatible with reality.

For example, no shoes will last forever, but perhaps those new plastic soles will last a good eighteen months or more, which is a lot more than leather, giving the basis for a good headline. In this instance, then, the wild, hypothetical promise has given direction to a realistic headline:

AMAZING NEW SHOE SOLES LAST 18 MONTHS OF ROUGH EVERYDAY WEAR.

The gasoline is another story, however. A gas that gives a thousand miles to the gallon may represent the epitome in a fuel, but when reduced to reality, the promise no longer has any appeal. Reduce a thousand to a realistic fifteen, for example, and what have you got but a rather unimpressive claim that even at its puny best still has to be qualified to be true.

Wake Up as Thin as You Like by Tomorrow Morning? Obviously impossible, but write

WAKE UP THINNER TOMORROW MORNING THAN YOU ARE RIGHT NOW

and you are on the track of what might develop into a good headline.

TEST FOR DETERMINING A GOOD HEADLINE

Your ability to gauge the worth of a headline is important. For one thing, a headline is usually indicative of the type of copy that is to follow. As a general rule, solid, reason-why copy rarely follows a cute, clever headline, and vice versa. The quality of a headline, then, is frequently an indication of the kind and quality of the copy.

Second, more important than its function as a mere indicator of the copy to follow, is the very definite fact that the difference between an ad's success or failure frequently hinges on the headline. No great ads are not preceded by great headlines.!

A simple, workable technique for testing headlines requires that you be able to answer yes to each of the following questions. If you can, in all probability you have a good headline. If you can't, it doesn't necessarily follow that your headline is not good, but it is a pretty good indication that something is wrong.

1. Does it pinpoint the audience you want to reach?
2. Does it make a strong enough promise to induce browsers to read your copy?
3. Does it tell the whole story in abbreviated form? Is it, in effect, a condensation of all that you are saying in your body copy?
4. Is it as specific as possible?
5. Is it as short as practicable?

HEADLINES, GOOD AND BAD

Okay, now you know what a headline should do. You have seen examples of good ones and bad ones. Take a look at the following and see what you think. Evaluate them yourself, then compare your observations with mine, and let's see how close we come.

_____ STOPS SUNBURN PAIN
Acts on Skin Nerves with Benzocaine
Used by Doctors. Amazingly Fast!

Pretty good headline. It flags down prospects and tells them just what the product does, and the subhead provides additional selling points. It might be improved, however, by taking one word, *fast* from the subhead and putting it in the headline like this:

_____ STOPS SUNBURN PAIN FAST!

If the medical evidence indicated the specific length of time it took for the product to work (doubtful) and that time period were a matter of seconds, the headline could be made even more effective by doing something like this:

_____ STOPS SUNBURN PAIN
IN JUST 27 SECONDS!

80

or better yet, put the product name in the body copy rather than in the headine. You can still make it prominent enough to be seen and remembered, and at the same time you help your headline to pop right out.

STOP SUNBURN PAIN FAST!

Now how about the following?

PROVED
ALL AROUND THE CLOCK
ALL AROUND THE CALENDAR
ALL AROUND THE COUNTRY
ALL AROUND THE CAR

Pretty awful headline. I've seen the ad a number of times in a number of places, but I still haven't got around to reading it. Why should I or anyone else, for that matter? This headline says nothing, does nothing, promises nothing, certainly offers no incentive for reading the ad. I couldn't care less about the technical machinations General Motors is involved in unless they can show me precisely how they relate to me and will benefit me!

HOW to WRITE IMPELLING LETTERS

LETTERS ARE IDEAL vehicles for conveying sales messages. They are personal and private, and they lend an aura of authenticity to their contents. They may not be an integral part of all direct-mail campaigns, but they certainly can be an important adjunct. As a matter of fact, in many instances the letter is the complete mailing! Prentice-Hall, probably the largest dollar-volume publisher in the United States and one of the largest and most consistently successful mailers, relies on little more than a letter and an accompanying postcard order form in virtually every one of its innumerable mailings.

Their theory is sound and simple. Since their mailings are all mail order, and since success in this area is measured in dollar profits, they do everything they can to keep production costs to a minimum. The lower the costs, the fewer orders required and, therefore, the greater the chance for success. To achieve this, Prentice-Hall prints its own mailings (usually by offset or multigraph) whenever practicable; hence, their predilection for letters which can be produced with relative ease.

Frequent testing over a period of many years has convinced them of the superiority of this technique. One could contest it in many specific instances, but no one can deny the overall wisdom of this method. It has certainly been a factor in their unusually vigorous growth.

If I had to make a choice between mailing a brochure or a letter, I would in most instances choose the latter. After all, there is nothing a brochure can do that a letter can't. Letters can be long or short, illustrated or not, and they have one plus—a good letter can establish a rapport between writer and recipient that is seldom achieved in any but the most skillfully written brochures. That rapport—that person-to person communication—is an important aspect of selling.

85

How to Write Impelling Letters

WHAT A GOOD LETTER SHOULD BE

There is no great mystery to writing strong, selling letters. Basically the same fundamentals that apply to copy apply to letters as well. You tell your story in a straightforward manner; you use only as many words as are necessary to do it, and you leave the cute stuff for your competitors.

Here, for example, is a device I have always used when writing letters and frequently when writing regular copy as well. Read it carefully and don't minimize its effectiveness. Copy, like everything else, comes out better when you are in the right frame of mind for writing it. This device will help to establish the proper mood. Try it. It has to help you.

Think of someone you know, someone you are fond of, someone you would like to help. Imagine that person sitting right across your desk as you start to write your letter. Don't write, "Dear Friend," or "Dear Sir," or "Dear Madam." Write "Dear Rosie," or "Dear Joe," or Dear whoever you are envisioning.

If you are selling something that can help that person—a drug remedy, a labor-saving device, insurance, books, a new washing machine, or whatever—adopt an attitude of commiseration toward him or her because he or she is not already blessed with your product or service.

In other words, think—don't necessarily say, but think—"What a shame. Poor Rosie. Poor Joe. If only you had this new, superduper whatever-it-is. If only you could see it, hold it, use it . . . what a world of difference it would make in your life!" And then, proceed to write your letter directly to Rosie or Joe, never letting his or her image fade until the letter is finished.

Corny? Of course. But don't scoff. It works! This device will never let you forget that you are communicating with a real, live human being whom you can help if you can convince him to use your product or service. Try it next time you have to write a selling letter. As a matter of fact, try it whenever you write any kind of copy. Personal communication, on a warm, human, specific, adult level, is an integral part of good copy, and this device will help you to achieve it!

86

How to Write Impelling Letters

THE SEVEN ELEMENTS EVERY GOOD LETTER SHOULD CONTAIN

Judging the merits of a piece of copy is a chore that you may some-day have to tackle. As you have probably suspected, this is never easy, but like everything else, it can be done and done well if a system is fol-lowed. Unless you are really expert, you don't, for example, merely pick up a letter, read it through, and say, "Yes, this letter will pull like mad," or "No, this letter is awful."

True, a reading does give you a general impression. You can decide with a fair amount of certitude that a letter sounds good or it doesn't, that it is strong or weak, impelling or not impelling; and on the basis of your judgment, you can hazard a guess as to what it will do on the firing line. But understand this: The guess you hazard will be no more than an educated guess. You may be right most often, which is great, but nobody can tell for sure.

You can, however, determine whether that copy has certain basic ele-ments that are terribly important to success. Here are the seven ele-ments a good letter should contain. With this list in front of you, you should have no trouble evaluating a letter. That is not to say that you will be able to predict with 100 percent accuracy how effective a letter will be, but certainly these check points will tell whether it con-forms to certain established standards. If any of these elements is miss-ing, you should make an effort to include them. Note, of course, that merely including these elements does not mean that you can abandon the other aspects of good copy. You still have to be direct, be specific, make promises, present proof, and so on.

1. You

Remember that your letter is not addressed to an amorphous mass. It is written to a specific individual. Just because you have never met him doesn't make him any less alive or human! Be sure this is reflected in your letter. Respect your reader for being a spe-cific individual and speak to him as such.

2. Personal

A letter is personal, a private, news-conveying communication

87

between writer and receiver, and that's just what it should read like! Make sure it is personal, private, and newsy. If your letter is cold, dispassionate, or too businesslike, you are negating its prime advantage and losing the opportunity to make a warm, informal, person-to-person appeal that often gets results where other methods fail.

3. Involvement

Involve the recipient of your letter with your product or service. Help the product come alive for him. Create a strong image of using the item and picture the immediate effect that use will have. (In the section on Pitches, beginning on page 213, note how the pitchman gives specific and detailed directions for using his product to an audience that hasn't even begun to purchase it. This is a time-tested pitch technique and a superb example of what is meant by *involvement*.)

4. Immediacy

Write the letter as though the product or service was already in the recipient's hands. Don't put the pleasures or benefits that will accrue into the future. Make them happen now by eliminating the future tense. For example, don't say, "You *will* enjoy this book," or "You *will* learn a great deal from it." Say, "You enjoy this book. You learn a great deal from it," and so on.

5. Superlatives

We live in an age of skepticism. People have been subjected to so many wild promises and exaggerated claims that they will be pretty much immune to whatever you say. So unless your copy is powerful, persuasive, and logical, much of it is going to be discounted right off the bat. Start strong, be convincing, and don't be afraid to use superlatives! If you think your product is best, say so!

6. Guarantee

Are you selling a good product? Do you have confidence in it?

Then say so! A guarantee is a powerful selling weapon. Use it! This is vitally important in mail order—really the guts of any mail-order offer—and it can be equally important in other kinds of solicitation by direct mail. Don't ignore or underplay it. Let your prospect know you stand behind your product. Tell him that if he is not completely satisfied in every way, he can get his money back immediately and without question. (Unless your product is absolutely hopeless—or expensive—relatively few people ever request a refund, although in the last two or three years the percentage of refund requests has risen to some degree.)

7. Close Strong

You've gone to the trouble and expense of sending a letter because you are trying to induce action on the part of your reader. Don't close without making that request for action emphatic. Motivate him and don't be afraid to use strong language to do it. Get him to do what you want and get him to do it *now*!

Those are the basic elements a good letter should incorporate. Eliminating any one of them must inevitably weaken its structure. Following is an excellent example of a successful letter that makes the most of all of those points. It was directed to agents who sell various items, usually on a part-time basis. The item being sold in this case was a small, inexpensive transistor radio. Read the letter and see what you think. Bear in mind, incidentally, that this offer was made in 1958, long before small transistor radios were generally available at anything even close to their current low prices.

Dear Friend,
 PICTURE YOU PERFORMING THIS MIRACLE. . . . You walk into a crowded room, take a small plastic box out of your shirt pocket, and place it on the palm of your hand. Then without uttering a word . . . without even opening your mouth, the miracle happens. The people in that room say, "How much?" and unhesitatingly reach into their pockets to buy that object from you!

Astounding? Not at all. Actually it happens all the time because that little case sitting on the palm of your hand happens to be one of the most sought after items in this country today . . . the world's lowest priced genuine transistor radio . . . the fabulous, all new REX Transistor Portable which *you* sell for the amazing low price of only $7.95 complete!

Think of it! A genuine transistor portable for a fraction of what anyone would normally expect to pay! It's beautiful! Has a gleaming plastic and gold case, plays like a dream, and is the perfect demonstration item besides! A flick of the switch, and wherever you go, crowds gather round and say, "I want one too!"

This is the dream of a lifetime . . . the self-selling, fast-moving, big-profit item you've hoped and prayed would some day be developed. And how our sales figures prove it! Our agents are chalking up record sales . . . selling REX faster, easier, and in greater quantities than anything they've ever handled before.

It's truly amazing! Hour after hour, day after day, new reports pour in. "Fabulous," . . . "Easiest seller I ever had," . . . "Making more money with this deal than anything I've sold before," . . . "Ship me more, more, more!"

It's a fabulous deal. The bonanza we've all waited for. Don't miss out on it. New men are joining up every minute. Get on the band-wagon now! There's no training, no special knowhow needed! You'll make big sales immediately . . . even bigger sales in the holiday season to come!

The REX is a "can't-miss deal" and here are the logical reasons why . . . First of all, it isn't a weird invention or an impractical gadget. The REX is a legitimate, wanted item never before available at such an incredibly low price. Second of all, you have no competition to worry about. Third, you have no involved pitch to deliver, no complicated demonstrations to give. And fourth,

THE MARKET IS VAST . . . over 10,000,000 radios sold in the U.S. last year alone!
THE MARKET IS VARIED . . . kids love them . . . teenagers are wild about them . . . sports-minded men want them for ball games, late results, etc. . . . housewives like them while they cook and sew . . . older folks use them for late-night listening.

90

THE MARKET CAN AFFORD THEM. This isn't a set that sells for $20, $30, or $40. . . . The REX is a genuine transistor portable radio complete for only $7.95!

Those are just a *few* of the reasons the REX represents such an outstanding money-making opportunity. So forget about the enthusiastic sales letters you've read. Forget about the guy in the magazine ad who says, "I make $99 an hour," or "I sell $700 worth of whosits a week," or "I earn $14,000 a year." Few if any of those hi-pressure items that supposedly sell so easily really have universal sales appeal. And that's the real reason the REX sells so much better! It appeals to everyone! Not just an automobile enthusiast or a housewife or a health-fanatic . . . but EVERYONE!

For example, right now there just happens to be a portable radio craze. Check with your local radio dealer. He'll tell you that everyone, male or female, young or old, wants a transistor portable . . . and the smaller, the better! Only one problem. Transistor portables cost 25, 35, 45 dollars and up. But stop and think a moment.

Suppose someone comes along at the right time with a genuine transistor portable so small it fits in a shirt pocket, and so inexpensive to own, it costs only $7.95 complete! And best of all, suppose that someone who has it for sale is *you*?

How can you miss? Here is the deal of a lifetime right at your fingertips! A proven item with proven sales appeal. These radios sell at a furious pace, and what's more they sell themselves! You don't go after the customers.

For the first time in your life, the customers go after you! To see one is to want one. Its' as simple as that!

And you don't have to take my word for it either! You can find out yourself without risking a single penny! Just order *one* REX radio now. Try it in your own home. Show it to your family and friends. If they don't agree it's the most amazing little radio they have ever seen . . . and still more, if they don't all want one for themselves, then forget the whole deal. Keep the set for your own amusement or send it back and I'll refund your money. You have nothing to lose but the few minutes it takes to mail the enclosed order blank.

Now surely that's a fair proposition. The rest is up to you. I've enclosed literature that tells you about the radio. I've enclosed a price list which outlines your deal. I've pointed out that this is a hot item in a hot market. If ever you've wanted a good deal, *this is it!*

You can find out for yourself by ordering your REX sample now. But don't put it off. Grab the bull by the horns! *This is the one that makes the money.* Send for your sample now!

Sincerely,
Sales Manager

What did you think of the opening paragraph? Good? You bet! It focuses on the reader, evokes his interest right from the start, puts him right into the action, and conjures up a situation every salesman dreams about. The rest of the letter flows along too, engendering interest and enthusiasm along the way. Check it off against the list and see.

The letter is *personal*, not gushy, but written in plain, straightforward, man-to-man language. It contains plenty of *you*, starting with the second word and continuing throughout the copy. In addition, it's fast moving, keeps flowing right along, and though long, isn't bogged down with extraneous detail or excess verbiage. There's plenty of *involvement*, too. The reader can easily see himself benefiting from the offer, and of course, the feeling of *immediacy* is apparent right from the start. It abounds in *superlatives*, as it should. It has a very strong *money-back guarantee*, and it has a *powerful closing* that urges the reader to action in no uncertain terms.

In short, it incorporates all those elements which combine to make a strong letter. But of course, in the final analysis the only objective criterion for this or any piece of copy is, *did it work*? Did it accomplish its mission? In this case, the answer was a resounding *yes!* It pulled a solid 9 percent on one good list and very close to that on a number of others. The overall average was around 5 percent, which is a fine return under any circumstances!

The other, and the major aspect of the portable-radio promotion was direct-to-the-consumer mail order, which was equally successful. Following is the letter used for that aspect of the operation. Note that it sells from the opening gun and continues to sell right through the postscript. This is a good letter and well worth studying carefully. It reiterates many of the selling points stressed in the brochure that accompanied it, but it does so in a more personal vein, as any good letter should. Most of its sell, however, is based on the guarantee .The letter urges the reader to see for himself, without fear of risk; and this, properly presented, is as powerful a persuader as can be offered.

Dear Friend,
    Without risking more than a few pennies . . .
How would you like to have a beautiful gleaming plastic and gold transistor portable radio sitting on the palm of your hand right now? A magnificent little radio . . .

    —so tiny, it fits in your shirt pocket or purse . . .
    —so cleverly designed, it plays indefinitely without tubes . . .
    —so economical to run, it uses just one 10¢ battery a year . . .
    —and so inexpensive to own, it costs just $7.95 complete . . .

Imagine! Not a toy, but a genuine transistor radio for a fraction of what you'd normally expect to pay! It's tiny; it's beautiful. You carry it with you wherever you go! You hear music, news, sports events, dramatic shows. Actually hold a world of glorious entertainment right at your fingertips!

It's a delight to own . . . a thrill to give as a gift because it's unique, unusual, plays so beautifully. Kids love it because it's so tiny, teenagers adore its beautiful tone, men want it for ball games and other sports events, housewives can enjoy it while they cook and sew, and the older folks appreciate it for private, late-night listening!

It's a magnificent set . . . a fabulous value made possible by the wonders of modern electronic science. And now this amazing radio can be yours to see, to play, to enjoy at a risk to you of only a few pennies!

Does this sound too good to be true? Are you wondering why we are willing to let you try this radio in your own home at such a small risk to yourself? Here are the reasons we make this unusual offer.

First of all, our radio is new, different, and we think, better-looking than any radio you've ever seen in your life. And, of course, it costs far, far less than you'd ever expect to pay for a portable transistor radio. It costs so much less, in fact, that we are afraid you may be suspicious. You may say, "How is it possible for this company to turn out a beautiful transistor portable radio for so much less than the giants in the radio industry have been able to do?" The answer is quite simple.

The REX is a blend of ingenuity and hard work. It utilizes the fabulous transistor and the germanium diode. It has a simplified circuit, it has fewer intricate parts than the average transistor radio, and it is sold by mail directly to you! In short, it is a wonderful radio . . . a wonderful value . . . a set you'll be proud to own.

But how are we going to convince you of it? How does one describe the sound of a radio in words? You see, big radio manufacturers have an advantage. Their radios are sold in stores from coast to coast. All you have to do is walk into any radio shop in America and say, "Show me all the Transistor Radios you have."

Unfortunately, we do not enjoy that advantage. We are a small company. We make only transistor radios. We don't have millions to pour into advertising. We can't afford TV shows or full page ads in expensive magazines. All we have to offer is this . . . the finest transistor portable radio, size-for-size, price-for-price, in the world today. But how can we convince you of this? What can we say?

Obviously we can't attach the radio to this letter. Nor can we send them out to people who may not be interested in a radio. That would cost a fortune. Our novel selling idea is this. We say, send for your REX now and we'll show you our appreciation for the faith you have in us by risking a lot more. We will ship this radio to your home for a 10-day no-risk trial. At the end of that time, if you're not absolutely convinced that this is the most wonderful radio you've ever used in your life, don't keep it. Simply return the radio to us and we'll refund your full purchase price immediately, no questions asked. Of course we couldn't make this offer if we weren't utterly convinced that you will enjoy using your REX radio and want to keep it always.

Now surely that makes sense, doesn't it? What better way is

there to find out about a radio than by trying it? But you must make your mind up immediately. Supplies are definitely limited, and of course the demand for radios of this type is enormous.

Why not mail the enclosed order coupon right now while it's still fresh in your mind? We know you'll be happy you did.

Sincerely,
Sales Manager

P.S. Remember . . . If someone near and dear to you has a birthday, wedding or anniversary coming up . . . or if you are the sensible type of person who plans ahead, and you want a Christmas gift that's really special, why not send for your REX now and lay it away for when you need it? If you don't you may be disappointed because these amazing radios are going so fast, they may be completely sold out when the gift season really begins.

In my estimation both these letters are superb examples of how to sell merchandise, and that contention is borne out by the sales figures.

Another very successful letter, which accompanied a reducing promotion, appears in chapter 14.

ADVERTISING ART

ART—PITFALLS TO AVOID

Except in rare and highly specialized instances, art should never dominate copy. It should be subservient to it in every respect. You will be safer if you always remember our basic premise—*the function of advertising is to sell goods!* Don't get rerouted. Winning awards for good-looking ads is fine if those ads sell. If not, forget it. If you are interested in art, buy paintings, go to museums, collect art books, but when it comes to advertising, don't finance fancy ads unless you are certain they are absolutely vital to disseminating your sales message—a circumstance that is rarely, if ever, the case.

Beware the Artistic Art Director

In order to better understand advertising art, to have a firmer grasp of what it is and why, it's a good idea to know something about the men who produce it. Who are they, what are they like, what motivates them?

Naturally, art directors aren't stereotypes, but people in certain professions often share certain characteristics. For example, virtually all art directors are more or less creative individuals. They are generally blessed with a certain sense of style, balance, and good taste. Frequently, however, they have well-developed egos, and that can sometimes be troublesome from your point of view. Pride in their ability is fine, but when they get carried away, look out! It's only natural to exaggerate the importance of one's role, but when it results in undue emphasis on one aspect of your ad, it's time to call a halt.

You have to be prepared to squelch ego. Your advertisement isn't a vehicle for artistic expression. If the art director must be an artist, be sure he doesn't take out his artistic frustrations on the advertising you pay for!

Ideally, an advertising artist should be capable of knocking out good, crisp, clean layouts. He should be reasonably fast, have a thorough knowledge of typography and production, and be a good artisan, dependable and workmanlike. And above all, he should realize that layout, design, illustration, typography, and so on—that is, advertising art—is not the end in itself, but rather a device that, in most instances, merely helps to make the message more palatable. That and nothing more!

If the advertising artist doesn't have enough self-control to keep his work from showing through, then you should control him. Let him get his fancy samples at somebody else's expense! Remember, you're the boss!

Beware the Complex Layout

The function of a layout is to present the components of an ad in the most readable and attractive manner possible in the smallest amount of space.

A good layout is one that helps to get the message across. That means no distracting elements, no diverse areas of activity vying with each other for attention. Keep it neat, simple, and sensible! Ideally, the reader should start at the headline and proceed uninterruptedly through the copy to the urge to action at the very end.

Think of it in terms of story telling. A good raconteur starts at the beginning and finishes at the end, always make sure that the message comes across loud and clear. Compare that with the inept story teller. In his attempts to embellish, he frequently goes off on a tangent, loses the thread of the story, and ends up losing his listeners entirely, or at very least confusing them.

In the same manner, complex layouts confuse the reader. They interrupt him, making it difficult for him to become absorbed in the copy story.

From the point of view of sheer readability, a short newspaper column is ideal. The headline attracts your attention and indicates whether the column will interest you sufficiently to induce you to read.

Once you start, there are no graphic devices to distract you. Down through the years a great many small ads have utilized this precise formula, apparently with success. (The fact that we see them repeated so often is our criterion.)

This basic concept is not confined to use in small space, however. The same principle works just as well for full pages. You attract with a provocative headline, start your reader at the beginning, and through the power of words—not graphic devices—carry him through to the end.

Beware the Promiscuous Use of Pictures

If you are like the average person and most advertising men as well, you are a victim of a major misconception that is distorting your view of what constitutes good advertising. I am referring to the baseless concept that all ads have to be embellished with a picture of some sort—that it is not advertising if it is not illustrated.

Essentially this notion exists because pictures attract attention, and attention achieved by any means is deemed to be an indispensable aspect of good advertising. As a consequence, it is automatically assumed that every ad has to have a picture. It is significant to note, for example, that virtually every time an ad man roughs out a projected ad, he automatically doodles in space for an illustration, often before he even knows what he wants to illustrate! He simply picks up a pencil, leaves a big space somewhere, says, "Picture goes here," and that's it! Mere habit accounts for an incredible and expensive array of unnecessary art!

Art can be a crutch of monster proportions. Think of it from the perspective of the men who have to produce the ads week in and week out, and you'll understand why.

Can't come up with a good idea? Throw in a picture. Nothing to say? Throw in a picture. Need a good attention getter? Writing a good headline isn't that easy, so why not throw in a picture? Trade publications are filled with pictures of pretty girls who don't relate to the printing presses or welding machines they are trying to advertise. Puppies, too, are used on occasion, and of course, the universal appeal of babies has never been matched. But advertising like this is most frequently utterly devoid of integrity.

Selling an advertiser an ad in which extraneous elements exist is like high pressuring an automobile buyer into a car with a fifth wheel. One has about as much function as the other. This is all the more reason why the advertiser should have a firm idea of the elements that determine whether an ad does need a picture.

Any magazine will furnish innumerable examples of the promiscuous use of advertising art. Most pictures are too large, do nothing to enhance the appeal of the ad, bear no relation to the product, or are just thrown in to attract attention—don't even do that particularly well.

With few exceptions, most advertising would be more effective if the space devoted to large illustrations were drastically reduced or, in some instances, eliminated altogether.

Bear that in mind if you ever have to evaluate an ad. Remember that from the point of view of good advertising procedure, one should start out on the premise that an illustration is *not* an intrinsic part of an ad. No advertisement should contain an illustration unless there is absolutely no question that one is required. If you run ads, see that the men responsible for producing them modify their thinking along those lines, and you as an advertiser will save a lot of money. Don't be dissuaded.

How to Tell if Your Ad Really Needs a Picture

Are you selling a fashion item—apparel, for example? Of course that item has to be displayed. Women's clothing and certain items of men's clothing provide one of the few instances in which the picture takes precedence over the copy. Here, the better—that is, the more flattering, the more enticing, the more appealing—the picture, the better the results.

Does styling provide much of the appeal of your item? Is it a car, a boat, a motorcycle, a typewriter, furniture, an appliance? Almost all hard goods depend upon styling to some degree, and since it is difficult to convey nuances of style in words, a picture is called for. But that doesn't mean the illustration has to be slopped all over the ad, nor does it mean that copy takes a back seat. On the contrary. The function of the picture in this instance is merely to show what the item looks like, to augment the words, which still bear the selling burden.

Do you sell a technical item? Is it a camera, an enlarger, or industrial equipment? A clear, plain picture of the item may be beneficial, but again, don't overdo it. Show it, not because you are trying to kill space, not because it will attract attention, but because you can tell it better with a picture than you can with words alone.

Don't make the mistake of overestimating the appeal of pictures. That old saw that one picture is worth a thousand words may be valid in certain rare and isolated instances, but for the most part it simply isn't true. To illustrate, let's take an extreme case—travel.

Now surely, much of the appeal of travel is visual. You travel to see things—white sand, aqua sea, fleecy white clouds, natural or man-made wonders, and so on. Certainly a good illustration can do much to make you feel those soft breezes blowing; but is that any reason to overlook the power of words?

If you walk into a travel agency and say, "Here I am, bored with winter," does the man behind the desk break out a picure and mutely wave it at you? Does he show you a series of pictures and display them without uttering a word? Of course not, because although the pictures may be attractive and stimulating and they may awaken a response, it takes words to be persuasive—and *to sell, you have to persuade.*

To be effective, that travel agent uses persuasive words, perhaps augmented by pictures. He gives you the information he feels you need and want, and he answers the questions he anticipates you may have. He points out the positive aspects of a winter vacation, he discusses the costs involved, and inevitably he sells along the way by emphasizing the many advantages you will enjoy. And that is precisely what an ad has to do!

Suppose, for example, that you and I had to write an ad for Jamaica. Jamaica is a fabulous island. It is 125 miles long and 30 miles wide. It has mountains seven thousand feet high and is ringed with beaches the likes of which few people ever dreamed existed—and that's just the beginning. It is a big, mysterious, fascinating island. It boasts some of the plushest, most tasteful hotels in the Caribbean, and until recently, it surely qualified as one of the dream vacation spots of this hemisphere.

In short, there are reams of fabulous material we could write about Jamaica (or any one of its Caribbean counterparts) and dozens of fascinating and appealing facts we could tell that would point up its worth as an ideal vacation spot.

Pictorially, nothing short of film would do Jamaica justice, but with words we can come a lot closer to telling the story. And of course, only with words—not with pictures—can we put the reader in the situation. Only with words can we persuade him to get up and go! What pictures, for example, can tell him he can be there just a few hours from right now? And what pictures can say it can be done for nothing down, five dollars per week (or whatever the terms happen to be)?

Now stop and think. Don't you agree that this is a better, surer way to sell the virtues of Jamaica than running a large, albeit lovely picture and a few sparse paragraphs of copy? Wouldn't you prefer to put your money on an ad that points up the specific advantages of a Jamaican vacation, rather than one that merely looks pretty but does little more than attract attention? And can't you see that if this technique is more valid for Jamaica—and it is—then it will also be more valid for whatever you are selling?

In conclusion, simply remember that pictures are valid, but unless you are selling merchandise whose basic appeal is style or appearance, don't let those pictures be the tail that wags the dog! Pictures come later, and then only to help the words.

If you have little or nothing to say, don't fill in the gaps wth pictures. Simply don't advertise.

Beware the Promiscuous Use of White Space

Among mail-order men, white space—that portion of an advertisement which is left blank or white—is generally abhorred. The reasons are basic. In mail order an ad has to produce measurable results, and since white space is never in itself productive, its use is beyond consideration. That is not to say that white space does not have a function. Actually, it has several.

First, white space helps to attract attention. It helps an ad to stand out on the page so that it will be noticed more readily and consequently have a better chance of being read.

Second, white space may be used to separate certain elements within a given ad, making those elements more readable than they would otherwise be.

Third, white space may improve the appearance of an ad. Judicious and tasteful handling of white space can enhance layout and design and thus improve the aesthetics of an ad, again making it somewhat more readable.

But now let's get back to number one. We say that white space helps an ad to attract attention, and this is perfectly valid. Every now and then someone takes out a full-page ad in the *New York Times* and puts a couple of lines of small type in the dead center, and it certainly does attract attention. But is this a good enough reason for buying all that space? Hell, no! White space isn't lying around waiting for you to use. It costs just as much money as if you had some productive copy of it!

If you want to attract attention, use a reason-why headline. Give your audience a valid reason for reading your ad, and you won't have to throw away a fortune on white space to achieve the same effect. Look through any paper or magazine and you'll see what I mean.

A full-page ad mostly white space, recently appeared on the back page of the *New York Times*. If the ad had been any smaller, it undoubtedly would not have been given the preferential back-page position. Essentially then, one could say that the promiscuous use of white space was justified in this instance because without it, the ad would probably have been relegated to the inside pages and hence would not have received the readership it did.

In rebuttal, I merely mention that it is a pretty sorry excuse for advertising that requires a client to throw away more than one thousand lines as a device to get his message read. Actually, if the major portion of the white space was eliminated, the ad would easily fit into one thousand lines without reducing one single element! As a one-thousand-line ad it would still dominate the page it appeared on and hence still be read by the same number of people. By merely eliminating the white space, this ad now becomes twice as efficient, since it now costs only half as much to get the same message across. (Incidentally, this company did not need a full page to gain prestige. They are extremely well known.)

How about using white space to separate the elements of an ad? Here, of course, the use of white space makes more sense, provided it is used sparingly. Use as much space as is necessary to keep one element from running into another, but that's all. (Incidentally, if you use a lot of small type in your body copy, try having this type set solid, indent the first line of each paragraph, and use leading only between paragraphs. This makes for much better readability.)

Now how about point number three? Does white space improve the appearance of an ad? If it is well-handled, yes, it does, at least to some degree. But why depend on white space to produce a good-looking ad? The trick is to utilize your space wisely, meaningfully, and economically and still come up with at least a neat, functional ad, if not a beautiful one.

Of course, if conspicuous consumption is your story, if you have so much money that you don't know what to do with it, and it tickles your fancy to impress the boys at the club or your wife's friends with blatant wastefulness and utter disregard for all the rules of sensible, effective advertising, then go! You can always delude yourself into believing that this is how you build up prestige for your company. But if you are trying to do an effective job, which means getting value for your advertising dollar, then think twice before you succumb to the lure of pretty white space.

Remember this, too. White space is easy to handle. The ad agency doesn't have to write words or draw pictures to put into it. And it pays just as much commission! From the agency's point of view, it is more profitable to sell you an ad with lots of white space than to fill that space with effective advertising. I am not inferring that this is consciously done, but it is a factor to be cognizant of.

To sum up, use white space sparingly. Let the art director handling your account know that you consider white space an abysmal waste of money, and maybe he'll be somewhat reluctant to use it indiscriminately. You'll still end up with some, of course, but not nearly as much as you might otherwise be stuck with.

CHECKLIST FOR A GOOD LAYOUT

Evaluating any aspect of advertising—copy, layout, headline, or whatnot—is essentially a question of "What am I trying to accomplish, and does this do it?" In virtually every instance, our goal is to sell something; therefore, the components of the ad must obviously make every effort to sell. In the case of the layout, we ask, "Is this layout helping to make my advertising message easy to read?" The following checklist should answer that question.

1. *Is it simple and straightforward?* If not, see that all extraneous and disconcerting elements are removed or toned down. If your eye jumps all over the ad, that ad is too busy and needs simplification.
2. *Does the headline pop right out at you?* The headline should be the dominant feature of the layout, immediately visible and easy to read.
3. *Is the type readable, neat, in harmony with the rest of the ad?* Running an ad with hard-to-read type is like driving a car with a dirty windshield. Don't do it!
4. *Is there a minimum of white space?* If not, reduce the size of your ad and keep reducing it until white space all but vanishes.
5. *Is the picture vital to your sales message, and if it is, is it necessary to have it this large?* If a picture isn't necessary, don't hesitate to run without one. If it is necessary, make sure it isn't any larger than it has to be.

If you can answer yes to each of the foregoing questions, it is fairly safe to assume that at very least, you have a reasonably good layout working for you. Precisely how good depends on the taste and good judgment with which the ad was put together, intangibles that no checklist can ascertain and that fortunately are not vital to an ad's success. If your layout conforms to the basic requirements, then you know it is doing the job for which it was intended, and that is what is important.

This isn't meant to imply that you are not to shoot for the ultimate. On the contrary. You want to come up with the best ad possible to produce. Suffice it to say, however, that it is far more desirable to have an ad that correctly utilizes the rudiments of good advertising procedure than one that goes overboard on handsome but meaningless detail.

DIRECT MAIL

Direct-mail advertising has always been a very effective way to get a sales message across and an ideal medium for mail-order sales. I have used it with extremely profitable results on many occasions. It is not my intention to become intimately involved in all of the highly detailed aspects of direct mail. However, I think you ought to know something about it.

Direct mail can be a great way to make money fast. It's not what it used to be, of course. Soaring postage rates and higher costs for paper, printing, mailing lists, and so on, have made it a far less attractive medium than when I was involved, but it still works with the right items, so let's take a look

WHAT IS DIRECT MAIL?

Direct mail is a means of delivering your sales message, via the mails, to an individual whom you assume to be a prospect for your product or service. Generally speaking, direct mail can be broken down into three broad categories:

1. *Mail order,* which solicits a direct and immediate sale, ideally with remittance enclosed, via the accompanying order form. (Examples are solicitations to subscribe to magazines, catalogs, specific offerings of merchandise, services, etc.)
2. *General dissemination* of information relating to a particular product or service with the object of stimulating the prospect to purchase it wherever it is sold. (Examples are coupon offerings, brochures, or other forms of sales literature sent in response to inquiries or mailed to prospects, etc.)
3. *House organs* and other institutional matter, usually mailed periodically to customers or prospects in an effort to enhance product name and image and thus ultimately create sales.

111

WHAT ARE THE ADVANTAGES OF DIRECT MAIL?

1. The prime advantage of direct mail is that ideally, you reach a specific, predetermined audience with little or no waste because you mail only to qualified prospects for your product or service.

2. You have practically unlimited space in which to tell your story. Your copy can go on for as long as you deem necessary to do an effective selling job. The only practical considerations are production costs. As your mailing increases in size, it becomes more expensive—longer copy, more type, possibly greater weight and therefore additional postage, etc. However, these considerations are generally relatively minor. If it is important to use long copy, then in all probability the advantages outweigh the relatively small increase in production costs.

3. Direct mail provides a more intimate and personal approach than does space advertising. Although some recipients regard direct mail as a bore and others as an infringement on their privacy, for the most part it remains a highly effective means of delivering a sales message.

4. A peripheral advantage, of practical consideration only in certain isolated instances, is the fact that with direct mail you can say things you might normally be prevented from saying in the general media. Within the bounds of propriety, the postal regulations, and your conscience, you are your own censor.

5. In certain instances direct mail can be used as a vehicle for testing copy or sales approaches, and even price setups, colors, styles, and other merchandising features.

IS DIRECT MAIL EXPENSIVE?

In terms of cost per thousand, direct mail is probably the most expensive medium. A black and white page in a leading magazine may cost a great deal—almost $ 50,000 in *TV GUIDE*, for example. But your message reaches millions of people, so your cost for each thousand readers is far less than the cost of direct mail.

Compare this with the approximately $250 and up that it costs to reach one thousand direct-mail prospects nowadays, and the difference seems vast. Actually, it isn't nearly as great as it appears, because unless your product has a very broad appeal, much of that magazine readership may be wasted. Not so with direct mail, because here you can usually pinpoint your audience with great accuracy and have virtually no waste.

If direct mail were not practical and profitable, it would have ceased to exist long ago. The volume of direct mail is steadily increasing, despite soaring postage and production costs; this is an indication of its efficacy as a selling medium.

WHERE DO YOU GET MAILING LISTS?

Mailing lists are rented from a large number of individuals and organizations known as list brokers. Prices range anywhere from twenty-five to thirty dollars per thousand and up, depending upon the strength of, and hence the demand for, the list, the degree of interest the list owner has in rentals, etc.

WHAT KINDS OF LISTS ARE AVAILABLE?

There are two general types of lists. One is the *compiled* list, which, as the name indicates, is a list of people in a specific category whose names have been compiled from directories, membership rosters, and other generally available sources. A list of doctors, for example, is compiled from medical directories; a list of Cadillac owners is compiled from the automotive registration files made available (for a price) by the various states, and so on. You select the category, and the list house does the rest. They obtain the latest directories and type the quantity of names you order on your envelopes or labels. Costs run in the neighborhood of twenty-five dollars per thousand or so, although some specialized lists run higher.

The second broad category comprises *mail-order lists*. These lists are composed of buyers of various mail-order products and services. They are available in an incredible array of classifications. It is probably safe to say that the name of anyone who has ever bought any product by mail reposes on some list somewhere.

Direct Mail

A good mail-order list—that is, a list whose names are particularly productive in terms of sales—is frequently a tremendous income producer for the owner. The average list now rents for about thirty-five dollars per thousand and may be rented anywhere from twelve to fifteen times a year, possibly more. Commissions run 20 percent, expenses run another 10 percent or so, and the rest is pure profit! Many mail-order operators are content to run break-even deals or worse, aware that their profits will show up in the form of list rentals.

Some names are particularly productive of sales and hence highly profitable. As an example, *Wall Street Journal* buyers, men who bought mail-order products advertised in the *Wall Street Journal*, are usually superb prospects for certain types of mail-order offers—books, interesting gadgets, and so on. For one thing, they are qualified mail-order buyers. The fact that they have bought by mail before is an indication that they are not opposed to doing so again and probably will if an intriguing offer comes along.

HOW DO YOU PREDETERMINE THE EFFECTIVENESS OF A LIST?

You can't, with any degree of precision, unless you have had recent personal experience with it or if you have absolutely reliable information from a previous user whose product or service is very similar to your own. Even then, factors such as recent mailings, particularly of a competitive nature, may render the list temporarily ineffective. The quality of a list can deteriorate rapidly. Always test. Never assume that because a list did well last time it is automatically going to repeat.

A good broker can tell you which lists are currently most effective. He bases his judgment on a number of factors:

1. Is the list generally sought after by mailers?
2. To what degree do specific mailers repeat the use of the list?
3. What results do they report with it? (Actually, knowledgeable users are rarely inclined to report results accurately, so usually the best or certainly the most objective criterion is whether they reuse the list for subsequent mailings.)

4. Is the list well maintained and administered?
    a. Are there a minimum of incorrect addresses?
    b. Is the list cleaned frequently? (Are persons who have moved or died recently culled out?)
    c. Are indiscriminate or excessive rentals avoided?
    d. Does the list owner maintain a sufficient interval between rentals to assure each mailer an adequate opportunity to make sales unimpeded by competitive offers?

Incidentally, the word of a broker is not necessarily to be taken at face value unless you know him well, unless he comes highly recommended, or unless you have some equally valid reason for accepting what he has to say. This is not meant to disparage brokers; however, in any business group anywhere, there are always individuals given to exaggeration or distortion. There is no reason to believe that brokers are any different.

Mail order can be a rough, tough, fiercely competitive business. Chicanery has been known to exist. Lists have been copied; the sources of names have been obscured or altered; lists have been salted—that is, good names mixed with inferior names to enhance the pull of the list in test mailings, to induce you to rent a continuation of the list; and so on.

Because so many possibilities for costly error exist, it should be obvious that despite the integrity of your list broker—and certainly a good one will give you much helpful advice—you must test carefully! Use relatively few names to begin with, and if the results warrant further activity, mail a larger segment, and so on, until a particular list has been exhausted.

One last word in respect to brokers. They are good sources of information, or at least they can be if they are so inclined. That isn't to say that you can walk into a broker's office cold and elicit precise information on the activities of a competitor's currently productive mail-order deals. However, brokers, particularly those who specialize in mail-order accounts, are aware of most of the important activity in the field. They maintain voluminous files replete with past and current mail-order deals and, in general, are focal points for news, scuttlebutt, and such.

Since it is their function to help you (the amount of business they do with you will be proportional to the amount of success you enjoy), you have every reason to expect whatever helpful information it is within the bounds of propriety for them to pass along.

There are a lot of salesmen in the field—for media, printers, letter shops, label manufacturers, and so forth—whose sole talent is their ability to elicit and disseminate information. This should clue you to one rather important aspect of the mail-order field. Since mail order is highly competitive, and since it usually doesn't require a great deal of effort to knock off a competitive deal or institute a similar operation, the fewer joyous tidings you spread in respect to your latest hit, the better off you will fare in the long run.

There is nothing more exciting than coming up with a winner, but why broadcast? Keep the details to yourself. There will be enough indicators of your success—the amount of printing you buy, the quantity of mail you send out, the lists you rent, the frequency with which your ad appears—all of which will soon become public knowledge. Why confirm your competitor's unhappy suspicions and whet his appetite? There's time enough to brag after your deal has waned and you are in the middle of your next success.

HOW DO YOU DETERMINE WHICH LISTS TO TEST?

The answer depends on what you are trying to accomplish. Are you trying to help elect your next-door neighbor to municipal office? Everyone in town over age eighteen is, to some degree, a prospect. Members of his political party are of course better prospects, but in any event, the names need not be highly qualified. Indeed, you don't have the time or the need to test. You put together the best mailing piece you can, send it out, and hope for the best.

On the other hand, suppose you are a national manufacturer about to embark on a nationwide sampling program. Once you have established the pulling power of your piece, you blast off with occupancy mailings. In this case your only qualifying criteria need be, do you have distribution in the geographic area in which you are mailing, and can the recipients afford to buy your product?

116

As you get into more specific areas, your problems mount. Suppose you have an item you wish to sell by direct mail. Your prime requisite is mail-order buyers. They are more productive than names on a compiled list simply because they are oriented to buying by mail.

Establishing an individual as a mail-order buyer, then, is the first qualifying step. Equally important is the question, a mail-order buyer of what? As a general rule, the closer an individual comes to being a purchaser of the type of merchandise you are offering, the better prospect he is for your product. If he bought books by mail, for example, you know he may be a good prospect for your mail-order book. And if the book he bought by mail happens to be on fishing, and you are selling a book on fishing, then he looms as an almost perfect prospect!

Let's consider the reducing field as a further illustration. Assume you are selling a reducing medication. Your prospects are overweight people. You call your list broker and ask for recommendations. He digs into his files and comes up with a set of five-by-seven cards on which are listed pertinent data—the name of the offer, its cost, the number of names available, a brief analysis of those names (sex, approximate age, etc.), and similar data of interest to you as a potential user. Among the cards you receive, there may be several that describe lists of mail-order buyers of similar reducing tablets, purchasers of various books on weight reduction, perhaps a list of mail-order buyers of large girdles or clothing, and so on.

As we have just mentioned, your best list will invariably be that of relatively recent purchasers of a reducing tablet similar to yours. Next will be the second most recent list of buyers of similar medication, perhaps followed by the latest list of large-girdle buyers. Conversely, the more remote the connection between your product and the names on the list, the less chance you have of making them customers.

List age is another determinant of a list's effectiveness. Approximately 20 percent of the population changes address each year. Deaths and other forms of attrition take a further toll. A list that is three or four years old may well have outlived its effectiveness. Then, too, the older a list, the more often it has been exploited and the less apt it is to remain productive.

Direct Mail

In the final analysis, your best guide—until you garner a great deal of familiarity with the lists in your field of interest—is your broker. Be sure he is reliable and knowledgeable! There is nothing more crushing—or costly—than to discover that the five-thousand-person test list that pulled an exciting 3 percent has suddenly dwindled to less than 1 percent when you followed with forty thousand more of what you presumed were names of the same quality.

HOW DO YOU TEST WITH DIRECT MAIL?

Direct mail is a made-to-order testing medium, and as such, it has been exploited in every possible way. Not only on copy, merchandising approaches, etc., but on every aspect of the mailing itself—size of envelope, use of stamps against metered mail, commemorative stamps against regular stamps, single-side letters against two-sided letters, first-class postage against third, and so on, ad infinitum. Since the mailer controls the medium, he is at liberty to utilize it in any fashion he sees fit.

The procedure is quite simple. On its most elemental level, it works like this. You order four thousand names from a list, for which you print four thousand mailing pieces identical in every respect but two. With two thousand pieces you include Letter A, and you key two thousand order forms or business-reply envelopes with "Department A." With the remaining two thousand pieces you include Letter B, the copy for which is different, and you key two thousand order forms or reply envelopes with "Department B." You then affix two thousand random names from List X on mailing A and the remaining two thousand on mailing B. You bring all four thousand pieces to the post office at the same time, and then you sit back and carefully tabulate the responses. At the expiration of 15 days or so, or after all significant quantities of return mail have ceased, you make an arithmetical evaluation. Whichever letter pulled best becomes the letter for your subsequent projection.

Simple? You bet! Effective? Probably, but not necessarily.

Unless the results in favor of one letter are substantially greater than those for the other, room for doubt exists. Ask any alert direct-mail practitioner and you learn that what often appear to be clear-cut differences aren't necessarily as valid as they appear.

Then too, Letter A may be better to List X, worse to List Y and even with List Z. If you had sent out ten thousand A mailings against ten thousand B mailings and discovered an emphatic difference between them, you would have had more substantial grounds on which to base a conclusion. The certainty would increase with the quantity tested. Better yet, for readily apparent reasons, if this larger test quantity were divided among a number of lists, and on each list Letter A outpulled Letter B, you could then conclude that you have conducted a valid test.

If you have more than one element to test, you must test each separately. If letter A was printed on blue stock and Letter B was printed on white, to what would you attribute the difference in pull—copy or color?

If the subject intrigues you, I suggest you read some of the current books on direct mail, which will fill you in on the intricacies and subtleties of the medium. Direct mail is a good way to go, but it is costly and tricky, so don't get into it unless you really know what you are doing or are involved with someone who does.

ANSWERS to SEVERAL BASIC ADVERTISING QUESTIONS

HOW LONG SHOULD COPY BE?

As a general rule, we can say that the longer the copy, the better the results. Obviously, your ad can't rant on forever, but the copy should be as long as necessary to make all the salient points. It should leave nothing to the imagination. Ideally, a piece of copy, like a painting, is finished when you can no longer do anything to improve it.

Of course, there are certain practical considerations. Space costs money, and there is only so much of it on a page. You can't devote endless quantities of it to any one item unless the economics are right, but that is a relatively easy decision to arrive at. The more your item sells for, the higher the markup, and the greater the potential market for that item, the larger your ad can be.

The situation is somewhat complicated if you are selling a repeat item, because then you may be willing to lose money the first time around in order to make customers. In this instance, it might be well to accertain how much a customer is worth to you and let that figure determine how much you can afford to pay for that customer. If your ad cost per new customer is less than the profit you will derive from him, you are in the black. If not, you have problems.

In any event, this aspect of advertising is academic. For the purpose of this book we assume that you know how to add and subtract. The decision whether to use large or small space depends to a great extent on the size of the market, the cost of the item, and how much you have to say in order to sell it. On the one hand, for example, we have automobiles. Here one can realistically write pages of copy of interest to any prospective purchaser. There is virtually no end of meaningful things to say, and of course, having such a high unit cost means that any given ad has to turn fewer prospects into buyers than an equally large ad for, say, soup. Automobiles, then, are obviously candidates for a large space.

At the other end of the pole, we have low-unit-cost items of somewhat limited appeal, like cough drops. At twenty-five cents a box, it is quite obvious that we can't begin to consider large space except under highly special circumstances (introducing a new product, trying to force distribution, and so on). Suffice it to say that you do best by using as much copy as you can comfortably fit into the size ad you have determined to run. This decision, because of the many variable factors, is best determined in concert with your advertising agency or possibly the space salesman and/or the examples set by your competitors, at least until you become sufficiently experienced yourself.

Again, if you remember that your ad is your salesman in print, you won't make the wrong decision. If you are selling locomotives, it might pay to let your salesman pitch for a week, a month, or a year! On the other hand, if he is selling penny whistles, look out if he does much more than shout, "Come and get them!"

HOW OFTEN SHOULD YOU ADVERTISE?

The answer depends on a great many factors. First, what kind of product are you selling? Is it seasonal? How big is your budget? Is it fixed or will it depend on the results of your ads? Obviously, circumstances dictate where you run, how frequently, and so on.

If you are running a mail-order deal, the success of your ad determines your schedule. If you have a hot ad, you run it whenever and wherever you think it will pay off. If the ad is a loser, forget it, the sooner the better.

If you manufacture a staple item that has appeal throughout the year, you advertise accordingly. If your item has gift appeal, you accelerate around Christmastime, graduation, or whatever time is appropriate to your product. Circumstances and your financial position dictate the frequency of your ad's appearance and the media in which they appear.

One thing is certain, however. If you understand the function of advertising, as presumably you now do, you should have a clearer conception of when to use it. *You should advertise only when you think you can successfully accomplish your purpose!* Let that be one of your guidelines, and you'll save a lot of otherwise wasted advertising dollars.

HOW FREQUENTLY CAN YOU REPEAT THE SAME AD?

If your ad is really a winner, then surely it bears repeating. As a general rule, it is probably safe to say that the smaller the ad, the more frequently it may be repeated, and conversely. There are a number of commonsense reasons for this. A very small ad has to sell a limited number of prospects to be worthwhile. A large ad has to produce a proportionately greater response to pay off, and since there are a limited number of prospects, they are sooner reached and exhuasted with large space than with small.

That is the classic pattern. Under normal circumstances—that is barring cataclysmic events—a large mail-order ad does its best the first time it runs and declines in effectiveness with each subsequent insertion. The extent of the decline depends on the interval between runs and on the initial pulling power of the ad. The longer the interval between runs, the more opportunity the ad has to recoup its lost vitality. Rarely, if ever, does an ad do as well the second or third time around. Suffice it to say that the pull of an ad is generally inversely proportional to the number of times it runs.

CAN GOOD ADVERTISING SELL BAD PRODUCTS?

Certainly. It happens every day. Faulty construction, inferior materials, bad design, and so on are hardly sales deterrents in the face of a powerful advertising campaign.

Unfortunately, the criterion for salability is not intrinsic merit, but rather superficial appeal. Is the product appealing? Does it look good, cute, interesting, amusing? Will having it enhance your appearance, will it increase your prestige, will it tickle your palate, will it make you more popular, more envied, more anything? These emotional appeals are more than sufficient to sell products.

The secret to selling any product, good, bad, or indifferent, is to utilize the *proper* appeals. Make the wrong sales points and you do an ineffective job on the best of products, and conversely.

HOW DO ADVERTISING AGENCIES FUNCTION?

Traditionally ad agencies derive their income from the publications in which they run ads. An accredited agency—that is, one that meets the requirements of the American Association of Advertising Agencies by maintaining a specified minimum bank balance and placing a minimum amount of advertising every year—is adjudged a good credit risk and is therefore granted a rebate of 15 percent of the gross cost of every ad it places. If the publication charge for space is one thousand dollars, the agency bills you for one thousand dollars, deducts 15 percent as their commission for placing the ad, and sends the balance to the publication.

In addition, the agency bills you for their actual production costs (art, type, etc.) plus an additional 15 percent, and if your account is small, they may charge you for other services as well.

HOW to EVALUATE ADVERTISING

I N THE FINAL analysis, you have to be capable of evaluating your advertising *before* it runs. Is it really a good ad? Will it do an effective job? Does it contain all the elements it needs to function as well as it should? This Ad Evaluator will help you to make those determinations. In essence it crystallizes the elements of good advertising contained in this book.

Obviously a chart of this type is bound to have some shortcomings. After all, advertising more closely approximates art than science and therefore doesn't especially lend itself to scientific evaluation. There are few if any blacks and whites. For the most part we are dealing with various gradations of gray, and trying to concretize them poses a great many problems. I am convinced, however, that if you use this chart properly, it can be enormously helpful. By breaking an ad down into a series of specifics, you remove much of the mystery, proceed with confidence, and have a firm basis for evaluating the components individually and the ad as a whole.

AD EVALUATOR
Layout

	YES	NO
Is it simple and straightforward?		
Does the headline pop out?		
Is the type neat and readable?		
Is there a minimum of white space?		
Is the picture vital to the sales message?		
Is it larger than necessary?		
If it shows the product, does it do so to advantage?		
Does it do justice to the image of quality and reliability you are trying to convey?		

Headline

Is it directed to your prospects? _____
Is the promise strong enough to make browsers readers? _____
Is it as specific as possible? _____
Is it as short as practicable? _____

Copy

Does it make strong promises? _____
Is it directed to prospects? _____
Does it contain enough logical reasons why? _____
Does it make comparisons? _____
Is the approach straightforward? _____
Does it present valid proof? _____
Does it contain a strong guarantee? _____
Are the statements specific? _____
Does it urge action? _____
Is the copy long enough to be convincing? _____

Ideally, all your answers should be yes. If there are any nos, there should be valid reasons for them. Sometimes it is impossible to shorten a headline for some products without weakening it considerably, or a guarantee isn't feasible under certain circumstances, or no valid comparisons can be made, etc., but by and large your ad will be more effective if all your answers are yes.

BASIC APPEALS

THERE ARE CERTAIN basic appeals that transcend time and place. Basic human needs and wants do not change readily. What was true a hundred years ago, and probably a thousand years ago, is still substantially true today. People want to be loved. They want to be respected. They want to be popular and sought after. They want to look good and feel good.

Fat people want to be thinner, thin people want to be fatter, bald men want to grow hair, and flat-chested women want to grow breasts. Short men want to be taller, and as a general rule, very tall men want to be shorter.

Men and women are always striving toward an ideal. That's part of the human drive, the human condition, and promoters are acutely aware of it. They are eager to cater to those human desires because therein lies great financial reward. Produce a product that genuinely satisfies any one of those basic needs, and mister, you've got it made!

Untold millions await the man who develops a product that really grows hair or really increases the size of the female breasts or genuinely reduces weight without diet and exercise or truly clears complexions or makes underweight persons heavier or removes wrinkles. No question about it. So far no one has even come close. Modern medical science, despite the fantastic success with which it has combatted so many serious diseases, hasn't even begun to find solutions to these basic human problems.

Of course, that hasn't stopped the promoters from trying. They were at it one hundred years ago and more, and they're still trying, still running the same old ads about reducing, backache, hemorrhoids, long, lustrous hair, lovelier complexion, more beautiful bust line, and on and on. Pick up an old newspaper or magazine from the 1870s or 1880s, and you'll be amused and amazed to see how little things have changed.

Similar ads are still running today. The copy isn't very much different, either. Human needs and desires may have been modified a bit by the passing years, but in essence they remain the same.

What can we logically conclude? Simply that substantial numbers of people have certain definite needs or desires. These people comprise vast markets ready, willing, and eager to be sold.

There are vast numbers of overweight persons who will buy anything they think will make them thin. There are vast numbers of bald men who will buy anything they think will grow hair on their heads. There are vast numbers of women who will buy anything that will give them a larger bustline, and so on, right down the list. Why am I going into this? Certainly not because I think these are areas in which you should be involved. Let's face it—your chances of coming up with a method to grow hair are obviously remote, and even if you did, you might have a hard time proving it.

Some years ago I knew a man who suffered a fairly serious heart attack. He was a diet faddist, and as soon as he got out of the hospital he went on a diet of his own creation. He lost a lot of weight and apparently enjoyed a good recovery from his coronary. He was so pleased with the results of his home diet that he concocted an organic medication based on it and proceeded to try to sell it with a direct-mail campaign.

Now, this man was perfectly sincere. He was truly convinced that his "Miraculous" recovery was a natural consequence of his self-imposed diet, and he said so loud and clear. His reasoning seemed perfectly plausible. He was overweight. He had a heart attack. He followed a special diet. He lost weight, and he felt better. If he could do it, so could anyone else, so why not say so?

The *why not* is quite simple. It's against the law. The Food and Drug Administration frowns upon claims for any drug product that are not substantiated to their complete satisfaction. They classify anything taken by mouth for purposes of health a drug, they require special licensing for its sale, and the requirements for that license are so stringent that you couldn't hope to get one without spending an absolute fortune in time and money.

134

My friend, despite his sincere belief that his diet was a blessing to mankind, was stopped cold and lucky he didn't wind up in the pokey.

You see, your conception of what is logical probably doesn't begin to coincide with what the Food and Drug people or the postal authorities think is logical. They have to protect the public, and they have laws to help them do it. Without these laws every food faddist and quack and unscrupulous character in America would be selling outlandish products to unsuspecting victims.

It used to happen all the time, and the public was much the worst for it. Before government regulations came into being, naïve men and women were being victimized to a pathetic degree. I was checking through an old 1902 Sears Roebuck catalog recently, and I could hardly believe some of the frauds that were being perpetrated . . . sure, guaranteed cures for everything from drunkenness to rheumatism, from obesity to pimples, from male "weakness" to the common cold. You name it, and that era had a medicine or a gadget that would cure it or grow it or get rid of it. No wonder the government had to step in!

Okay, if government regulations are so rigid, why do we constantly see advertising for questionable products? A few paragraphs ago we agreed that no known product will help a woman's breasts grow larger or shapelier; nevertheless, bust-development ads abound. One mail-order operator on the West Coast appears to have made vast sums of money from such ads. His customer list (which he rents) consists of many hundreds of thousands of names, each of whom has sent him at least $9.95.

What is he selling? First of all, he is not selling anything that will make breasts grow larger, nor does he claim to. His ad promises a larger, lovelier "bustline," and it is embellished with before and after photos of well-endowed young ladies. Now, you measure the bustline by placing a tape measure around the entire chest. The measurement includes the back, the pectoral and lattimus muscles, and the breasts. If the size of the pectoral and the lattimus muscles is increased, the size of the bustline is increased and the promise made in the ad is fulfilled.

To accomplish that, this man sells an exercise device—a little spring-

135

like gadget that, if used as directed, will ultimately increase the size of the bustline. And that's how its done. Now I am not relating these facts because I want to pass judgment on the ethics involved. In all probability, if a woman does increase her overall dimensions, she will look better in sweaters and blouses and so on, and if she looks better, she'll feel better psychologically and be more than satisfied that her $9.95 was well spent. I am sure that this man's files are filled with glowing testimonials. And by the same token, I am sure that he has made countless refunds to women who were not satisfied.

I am going into these details because I believe you should know and understand the means by which a great many fortunes are being built.

Another mail-order outfit, also apparently exploiting the bust-development market successfully, is selling a gadget consisting of a wire-cup-like device that fits over the breast. The user hops into the shower or bath, hooks the attached hose to the water faucet, and turns the knob. The water pressure whirls a propellerlike device in the cup, spraying the breast with fine jets of water, in effect giving the breast a water massage. I am not sure exactly what the benefits are, but you can be sure the promoter is making every claim he can legally support.

Why do advertisers keep selling products whose merits are questionable? Because those products have basic appeal. Because people want the effects those products promise and they are willing to risk their dollars, and sometimes even their health, in an effort to find them.

The ideal situation from the seller's point of view is, and always has been, to find an honest, effective product that has broad general appeal.

MAIL ORDER

WHAT ABOUT THE mail-order business? Is it really all it's cracked up to be? That depends on where you are sitting at the moment. If you have just had a series of flops, it's a rotten bussiness to be in. But when you have a real winner, it can be the most exciting, most intriguing, most fascinating business in the whole world!

I remember going to the post office one Monday morning when there were so many sacks of mail that I had to put down the top of my convertible to get them all in. I have forgotten how many thousands of orders I pulled on that one day (somewhere in the neighborhood of six thousand), but compared to what some of the TV boys are doing today, that was small potatoes. I have heard that some of those record-album offers you see advertised on TV pull sixty and seventy thousand orders and more in a single week! I have heard that one recipe-card deal on TV—which is really the powerhouse medium of all time—actually did a gross business of fifty-two million dollars in about three years.

Now, perhaps the figures I heard were exaggerated, although I got them from a reliable source. But suppose they were? Suppose it wasn't fifty-two million dollars. Suppose it was only forty-two million, or thirty-two million, or, for that matter, ten million. That wouldn't be too bad, would it?

Sure, mail order is a great business when you have a winner, but for every deal that works there are twenty that don't. For every ad you see repeated, dozens fizzle out after the first crack. For every guy who made it, a hundred are lucky to eke out a scanty, risky living.

It's easy to sit back and envy the other guy's good fortune, but can you imagine the effort involved in putting a successful deal together? Have you any conception of the time and money that are often poured into a deal? I ran into an old mail-order friend the other day—a man who has made a comfortable living for a lot of years—and during the conversation he said that he was glad to test twenty ads to come up with one solid winner. That's a worse percentage than drilling for oil, and you know how risky that business is.

Mail Order

In mail order you dream up the deal, assemble all the materials you need for it, and possibly even manufacture the item yourself. Then you spend days—or sometimes weeks—pounding out the copy, risking a great deal of money on test ads; and then, despite your confidence, despite your expertise, despite all the thinking and the scheming and the effort . . . you may well bomb out! Cold failure and frustration!

Losers are damaging not only because you've wasted time and lost money, but psychologically, too! It's never easy to accept defeat. It's not easy to admit that you were dead wrong. There are no excuses in mail order. You lay it on the line, and either the orders come in or they don't. It's as cut and dried as that. But when your ad pays off, there are few things more exciting! Once you've had a winner, you're hooked for life.

I've jotted down a few random bits and pieces of information on the mail-order business that I hope you will find informative, interesting, and helpful. Whether you get into mail order or not, consider them part of your get-rich education.

Ads in newspapers and magazines are called *space ads*.

•

Ads delivered by the postman are called *direct mail*.

•

TV is the most potent mail-order medium today, but only for products that lend themselves to quick visual presentation.

•

It is getting increasingly difficult to buy TV time for mail-order ads. TV business is good, and the stations would rather sell time to regular advertisers than to mail-order operators. Then too, the success of TV mail-order advertising is attracting more and more competition, so the laws of supply and demand are driving prices for time higher yet.

•

Record offers are ideal because they show a high profit. An album for which the public is accustomed to paying five or six dollars costs eighty cents or so, sometimes even less.

140

With a few exceptions, books have failed to sell well on **TV.**

•

Most TV promoters buy large blocks of time at cut-rate prices. The larger operators invest fortunes in anticipation of deals they haven't even begun to put together. You pay much more for time when you buy just a few spots. In any case, deals are invariably made. The key here is the time salesman or the sales manager. Get friendly, ask for his opinion and advice, and try to elicit as much information as you can. Under certain circumstances, buying time is like horse trading—the better trader you are, the better deal you are going to get.

•

All publications issue a rate card on which are printed the rates for space in the various sections of the publication. Most magazines (with the possible exception of the most successful) sell for substantially less than their card rate. You can bargain with space salesmen. The quantity and frequency with which you buy and the amount of space a magazine has open for an edition determine the degree to which they are willing to negotiate. Sometimes, when they are about to close the publication and go to press, they offer unsold space at bargain rates. In any case, don't plunge in and buy at card rates unless you are sure the medium absolutely won't sell for less.

Many magazines have space representatives who sell space for them. Representatives frequently buy up large blocks of space, which they sell for what the traffic will bear. Often they will put their own deals into magazines, which explains why you frequently see the same mailing address repeated for various offers.

•

P.I. stands for *per inquiry*. If you have a deal that looks promising, a representative of a magazine, many radio stations, and even some TV stations will work with you on a P.I. basis. They will run your ad in their medium at their expense and sell you the resulting orders at a previously agreed-upon price. You fill those orders, answer inquiries, make refunds if necessary, and do everything else necessary to run your business at your expense. Their responsibility ends once you have the order.

To illustrate further, suppose you are selling a book for $6.95 that costs you $1.50. A P.I. operator offers to sell you orders for $4.00. He runs your ad at his expense. Every time he receives an order he takes $4.00 off the top and gives you the balance of $2.95, along with that order. Out of that $2.95 you pay $1.50 for the book and $.50 for packaging, postage, labeling, and handling. In addition, you can expect a refund factor of anywhere from 5 to 10 percent, depending upon how well your buyers like the book. If you figure 5 percent for refunds, that adds another $.50 per order to your costs. At that rate, your deal has done a little better than break even. You make $.45 per book not counting your overhead.

Is that a good deal for you? It depends on the type of operation you are running. If it is a one-shot promotion and you aren't looking for repeat sales, have no other books or merchandise to sell your customers, and are not interested in building a mailing list either for your own subsequent use or for rentals, then obviously you are involved in a near loser and your alternatives are clearcut. You tell whoever is running your ad that you are not making out, and he will either charge you less for each order if he can afford to do so, or, if the ad is not pulling well enough to warrant his continued participation, he will simply cancel the deal.

On the other hand, you may find that if you have a solid book business, every customer you can get is worth three or four or five dollars or more to you. Many advertisers are happy to break even or lose on their initial sale. They make their profit from subsequent sales to those same buyers. The larger the core of solid customers they have, the more lucrative their business is over the long haul.

To sum up, one-shot offers have to pay off on their own. Deals in which repeat or additional sales are likely can afford to come in at less than the break-even point.

●

Don't pioneer. Better to be sure by going into a deal for which you know a market exists, rather than take a chance in a new area that may not appeal to potential buyers.

To find the type of mail-order items that traditionally sell well, browse over magazines that run lots of mail-order ads. List the items that appear most frequently, and you have a good idea of what sells and what doesn't.

•

Free-bonus offers increase the pull of your ad. If you can offer your audience a free bonus gift, do.

•

R.O.P. stands for *run of paper*. It means your ad will appear any-where the newspaper chooses to run it. R.O.P. ads frequently get lost! It usually makes sense to pay a premium to get your ad in a section where it will be seen. Many media experts think the TV page is tops. If a paper runs a mail-order section, that is generally the best place to appear because readers interested in mail order turn to that section.

•

Never fall in love with your own product. Emotional involvement with your own product or idea makes for faulty judgment. All your decisions should be cold, calculating, and objective!

•

Keep accurate records and maintain them daily. They are vital. Without them you don't know whether your item is paying off.

Write the name of the medium, the date the ad ran, the key number of the ad, the cost of the ad, and the number of orders required to break even at top of the page. Then, each day without fail, record the number and type of orders received.

•

Small ads can be run with some degree of regularity, but large ads soon exhaust a medium.

•

Names and addresses of publishers' representatives may be found in the Yellow Pages under the headings "Advertising—Newspaper—Pub-lishers' Representatives" and "Advertising—Periodical—Publishers' Rep-resentatives."

•

Keep a file. Familiarize yourself with what is going on in mail order by reading magazines, Sunday supplements, newspapers, etc. Cut out and file ads you see repeated, and you'll soon acquire a feel for what will and what won't sell.

•

Since the demise of the general magazines such as *Life* and *Look*, many mail-order operators are dreaming up deals for the specialized audiences reached by the specialized magazines. These include sex deals for the sex magazines, fishing deals for the fishing magazines, sewing deals for the sewing magazines, etc.

•

High-priced, high-profit items generally do better in direct mail nowadays than low-cost items because it takes fewer sales to cover the ever-increasing costs of printing, handling, and postage.

•

Don't get in the "drop-ship" mail-order business you see widely advertised. Buying stock catalogs with your name imprinted is time and money wasted. If you could sell enough merchandise to make out by mailing those catalogs, so could the guy who prints them, and what would he need you for?

The mail-order-catalog business is difficult, demanding, and highly competitive. It requires substantial backing to run successfully. A lot of very clever merchandisers have fallen by the wayside when they became involved in it. It would be naïve of you to think that you could buy catalogs (which include a large profit to the seller and cost you much more than your competition pays for theirs), mail them to lists you rent, and have them pay off.

•

You can tell it's a hot ad if you see it repeated. Nobody repeats a loser.

Beware of barely-break-even offers. If your ad pays off, you know you have to repeat it. If it flops, you know you have to abandon it. But if it breaks even, you have a problem. Maybe you can improve it, maybe you can't. Sometimes you can "break even" yourself into the poorhouse. Most mail-order men would rather write off break-even deals and concentrate on trying to develop winners.

A SUCCESSFUL
MAIL-ORDER DEAL

A LONG TIME ago, when I was relatively new to the mail-order business, I was involved in a deal that was extraordinarily successful, to say the least. In those days, as today, the first step was to find—or create—a deal. Ideally, you would like a product that has proven sales appeal and a potentially substantial profit margin and is readily available or can be easily produced and conveniently packaged and mailed. Drug products have always been appealing for these reasons. Pills are small, light, and generally easily and inexpensively manufactured, packaged, and mailed. If they really perform the function for which they are designed, and if proof in the form of actual doctor-conducted clinical tests exists, you might have yourself a deal—provided you can put together a winning ad and without making exaggerated promises or exorbitant claims.

Some people with whom I had once been associated had precisely such a product.

There were, and I am sure still are, chemists who develop drug and cosmetic products. They get an idea just the way an inventor does. They experiment, compound samples, and turn them over to doctors who test the drug in hospital clinics on as many patients as the chemists specify and pay for. The test must, of course, be conducted in an impartial, objective, medically accepted manner. At the end of the test period, which may be weeks, months, and in some instances years, the information is collected and analyzed. If the results indicate that the product works, it is offered to the trade—that is, drug wholesalers—on a royalty basis just the way any invention is offered to manufacturers.

In this instance my friends were certain they had a product they could market profitably, and as events later proved, they were quite right. Accordingly, they signed a contract with the chemists and for a small advance payment and a royalty of 5 percent of the wholesale price or, in the case of mail-order sales, for 2½ percent of the retail

147

price, they had the right to produce and market the product however and wherever they could.

The product was a reducer. In those days—the mid-fifties—the Food and Drug Administration accepted the premise that reducing products could be effective. So if you had a product that worked and could prove it with valid medical evidence, and if you sold it with a reasonable amount of restraint, you were in business.

In this case the product had a very impressive record. It had been thoroughly tested by a reputable medical doctor, and the clinical tests indicated that when taken and used as directed it did help to reduce weight and, in some instances, to a fairly considerable extent.

I checked out the medical evidence, and it looked very good. The product was safe and effective, and based on the clinical tests the doctor had run, some very positive claims could be made for it.

Now, before you envision yourself in the role of a reducing tycoon, allow me to interject a few words of caution. As far as I know, no known substance actually reduces or melts or dissolves or attacks or dissipates or burns off fatty tissue on its own merits.

Fat accumulates on your body because you ingest more calories than your body needs to live on, and those excess calories are converted into fat and stored in various parts of your body. The only way to weigh less is to eat less, forcing your body to burn off that accumulated fat in the form of energy.

That's it, period!

All any reducing product can do is help you to eat less, and this is accomplished in various ways. Some products bulk up in your stomach, making you feel fuller and thereby curbing your desire to overeat. Others claim to work directly on your appetite-producing mechanism. The prescription products your doctor puts you on (generally amphetamines) work like that. One reducer, popular for years, is nothing more than low-calorie candy that helps to dull your appetite and, hopefully, your desire to overeat. Sometimes a reducer is no more than a vitamin to keep up your strength while you follow a diet.

Incidentally, virtually all reducing products sold without prescription include a plan or regimen that is really no more than a low-calorie or low-carbohydrate diet. The pills make it easier to stay on the diet, and the diet helps you to lose weight.

Check out some of the reducers you see advertised. Notice that although they may create the impression that they are composed of some potent substance that makes fat disappear, they rarely fail to mention that the product has to be used in conjunction with a plan.

This is a sensitive area. We live in an age of flourishing consumerism, and I think that's good. The public has been ripped off too long and too frequently, and I think they need protection. Sometimes the protective government agencies may be somewhat overzealous in their efforts, but I suppose if they didn't get rough on occasion, unscrupulous operators would go wild. You have to be very careful about what you say in a medicine ad. Just because it sounds sensible and logical and truthful to you doesn't mean that it may not be interpreted in an entirely different light by some government attorney, and the penalties can be severe.

When I was involved in this deal the situation was considerably different. If the government felt that your copy was overstated, they told you precisely what they objected to and gave you a chance to defend your position before a hearing examiner. If you could present enough evidence to validate your claims and the hearing examiner agreed that your position was sound, or if you agreed to modify your claims or change them to conform with what the government felt was fair, you could continue in business for as long as you liked.

On the other hand, if you failed to defend your position to the satisfaction of the examiner and no compromise could be reached, you were obliged to go out of business. This could be a disastrous situation if you had a lot of advertising running or about to run in various publications, of if you had large quantities of merchandise on hand or in stores; but at least you didn't go to jail unless you were a repeat offender, in which case you probably deserved it.

Nowadays the situation is quite different. The government takes a very dim view of reducing products, no matter how many plans accompany them. This is especially true if they are sold by mail order. If the government believes your advertising claims are exaggerated or untrue, you may not be brought up before a hearing examiner. You may be indicted on criminal charges, and if you don't defend yourself successfully, you may very well end up in jail.

Now, I am not about to judge the system. I suppose if unscrupulous operators hadn't taken advantage of the public, there wouldn't be a need for stringent laws. All I know is that all advertising is rife with exaggerations (the advertising industry calls it puffery) and misleading statements. Lies by omission and commission are commonplace, and it's not just the little mail-order guys who are guilty. If you took the trouble to go through the Federal Trade Commission files you would be overwhelmed by the sheer quantity of large, reputable firms that have been cited for false and misleading advertising. But just because the big companies do it doesn't make it legal. It just means that they have more money with which to fight than you do.

If you plan to get involved in any type of drug operation don't make a move without the advice of a good lawyer. Be sure he understands this highly complex field (most of them don't) and be sure he checks out your copy, word for word. Just because the other guy makes strong or unfounded claims is no excuse for you to. Besides, he may end up in jail for doing it.

Okay. Now you have some conception of what's involved. Like everything nowadays, the drug business is very complex and getting more so all the time. It can be a good business and a lucrative one, but it takes a lot of know-how to make it work, and it is fraught with danger for the naïve and uninformed. When I was involved, life was less complicated. We had a product that we really believed in. Our clinical tests convinced us that it was more effective than anything then on the market. We felt we could substantiate that point of view, and we had the advice of the top lawyer in the field.

Our product worked two ways. First, it was an anorexogenic . . . that is, a substance that can dull the appetite, making it easier to eat less. Second, it was a diuretic. It removed water from the system, decreasing bloat and weight, and it did it quickly. On the basis of the product, and the claims we felt we could honestly make for it, we were confident that the deal would work. But of course, you can't tell until you test. True, some areas are traditionally better than others, and as we have already discussed, reducing happens to be one of them.

We knew there was a reducing market out there. We knew there were literally millions of overweight folks desperate to lose weight. We were sure we had the product to help them, and we were confident we could come up with an ad good enough to convince them of it. The situation was made rosier still because there were more than two million and a half good reducing names for rent at fifteen dollars per thousand, the standard rate at the time. With visions of all those fresh names dancing in our heads, we opted for direct mail, and accordingly I went to work.

I rented a large, clean loft for seventy-five dollars a month, bought a used desk for fifteen dollars, and set up my trusty typewriter, and we were in business. Or almost. I spent three solid weeks alone in that big, empty loft banging away at the copy. But when I was done I had a mailing piece that looked very promising indeed—so promising that we planned to go for broke. We had access to two hundred thousand names that we knew were all fresh mail-order reducing buyers, and because we were anxious to get fast returns and because I felt it made sense to use first-class mail (if the addressee has moved, first-class mail gets forwarded, so a greater percentage of your mail gets delivered), we took the plunge.

First-class postage was then three cents (as opposed to third class, which cost one and a half cents), so we needed six thousand dollars for stamps alone. No matter how good your credit is, no printer or mailer will spring for postage; but my associate came up with the cash, I put my house up for security on the printing, and we were on our way. You should know, incidentally, that mailing two hundred thousand pieces without a test was a very dumb move. The whole secret to mail order is careful testing. That's its primary advantage. If your mailing or your ad doesn't make it, at least you keep your loses to a minimum. But we were young and dumb and brave, and in exactly one week from the time our mail went out we knew we were rich too!

A Successful Mail-order Deal

Our deal turned out to be nothing short of fantastic, to say the least. I had been involved in a couple of mail-order winners previously, but this mail poured in like there was no tomorrow. There was just no quitting, and every list we mailed did just as well. The arithmetic is interesting. It worked something like this:

As I recall, the entire mailing, first-class postage and all, cost approximately eighty dollars per thousand pieces mailed. The breakdown went as follows. All figures are based on one thousand units.

Postage (1000 @ 3¢)	$30
Mailing list	15
Brochure	12
Letter	7
Envelopes	6
Inserting and mailing	10
	——
Total cost per 1000	$80

The product came in two sizes, selling for three dollars and five dollars. Average sale was four dollars.

3% return per 1000 equals 30 orders @ $4		$120 Gross
less mailing cost	–$80	
less refund factor of 5% of $120	–6	
less cost of merchandise		
(average cost of 50¢ X 30 orders)	–15	
Less total costs		–101
		——
Profit per 1000		$ 19

At 3 percent return we have a profit of $19 per thousand. Multiply that by two and a half million names, and the profit is $47,500.

At 4 percent the picture starts to change drastically; 4 percent return is $54 profit per 1000, or a profit of $135,000 for the entire mailing.

152

At 5 percent the profit is $85, or a profit of $212,500 for the entire mailing.

I don't recall what average return was, but I fondly remember that one list of 150,000 names pulled a staggering 13 percent!

All told, the mailing was very successful, and when I translated our direct-mail piece into a space ad, which we ran in newspapers and magazines across the country, results were just as exciting. Repeat business, the best indication that the product was effective, was exceptionally gratifying.

It was a superb deal right down the line—very exciting, very profitable. After we had the business for about a year, we sold it for $200,000 to a man with a genius for buying businesses and making money with them.

Ultimately, I am sorry to say, the Post Office Department found fault with some of the copy claims, and rather than fight the issue or compromise on the copy, our successor, who had more than recouped his investment, closed down the business.

All in all, it worked very well, and following is the copy that did it. Please note that the identical hard-sell principles utilized in this copy, and in all the copy I have ever written, are carefully presented for your use in this book.

This is the letter that accompanied the mailing piece. It was multigraphed in red and black and had a gray signature and letterhead.

IMPORTANT NEWS FOR FOLKS WHO SWORE THEY WOULD NEVER TRY ANOTHER REDUCING PRODUCT:

Dear Friend:

Here's electrifying news about the most revolutionary reducing regimen ever developed! It's brand new, completely different, proved by doctors to be more effective than ANY OTHER REDUCING PRODUCT YOU HAVE EVER TRIED OR EVER HEARD OF!

It is called _____

_____ is just like a doctor's prescription! It is a new formulation of medical ingredients never before used in a reducing product. Here is how it works three ways to help you reduce *more* pounds *more* quickly than ever before . . .

1. _____ curbs your appetite so effectively, YOU NEVER SUFFER HORRIBLE HUNGER PANGS from morning to night.

2. _____ works directly on your ugly fat. It helps nature to DIS-SOLVE fatty bloat and turn it into liquid waste which your body eliminates. YOU REDUCE FASTER THAN EVER!

3. _____ picks you up . . . gives you a lift! Helps you feel better, peppier, more alert while that fat is coming off!

With the amazing _____ you'll find it surprisingly easy to lose as many pounds as you should lose! You can reduce up to 6 POUNDS THE FIRST 48 HOURS, up to 11 POUNDS THE FIRST 7 DAYS, up to 49 POUNDS IN A LONGER PERIOD OF TIME! Even more if you like!

And you still enjoy eating . . . still enjoy luscious roasts, steaks, chops, desserts and other favorites! You won't be endangering your health with impossible-to-keep fad diets, dangerous drugs, or exercise . . . won't take huge pills and capsules three and four times a day!

You simply take two tiny tablets (one smaller than an aspirin, one slightly larger) before each meal for the first three days. After that you cut down to only one tiny tablet before each meal! What a difference between _____ and other products!

HOW _____ WAS DEVELOPED

Doctors have long known that present day reducing methods are impractical, and often impossible to keep up. They recognize the need for a new, different reducing regimen that is safe, sure, inexpensive and easy to follow . . . a method that doesn't require great will-power, fad diets, constant dosing with huge tablets, or expensive steam baths or massage. And now, for the first time, that's EXACTLY what has been developed.

You see, doctors know overweight is caused by overeating. To weigh less, you must cut down on the powerful appetite that is forcing you to eat more food than your body needs. Then, and only then, your weight will come down.

But how can you cut down on your appetite without filling your stomach with expanding pills or sickening-sweet candy-wafers all day long?

Amazingly enough, doctors had the answer right in their medicine cabinets . . . an astonishing drug which helps you to reduce more quickly and more easily than perhaps any drug known to medical science! Many doctors agree it is the very best weapon medical science has against overweight!

If this drug is so wonderful, why don't doctors prescribe it for all their overweight patients? Doctors would prescribe this drug more often if it didn't tend to make you nervous, jumpy and irritable.

But what if this drug could be improved? What if it or another with similar good features could help you rid yourself of ugly fat WITHOUT making you jumpy, cross and irritable? Wouldn't that be a blessing?

Now, after years of research and development, *exactly that has been done*! An amazing new combination of drugs has been compounded which has all the good features but none of the bad effects . . . a wonderful drug just like the one your doctor has, that will do a better job for you than anything you ever dreamed possible! It is so safe that it has been approved for sale without a prescription! And that's only half the story . . .

Included is an amazing ingredient that acts directly on the bloating water in your fatty tissue! It removes that water right at the start so that you see almost immediate results! You lose up to 6 pounds in the very first 48 hours, up to 11 or 12 pounds the first week!

Now you'll have to admit nothing you have ever tried, nothing you have ever even heard about, is this effective! Clinical tests conducted by doctors prove it! In the enclosed brochure, for perhaps the first time ever, we have printed the *actual results of those clinical tests*. They prove astounding weight losses far greater than those shown for other reducing products.

So even if you've had failures in the past . . . even if you swore you would never try another reducing product, do yourself a favor and try _____. This may be the product you've hoped and prayed science would some day discover! Don't pass it by! Let us send you a Free package to use in your own home. If _____ doesn't prove to your entire satisfaction that it is far and away the finest product you have ever used in your life, it won't cost you one single penny! But this Free trial offer is limited! You must send now!

With every regular 10-day supply you order at the regular price of $3.00 we will include a second 10-day supply at no extra cost! You get the two full-size packages for the cost of one . . . a regular $6 supply for only $3.00! And you try it at our risk! If, after 48 hours you have not lost up to 6 pounds . . . if at the end of 7 days you have not lost up to 12 pounds . . . if you don't look better and feel better, return the unused package for a full refund, no questions asked! You try before you buy! If it doesn't work the way we know it will, it costs you nothing!

This offer may be withdrawn soon. To get your FREE package send today! We'll rush your Free full-size package of _____ to you by return mail!

Sincerely,

_____

P.S. Save even more money! Order a 20-day supply of _____ (regular $5.00 package) and we will send you, absolutely FREE, a second 20-day package. That's $10 worth for just $5. You save $5. But you must act now!

Following is the copy that appeared in the brochure. It was printed in two colors, dark blue and green, on white stock. It measured seven and a half by fourteen inches and had three folds that brought it down to three and a half by seven and a half, so that it easily fit into a number-nine envelope. A separate order form and a business-reply envelope completed the mailing.

BRAND NEW!
DIFFERENT! Like nothing you have ever tried before!
NOW AVAILABLE FOR FIRST TIME!
FLUSHES FAT RIGHT OUT OF YOUR BODY!

Reduce . . . up to 6 pounds the first 2 days . . .
          up to 11 pounds the first week . . .
or pay nothing!

●

JUST LIKE A DOCTOR'S PRESCRIPTION (proved safe, proved effective)

A REVOLUTIONARY NEW REDUCING REGIMEN THAT GUARANTEES . . .
    REDUCE UP TO 6 POUNDS THE FIRST 48 HOURS . . .
    REDUCE UP TO 11 POUNDS THE FIRST WEEK . . .
without fad diets, without intense hunger, without exercise OR PAY NOTHING!

Just released! An amazing scientific discovery that melts off up to 49 pounds of ugly fat! You lose up to 6 pounds the first two days . . . up to 11 or 12 pounds the first week . . . up to 40, 50 pounds or more in a reasonable length of time, *without* A SINGLE HUNGRY MOMENT, WITHOUT GIVING UP THE FOODS YOU LOVE . . . or you pay nothing!

Yes, it's the amazing discovery you've heard about . . . the product you've wanted to try . . . now available for the first time ever!

It's amazing! It works all the time . . . while you eat, while you sleep, at work or at play, at home or away! Positively fantastic . . . so effective, your friends may barely recognize you as little as ten days from now!

Sound too good to be true? Don't take our word for it! *Prove it to yourself!* Try this amazing plan for 10 days entirely at our risk! It must work for you! Must produce the same fantastic results on your body as it has on countless others in Doctor-supervised clinical tests, *or you don't pay one single penny!*

You have nothing to lose but ugly fat! See for yourself! You be the judge! Read these scientific facts. Then take advantage of this fantastic no-risk offer!

STOP TORTURING YOURSELF! HERE'S WHY OTHER PRODUCTS DON'T WORK!

157

Here are the facts! Straightforward, hard-hitting facts . . . *just as your own doctor would tell them to you.*

Ordinary reducing plans . . . the very kind you are probably familiar with . . . cannot, of themselves, reduce your weight! *You* have to furnish the will power. *You* have to do the starving! *You* have to cut down on the foods you enjoy eating! Then, and only then, will you lose weight!

In other words, the very reducing plans you have paid $5 and $10 for, do nothing more than appease or dull your appetite! *You have to do the rest!* And it's not hard to see why. . . .

Not one of those passive reducing plans actually works on the root of your problem . . . your fatty tissue itself! Not one of those products helps *to burn up ugly fat . . . to oxidize fat . . . to actually melt that fat away forever!*

And you know it! When you took those products, you did all the work! You took pills and capsules three and four times a day! You turned down delicious foods you loved so well. You suffered week after weary week! And the results? Perhaps if you were very lucky, you lost 5 or 6 pounds.

But how long could you keep up that starvation diet? How long before you sneaked in a snack here and a snack there? How long before you were eating as much as ever? And how long before those ugly ounces and pounds of dangerous, deadly overweight came back to make your life miserable?

What next? If you are like the average overweight person, you tried another plan, and still another. And the results? Always the same heartbreaking story! Little or no loss in weight! Little or no lasting effect. Then what did you do? Were you like the men and women whose utterly amazing case histories were reported in our clinical tests? Did you discover a better, more effective way to reduce? WITHOUT TORTURE? WITHOUT FAD OR STARVA-TION DIETS? WITHOUT THE NEED FOR TREMENDOUS WILL POWER?

THANKS TO THIS AMAZING DEVELOPMENT, YOU CAN REDUCE FASTER AND EASIER THAN YOU EVER THOUGHT POSSIBLE!

Doctors had the answer . . . a reducing regimen identical in principle to the one more doctors prescribe than any other . . . an amazing combination of ingredients medically proven to be the greatest aid for the elimination of excess fat ever as proved in astonishingly successful clinical tests!

Not a bulk-producing agent . . . *not* a sweet wafer supposed to "kill" your appetite . . . *not* giant pills or capsules, this astounding compound is *like nothing you have ever tried before,* because it has just been made available for the first time ever!

It is guaranteed safe, guaranteed effective, guaranteed to perform not one, not two, but all *three* functions necessary for quick easy, *comfortable* weight reduction! This is what it does . . .

1. _____ flushes away the bloat-like water that makes up to 70% of your fatty tissue! It goes to work the very first day . . . removes that water . . . makes you lose weight fast! Makes you see and feel results almost instantly!

2. _____ actually gives you a boost . . . makes you feel peppy and alert. Helps you overcome that tired, dragged-out feeling. Actually may help you feel more vibrantly alive than you have felt in years!

3. _____, without filling your stomach with sluggish bulk, works internally on the true center of your appetite! You still enjoy your food, but you have less desire to overeat, and you find it easier to do without fattening, unwholesome extras that are making you fat.

No wonder that when _____ was tried on overweight patients in hospitals, results were so astonishing!

POUNDS GONE FOREVER!

Here are the amazing facts! Read them carefully. Think of what they mean if you are a person who must lose weight!

When doctors testing this amazing product on overweight patients, they did not tell those patients to go on a diet! They did not tell those patients what to eat! They did not tell those patients how to eat!

159

Those patients lost pound after pound of ugly fat . . . up to 12 pounds the first week . . . up to 39 pounds the first month, up to 49 pounds in a longer period of time! Day by day, safely and more quickly, more easily than ever before, their ugly, health-destroying pounds started to melt away!

While they were eating three delicious meals a day, they were losing weight. While they were enjoying mouthwatering steaks and chops, juicy roast beef, vegetables and deserts, bread and butter . . . while they ate the foods they liked, off came ugly inches from waist, hips, thighs, everywhere!

And best of all, in case after case, they actually said they felt better . . . had more pep, more energy, more vitality than they had in years!

And when the tests were over, those men and women showed remarkable weight losses. And they did it without discomfort, without diets, without horrible hunger! It was like a wonderful dream come true! They had actually turned back the clock . . . made themselves look more youthful and even feel more youthful than they had in years!

And what's more, they could stay that way! . . . could continue to keep their weight under control, for as long as they wanted to . . . even the rest of their lives! Because now they had an active fat-reducing regimen available that would actually help keep ugly fat away!

PROVE IT TO YOURSELF! TRY FULL PACKAGE ENTIRELY AT OUR RISK!

Now you can try this very same tested and proven plan in the privacy of your own home without risking one single penny!

This amazing plan must melt up to 6 pounds of ugly, excess fat right off your body in the first two days . . . up to 11 pounds in the first 7 days . . . or you don't pay one single penny!

These are not idle claims. These are not exaggerations. Your own doctor will tell you the same thing! This plan was proven almost 100% effective in doctor proved hospital tests! It worked for countless other normally healthy overweight folks and it will work for you!

A Successful Mail-order Deal

For the sake of your health, for the sake of your appearance . . . even to prolong your life . . . you owe it to yourself to reduce! And in the opinion of our experts the very best way to do exactly that is with the aid of the _____ lo-calorie plan.

Now we have done everything humanly possible to make it easy for you. We have presented you with the opportunity to obtain, for the first time ever, the same type of medication doctors prescribe for overweight patients. The rest is up to you. If you really want to reduce, you can. So right now, fill out the enclosed order form, and mail it in the postage-paid envelope provided. You'll be happy you did! If you are not absolutely delighted, your money back, no questions asked. You have nothing to lose but ugly fat!

•

READ THESE ASTONISHING RESULTS OF CLINICAL TESTS CONDUCTED BY DOCTORS!
No other product ever prints actual clinical test results, because no other product can show such astounding weight losses!

1st week up to *12 pounds lost*
2nd week up to *24 pounds lost*
4th week up to *39 pounds lost*
6th week up to *44 pounds lost*
8th week up to *49 pounds lost*

These tests were conducted by doctors on average, normally healthy overweight persons. Those men and women were NOT told to diet . . . were NOT told what or what not to eat! All they did was TAKE ONE TINY TABLET SMALLER THAN AN ASPIRIN, BEFORE EACH MEAL . . . yet their weight losses were almost unbelievable!

THIS IS THE MOST POWERFUL PROOF YOU HAVE EVER SEEN FOR *ANY* REDUCING REGIMEN! NO OTHER PRODUCT SOLD IS AS EFFECTIVE AS _____. SEND NOW AND SEE!

•

_____ IS SAFE!
_____ is a safe, tested product proved effective by doctors. It cannot harm your heart, lungs, liver or other vital organs. Any nor-

161

mally healthy person may take _____ as directed, with complete confidence, content in the knowledge that it cannot be harmful.

•

HERE ARE FACTS YOU SHOULD KNOW ABOUT _____.

WHAT IS IT? _____ is a scientific combination of safe drugs which works just like a doctor's prescription to help you lose weight.

HOW DOES IT WORK? _____ works three ways to help you reduce quickly, safely and easily.

1. _____ draws off and flushes out the weight-adding bloat-producing water that makes up to 70% of your fatty tissue.

2. _____ inhibits your appetite without bloating your system with bulk material.

3. _____ makes you feel better, more peppy and alert . . . actually gives you a life while those pounds are coming off!

HOW DO YOU TAKE IT? _____ is a tiny tablet smaller than an aspirin tablet. For the first three days you take two tablets before each meal. After the first three days, you take only *one* tablet before each meal.

IS IT SAFE? _____ is not a dangerous drug, not a laxative, not a thyroid extract, not a bulk-producing medicine! It is a safe, doctor-tested product made of pure, medically approved ingredients. Any normally healthy person may take _____ as directed with complete confidence because it cannot harm you in any way.

When you follow the _____ plan, you do not have to do backbreaking exercises, you do not have to go on a fad diet, you do not have to give up all the foods you love to eat, you do not have to take giant pills and capsules, powders or sweet wafers all day long!

You simply take one or two tiny tablets (smaller than aspirin tablets) before each meal! No other product is so easy to take!

•

WHY YOU SHOULD TRY _____ . . .
EVEN IF YOU PROMISED YOURSELF YOU WOULD NEVER TRY ANOTHER REDUCING REGIMEN AGAIN!

Are you a person who has tried everything? . . . giant pills and

162

capsules 3 and 4 times a day? . . . fad diets? . . . powders and sprinkle on food? . . . exercise? . . . gadgets and gimmicks? . . . everything and anything that promised freedom from those extra pounds of fat that are spoiling your figure and endangering your health?

Are you a person who swore you'd never try another reducing plan? Stop and think a moment. Wouldn't it be a shame if _____ was really the one product that could help you, and you didn't at least try it?

You see, regardless of what you think, regardless of how many times you have been disappointed before, _____ really works! Really does everything we claim it will! It's safe, it's quick, it's easy! In doctor-supervised clinical tests, it was proven to be astonishingly successful!

And no wonder . . . For it is the only reducing regimen sold that is really like a doctor's prescription. It flushes away bloat, it keeps you from feeling hungry, and it actually picks you up and makes you feel better than usual while those ugly pounds are coming off! And how they come off—actually faster than ever before!

So don't miss out on this opportunity! Don't turn back now! Even if you have been disappointed before, now you are within sight of your goal. Think of how wonderful it will be to look better and feel better . . . to really be slimmer and trimmer than you have been in years? That's the opportunity that now awaits you! And you can do it all without risking one single penny! Simply send for _____ now.

Try it for as long as you like. If you are not satisfied, you are under no obligation to keep it. All you do is mail back the unused portion and get your money back immediately, no questions asked. You are trying, not buying. If you don't get the results you hoped for, you have paid nothing, and at least you have had the satisfaction of trying this amazing new product. You have nothing to lose but ugly fat!

So don't put it off. Act on that impulse! Determine to help yourself . . . determine to have the slim, youthful-looking figure that amazing new _____ can help you obtain. And do it now! It only takes a minute to fill out the enclosed card and mail it in the postage-paid envelope provided. If you are not delighted in every way, all you will have lost is a few minutes of your time. You know we must have great confidence that _____ will help you or we could never afford to make this spectacular no-risk offer. So why not send now?

•

MONEY BACK GUARANTEE

Use a whole package of _____ in your own home at our expense!

If the _____ plan doesn't help you lose up to 6 pounds in the first 48 hours . . . up to 11 pounds the first week . . . If it doesn't make you look better and feel better . . . If you aren't completely convinced this lo-calorie regimen is the quickest, best way to reduce you have ever tried, don't keep it! Return the unused portion and we refund your money immediately, no questions asked!

It must work just the way we say it does, or you pay nothing!

•

SPECIAL *FREE* INTRODUCTORY OFFER . . .
BEFORE _____ IS SOLD IN DRUGSTORES FOR REGULAR PRICE OF $3.00 & $5.00

buy 10-day supply (regular price)	$3.00
get FREE 10-day supply (regular price)	$3.00
TOTAL VALUE	$6.00

YOU PAY ONLY $3.00
YOU SAVE $3.00
or

buy 20-day supply (regular price)	$5.00
get FREE 20-day supply (regular price)	$5.00
TOTAL VALUE	$10.00

YOU PAY ONLY $5.00
YOU SAVE $5.00

OFFER GOOD FOR LIMITED TIME ONLY!

IF NOT DELIGHTED IN EVERY WAY, MONEY BACK IMMEDIATELY, NO QUESTIONS ASKED!

INVESTORS INTELLIGENCE— FROM 0 to 25,500 SUBSCRIBERS at $36 PER in FOURTEEN MONTHS

SOME YEARS AGO I was the principal in Investors Intelligence, which, if you have been in the stock market, you may remember. It was a "comprehensive and authoritative semimonthly summary of all outstanding features reported by the leading investment services." In short, kind of a *Reader's Digest* of current stock-market opinion culled from various investment services, condensed, and sent to subscribers every other week.

It was a superb idea, as you can plainly see, the brainchild of a good friend of mine who happens to be not only an excellent and most prolific copywriter, but probably the leading authority on financial and related advertising anywhere.

Up to this point I had never written any financial copy, not that it mattered. I believed then, as I do now, that copy is copy and people are people, and hence no special techniques or approaches are required. In this I was hotly disputed. The experts in the field advised me that buyers of financial services were more sophisticated, more intelligent, more this and more that. I never doubted the wisdom of these erudite pronouncements, but the fact remained: Market speculators were still people and hence still motivated by the same basic appeals.

With this firmly in mind the copy was written, the ads were placed, the direct mail was sent out, and the results poured in! The copy worked extremely well. In direct mail the better lists pulled as high as 3 percent and better, which is a very gratifying return.

The arithmetic makes interesting reminiscing. At 3 percent we grossed approximately $1,080 per thousand brochures mailed. Subtract $80 per thousand for the mailing costs (which included printing, inserting, postage, and mailing), and that leaves us with a round figure of $1,000. From that subtract the cost of fulfilling each of the 30 subscriptions we sold. They cost around thirteen dollars each over the course of the year, or $13 times thirty. That's $390 for fulfillment, leaving us with approximately $610. Deduct 5 percent of the gross figure for refunds (around $50, although actually the figure was substantially less), and at 3 percent we come up with a net profit of approximately $560 per thousand brochures mailed.

Of course, all lists weren't that productive. The overall average on the first mailing of about 250,000 pieces was around 1½ percent, still a mighty healthy return. Subsequent mailings with the same copy to the same lists and to weaker lists, which were normally marginal at best, still produced substantial although gradually diminishing returns. It is interesting to note that in a little more than a year we built a membership of some 25,500 investors, which made us one of the three or four largest investment services in the world!

The point, of course, is that good copy can be eminently rewarding. Read it and see what you think. Note that this copy is hardly what you would call sophisticated. It is typical, hard-sell mail order, and there is plenty of it, plenty of detail, plenty of reason why. Nothing is left to the imagination, and nothing should be. After all, when you are asking people to send thirty-six dollars to a company they never even heard of, you have to motivate them strongly, and that is precisely what this copy does.

All the arguments—and there are plenty of them—are simple, basic, and logical. No concessions are made to the alleged affluence or intelligence of the audience. It was assumed that as investors they were interested in making money in the market, and they were approached from that point of view and no other.

As an extra convincer, and to bolster their confidence, they were offered a solid, money-back guarantee. *"If not delighted anytime during the entire year, your money back completely and without question."*

The theory, which was subsequently borne out, was that a year's guarantee was no more risky than a month's guarantee. If a customer was dissatisfied, it was believed that his dissatisfaction would manifest itself early, perhaps after one or two issues, and in this we were substantially correct. There were few refund requests, and most of these occurred in the early stages of the subscription. In any event, we were sure that the generous nature of the guarantee helped create far more sales than might normally have occurred.

The mailing consisted of a two page letter, order form, business reply envelope, and the following brochure which was approximately seven inches high and fourteen inches wide. Three folds brought it down to a neat three and one half by seven inches in size.

(a)

NEW

INVESTORS

INTELLIGENCE

(b)

**CONDENSES OUTSTANDING RECOMMENDATIONS
OF ALL LEADING SERVICES AND
BROKERS IN ALL FIELDS OF INVESTMENT
INTO ONE COMPREHENSIVE REPORT!**

(c)

**OVER $4000 WORTH OF SERVICES PER YEAR
. . . NOW YOURS FOR A FRACTION OF WHAT YOU
WOULD PAY FOR JUST ONE SERVICE ALONE!**

(d)

**FULL YEAR'S NO-RISK TRIAL
AS EVIDENCE OF OUR CONFIDENCE IN THE VALUE OF THIS
UNIQUE NEW SERVICE, CHARTER SUBSCRIBERS ARE OFFERED
A FULL YEAR'S GUARANTEE**

(e)

**PLUS
SUBSTANTIAL CHARTER SUBSCRIPTION SAVINGS!**

(f)

INVESTORS INTELLIGENCE GIVES YOU A THOROUGH, AUTHORITATIVELY EDITED DIGEST OF RECOMMENDATIONS FROM LEADING INVESTMENT SERVICES, BROKER'S NEWS LETTERS AND OTHER SOURCES

(g)

If You Had Received Investors Intelligence This Morning, You Would Know Which Are Now the Most Highly Recommended Stocks, Which Special Situations Are the Most Promising, What the Funds and Institutions are Buying, and Everything Else of Special Importance In the Field!

(h)

At last! No more jumping from service to service! No more wondering whether the information you get is really valid! No more wondering whether you are missing out on important new market developments!

Now you can get a thorough digest of *all* the leading investment services . . . all the vital information they provide, the special advice they offer, all the important recommendations and opinions they come up with, yours not for the $4,000 or so it would cost if you bought those services individually, but for a fraction of what you would pay for just one service alone!

This is the first truly comprehensive service to come along in years. . . . It's new, different, now being offered to a limited number of subscribers for the first time ever!

EASY TO FIND WHATEVER YOU WANT!

Whatever your interests, here you find the vital, profit-making facts you need right at your fingertips! Are you interested in special situations? Scan the Special Situation section and you have the best of all the available information right at hand. Want to know which stocks are currently most highly recommended by the services? Turn to the Most Recommended section, and there it is right before your eyes. Looking for a stock with real capital gain poten-

170

tial or a solid long-term stock for income? Do you dabble in warrants? Does the commodity exchange intrigue you? Would you like to know a little more about tax-free bonds? Here it is . . . all the solid, useful information you need for sound, money-making investment!

No wonder the editors of INVESTORS INTELLIGENCE are so excited about this unique new service! No wonder investors who have examined advance copies are so enthusiastic! For here, between the covers of each issue, is a wealth of information and advice never, ever before available from any single source!

THINK OF WHAT INVESTORS INTELLIGENCE CAN MEAN TO YOU!

Imagine! Every two weeks you get a thorough summary of the best recommendations of the leading investment services! You get the best of their expert advice on all the subjects they cover such as:

- Stocks to buy for Speculation, Capital Gains, Income
- Special Situations
- Stocks Most Recommended by the Analysts
- Rights and Warrants
- What the Brokers are Recommending
- What the Funds are Buying
- Bonds
- Current News
- Technical Background
- Commodities, plus a wealth of other valuable data

You get all the facts, all the vital information on every phase of the investment field, wrapped up into one complete package and placed in your hands every two weeks, for less than the cost of a single good service alone!

And most important to you, this vast wealth of data is edited by experts . . . men whose intimate knowledge of the field, whose experience, mature judgment and critical eye can pick the wheat from the chaff, detect trends and help guide you down the path towards successful investment.

Think of what that can mean to your profit picture! *One service that reviews and edits for you the best features found in all the*

171

others . . . so comprehensive, you'll never have to go to another source for financial information again, so reliable, you'll be able to buy and sell with complete confidence, secure in the knowledge that no angle has been overlooked, no stone left unturned!

LIKE HAVING YOUR OWN STAFF OF EXPERTS!

Having this service mailed to you regularly is the same as hiring a personal staff of experts. . . . The same as saying to those experts, "Subscribe to all the leading stock services regardless of cost. Find out what the brokers are recommending and what the funds and institutions are buying. Save the important advice and throw away the padding. Compile this data, summarize it, evaluate it. Then transpose it into neat, plain language. List the recommended stocks and the reasons why. Tell me how many experts are for and how many against. Give me their advice on special situations, rights and warrants, convertible bonds, etc. Report on everything you think is important in easy-to-understand, plain language! I don't want vague, wishy-washy general information! I want specific facts . . . solid, concrete advice I can put to work to make money for me!"

Having INVESTORS INTELLIGENCE at your finger-tips is just like that! No wonder it can do more to help you than any service you've ever subscribed to before! You don't get just one group's opinion . . . you get the pick of the opinions of the top experts in the entire field! And that can be vitally important!

Suppose, for example, that you now subscribe to a good service that recommends a particular stock, but at the same time, four equally reputable services rate the stock low. Unless you happen to subscribe to all of those services instead of the one, you might buy in, never knowing that *most* of the experts don't think much of your chances.

Having INVESTORS INTELLIGENCE would have made that situation crystal-clear for you!

Or suppose the reverse was true. Suppose, as a subscriber to INVESTORS INTELLIGENCE you see that seven or eight services recommend a given stock. Wouldn't you buy with a lot more confidence than you would if you only subscribed to one service?

SOME SERVICES CAN'T SEE THE
FOREST FOR THE TREES

Stop to think for a moment, and you'll realize this makes good sense. For example, do you remember the story of the three blind men who were asked to describe an elephant? The first, fingering the trunk, described the elephant as a great, writhing serpent. The second, running his hand over the elephants' side, described the animal as a huge, rough wall. And the third, holding the tail, was certain the elephant was a thin, snake-like creature. All of those men were sincere. All meant well. *But each was a little too close to a particular part of the beast to give an accurate evaluation of the animal as a whole!*

How often is that true for the particular investment service you subscribe to? Does your service tend to be a bullish or bearish? Do they favor blue-chips or recommend speculations? Are they naturally optimistic, or are they purveyors of doom? *Their* likes or dislikes, *their* prejudices or quirks, can cost *you* money!

Isn't this area too important to depend on just one service for advice? Doesn't it make sense not to put all your eggs into one basket? Just as you diversify your holdings, shouldn't you also diversify your sources of information?

Now, you can do exactly that for just a fraction of what it would normally cost! We, in effect, sort out and condense the advice of the experts for you! We cull out the good and throw away the bad. We present you with the nuggets of solid information you need and discard the rest!

If you did that yourself by subscribing to each of these services individually, your yearly cost would be well over $3,000. But now you get this very same information stripped of excess verbiage, stripped of obtuse meanings, objectively analyzed and succinctly presented in plain, unmistakable language for just a fraction of what you would normally expect to pay. It's the solid, money-making information you need and should have right at your fingertips! Information that can help make a fortune for you!

And best of all, it is now available to you at a substantial savings! As one of a limited number of Charter Subscribers, you will actually save a full 25% over the regular yearly subscription price!

FULL YEARS NO-RISK TRIAL

To prove our sincerity . . . to demonstrate the tremendous confidence we have in this unique service, we make this unprecedented offer. . . .

Become a Charter Subscriber to INVESTORS INTELLIGENCE now! Use your valuable reports for a full year. Then if you don't agree that INVESTORS INTELLIGENCE is far and away the most valuable service you have ever subscribed to . . . if it hasn't been worth every penny you paid, or if you are dissatisfied for any reason at all, simply let us know and we will refund your full purchase price immediately, no questions asked. You must be completely delighted in every way, or even after a full year's subscription you can have your money back and INVESTORS INTELLIGENCE has cost you nothing!

Now surely you'll agree that is a fair proposition. We certainly wouldn't make the offer if we weren't sublimely confident you will appreciate each issue. The rest is up to you. If you would like to participate in this unique service, don't hesitate or delay. Right now, while it is still fresh in your mind, fill out and mail the enclosed Charter Subscription blank and mail it at once in the postage-paid envelope provided.

●

(i)

HERE IS THE SPECIFIC INFORMATION YOU GET IN INVESTORS INTELLIGENCE!

STOCKS

Stock coverage is comprehensive. You get multi-faceted information and advice on every phase of the subject as reported by the leading investment analysts. These regular features include . . .
- Stocks for speculation
- Stocks for long-term capital gains
- Stocks for appreciation
- Outstanding current buys
- Stocks most frequently recommended by the various market letters in the past 2 weeks.
- Investors Intelligence's own detailed recommendations based on thorough studies of all data presented by the various investment services.

174

You actually get more thorough, more comprehensive coverage than any single service could possibly give you.

BONDS

You get a complete breakdown on convertibles, tax-free bonds, municipal issues, etc. . . . which are considered best buys, and why!

SPECIAL SITUATIONS

Each issue of INVESTORS INTELLIGENCE contains a section devoted to special situations. Here you will find comprehensive coverage of at least one special situation whose profit potential is considered sufficiently attractive to merit inclusion. Additional special situations are included when warranted.

RIGHTS AND WARRANTS

A full section on rights and warrants appears in every issue.

These frequently attractive offerings are of special interest to the sophisticated investor. The huge profit potential possible in a relatively short period of time dictates their inclusion in INVESTORS INTELLIGENCE.

THE FUNDS AND WHAT THEY ARE BUYING

This feature can be quite profitable. For here you see exactly what the Mutual Funds with their huge resources are buying. This keen insight into the buying patterns of some of the shrewdest analysts on the street can prove of incalculable help in your own investments.

WHAT THE BROKERS RECOMMEND

This exclusive feature condenses the best of the advice and information appearing in the dozens of news letters and services issued by the leading brokerage house to their private mailing lists. An invaluable aid, it rounds out your financial picture . . . provides you with timely tips, and in general acquaints you with the basic thinking of these knowledgeable professionals.

NEWS BRIEFS, ECONOMIC BACKGROUND, ETC.

Here you find timely and interesting tips and information calculated to paint a broad picture of market conditions in general and of certain issues in particular.

Also included are sections on COMMODITIES, PUTS and CALLS, STOCK-SPLIT CANDIDATES, FORMULA PLANS and much other information of interest.

●

(j)

THE SELECTED ADVICE OF OVER $4000 WORTH OF MARKET SERVICES

Annual Cost of

60 Investment Services $3715
22 Financial and Business Periodicals 315
75 Broker's News-Letters ....—

TOTAL COST $4030

YOUR CHARTER RATE—$36 for Investors Intelligence, Inc.
CHARTER SAVING and 1-Year No-Risk Guarantee

Under this Charter Offer you not only save 25% from the established $48 annual fee—but you risk not even the low Charter Rate.

Full refund is guaranteed anytime during the year. Send for your No-Risk Charter Subscription today!

Full Year's
NO-RISK TRIAL

Send for INVESTORS INTELLIGENCE now! Use it for one full year. If you are not absolutely convinced INVESTORS INTELLIGENCE is far and away the most valuable investment service you have ever used. . . . If it isn't everything you have expected, or you are dissatisfied for any reason, your full purchase price will be refunded at anytime during the next year. You must be completely satisfied or you pay nothing!

INVESTORS INTELLIGENCE, INC.
2 East Avenue, Larchmont, N.Y.

Please enroll me as a Charter Subscriber to INVESTORS INTELLIGENCE for one year at the special Charter Rate of only $36 (I save $12). I understand that if I am dissatisfied for any reason—even after a full year—you will refund my full subscription price, no questions asked!

(Please Make Checks Payable To
INVESTORS INTELLIGENCE)

☐ Payment enclosed. (Extra month FREE because by enclosing payment I save you billing expense, etc.)
☐ Bill me.

(PLEASE PRINT CAREFULLY)

NAME _____

ADDRESS _____

CITY _____ ZONE _____ STATE_____

●

(k)

AN UNPRECEDENTED
NO-RISK OFFER!
PLUS
BIG CHARTER SAVINGS OF 25%
Because we are convinced INVESTORS INTELLIGENCE
will do more to help you realize greater
investment profits than any service you
have ever used, we made this unusual offer . . .
NO-RISK TRIAL
for a
FOR A
FULL YEAR

Regular Subscription $48
Charter Subscription 36
YOU SAVE $12
You get 24 issues plus extra bulletins, etc., whenever warranted!

AN ANALYSIS OF THE INVESTORS INTELLIGENCE COPY

It should be immediately apparent that the nine important copy elements previously discussed are plainly evident here. The solid, *reason-why* copy makes a strong *promise*. It is unmistakably *aimed at prospects*. It is certainly *straightforward* and *specific*, makes frequent *comparisons* to other services, attempts to *prove the claims* it makes, *urges action* in no uncertain terms, and wraps it all up with an emphatic and liberal *guarantee*.

Superficially, then, this piece complies with our basic requirements for good copy. The sum total is persuasive. It does a strong selling job, which is precisely its function. Now let's take it a step further and see what actually motivated each segment of the brochure.

To begin with, this format was chosen for several reasons. For one thing, I believe it lends itself to easy, uninterrupted reading. It starts at the beginning and ends at the end. The reader's progress is unimpeded by fancy folds, tricky art, other diversions. Then, too, I believe that this format has retention value, or at least greater retention value than other, larger formats. I have nothing to base this contention on, however. It is prompted more by feeling than by scientific fact. I suppose that because it is neat and small and somewhat resembles a booklet, I feel it is less likely to be quickly discarded than a more cumbersome folder. This is a plus, perhaps minor, but a plus nevertheless. Incidentally, it is interesting to note that a surprising number of orders was received on the brochure-attached form, which seems to lend credence to the theory that the brochure itself was retained after the rest of the material was disposed of.

a) The average investor is deluged with investment-service offers. It was important that he realize this was a *new* offer, one he had never seen before. The name *Investors Intelligence* prominently displayed would help achieve this end.

b) Tells the essential nature of Investors Intelligence and precisely what it can do for the reader.

c) A strong and provocative selling statement, it tells the reader a little more specifically what he is going to get and it emphasizes the bargain aspects of the offer.

d) The exceptional nature of the guarantee—a full year—builds confidence in the offer and in the fairness of the company making it.

e) Just a little more sell again emphasizing the bargain aspects of the offer. (In this day of discount merchandising, few are the individuals who don't enjoy—or expect—bargains, some because they need them, others because if they don't get them, they feel taken).

f) Again, but in different words, a succinct and complete summation of the offer. If the reader were to stop at this point, he would still be completely apprised of the nature of Investors Intelligence.

g) Involves the reader directly, gives the entire situation a sense of immediacy, enables him to envision the benefits of being a subscriber.

h) The copy reads fairly well, races right along, and tries to anticipate the reader's desire and answer his objections. Note, too, that this is more than a mere delineation of facts and figures. Throughout, an intense effort is made to convince the reader that Investors Intelligence will help him, and he is urged to take advantage of this help by subscribing.

Note, also, the strong closing. We made a firm and impressive guarantee, and we wanted the terms and advantages of that guarantee firmly implanted.

i) This panel itemizes all the information and advice the subscriber will find in Investors Intelligence. It is important for several reasons. First, it sums up precisely what the buyer is going to get for his money. Second, it substantiates the contention that Investors Intelligence is thorough and all-embracing by demonstrating just how far-ranging it actually is. Third, it appeals to readers who may not care for the overall concept but who may have an interest in a specific aspect of the market about which they would like more advice. By listing all the features, we thus increase the possibility of making customers who might otherwise have been lost.

j) This is a duplicate of the regular order form that accompanied the mailing. Unless I have copy of importance for which there is no room elsewhere, I generally repeat the order form on the brochure for three reasons: (1) In a sense, it reiterates the offer in specific terms, and it includes the exact guarantee; (2) if the brochure is passed on to a friend, the order form is available; (3) if the regular order form is lost or the inserting machines fail to include an order form in the mailing (a rare but occasional occurrence), no problem ensues.

k) These panels merely spell out the offer in a more graphic fashion. Although neither panel is essential to the mailing, their inclusion can't possibly hurt. There is no harm in repetition. There is in omission.

When the same copy was run in the financial section of the *New York Times*, it did fabulously well again. We used a number of approaches, both in direct mail and space, but nothing ever pulled with the vitality of this copy.

179

THE
DEPRESSION BOOK

IN 1972 I BECAME involved in a book deal that worked out rather well. If you read financial newspapers or magazines, you may remember it. The book was called *How to Beat the Depression That Is Surely Coming*, and it was written by Doctor Robert Persons, Jr., a Ph.D. in economics and an unquestioned authority on the subject.

Although the depression book was not an overwhelming mail-order hit, we did sell fifty thousand copies at ten dollars each, and that is considered pretty fair for a book.

How was the project born? What sparked the idea, and then, how did the book get off the ground?

Early in 1972 members of the financial community, economists, and even the general public were becoming aware of the inflationary trend that was creeping into the economy. At about that time an associate and I were kicking around ideas we felt might have mail-order potential. During the conversation, certain facts emerged that seemed to indicate that the country was heading toward hard times. Not only was inflation underway, but some economists were predicting that it was going to be serious and prolonged. Prices were zooming, salaries were rising frantically in an effort to catch up, and business conditions just weren't as healthy and as vigorous as they had been.

In addition, other elements—the rising crime rate, soaring taxes, the large cities' inability to cope with basic problems, and the increasing unpopularity of the Vietnam war—were contributing to the low spirits that seemed to be pervading the nation. Nothing good seemed to be happening, and we felt that if we were concerned about the possibility of a depression, there were probably plenty of others who agreed with us.

There are always negatively inclined individuals. Several investment-advisory services had been purveying doom for years and making a fortune. At least two that I know of, and possibly more, consistently

183

forecast economic doom. Even while the market was rising—during the very period when investors were making fortunes buying stocks and bonds—these doomsayers were urging their readers to liquidate their holdings. The better the market got, the more pessimistic they became, the more readers they attracted, and the more money they made!

With that in mind, we decided that perhaps a book that warned about the strong possibility of depression and gave the reader positive steps to protect himself might not only fill a strong need, but turn a profit.

This is a big country. There's a market for everything, if you can find it, and we thought we could. Accordingly, I contacted Doctor Persons, who had been my editor-in-chief at Investors Intelligence. He is a professor of finance and banking at a large university, and I had always held his judgment in very high regard. We got together and discussed the economic climate in general and the possibility of depression in particular. Along with a great many economists during that period, he felt that a depression was a distinct possibility. He believed that when the depression did strike, it would be somewhat fragmented. Instead of a general, all-out depression like the one during the thirties, he thought that only certain industries and the areas in which they were situated would suffer, while other businesses prospered. Events proved him to be quite correct.

When we felt sure we had the basis for a good book, I proceeded to rough out the ad, the final version of which appears at the end of this chapter. The premise of the ad—and of course the book—was that a depression was surely coming, but there were steps that alert, intelligent persons could take, not only to protect themselves, but possibly to profit from it as well, and this book would show how.

Now, certainly that was a logical, reasonable point of view. If one is alerted to any impending dilemma in advance, given enough time to prepare, and told how to do so by an expert, then surely that person has a much greater chance of weathering the storm than the individual caught completely off-guard.

While writing the ad, I came up with a headline, "How to Beat the

Depression That Is Surely Coming," and because it was provocative and made a strong promise, we decided to use it as the title of the book. Working on the ad before the book was even written made a great deal of sense. Since the book was nonexistent, I wasn't hampered by what I could or could not say about it. I included whatever sales points I thought would be interesting and helpful to the potential audience. For example, it occurred to me that men anxious to protect themselves and their families from the ravages of a coming depression would probably find it interesting to know how some clever individuals managed to turn the great depression of the thirties to their advantage and, in some instances, even make a fortune from it. That was one point I made in the ad, and it was subsequently included in the book.

I promised our potential buyers that this book would tell them how to handle their real estate in the event of a depression, on the theory that many of them would be concerned about what to do with their homes and other property, and I included as many other points as I thought would be of interest and concern to our eventual readers.

When the ad was completed, I turned it over to our author and elicited his comments. In some instances he had already planned to include the points the ad made, and in others he felt he could supply valid information. In a few instances, however, he felt that there was no way he could furnish valid material of the type I had said the book contained, and those promises were deleted from the ad.

This is a sound way to proceed with creating a book that is really designed to fulfill the needs of its readers. We made no attempt to dictate content, nor could we have even if we had wanted to, but we did request that if possible, we would like to have the book include in-depth coverage of those points which we felt readers would find helpful. In that way, all the promises the ad made would be legitimately fulfilled, and the book would be all the more complete for having included that material.

We were very pleased with the ultimate results, and so were our readers. *How to Beat the Depression That Is Surely Coming* turned out to be a fine book. It was well written in plain, straightforward, easy-to-understand language and contained a wealth of interesting and eminently helpful information and advice.

We tested the copy and the appeal of the book by direct mail. We sent out the mailing you see reproduced here—a five-page letter printed in red and black, along with an order form and a business-reply envelope. We made no effort to do an elaborate mailing. My theory—and it is no more than that—is that a simple, unadorned format helps to convey the impression that the message is so honest and sincere that it doesn't require fancy art or expensive printing.

Here is the copy . . .

HOW TO BEAT THE DEPRESSION
THAT IS SURELY COMING

Ingenious, Tested Techniques Not Only Help You Weather The Coming Financial Storm But Help You Make A Fortune Out of It Besides!

Dear Friend:

How would you like to beat the coming depression . . . to live securely and well during it (while everyone else is going under) . . . and perhaps make a fortune from it besides?

Sound hard to believe? Regardless of what you think, it can happen to you!

You don't have to be a millionaire to live better than ever during a depression. You don't have to be a financial wizard to profit enormously from it! Thousands of men did it during the thirties. For many of them it was an era of golden opportunity. It can be for you too, and there are several very logical, very sensible reasons why. But let's start at the beginning. . . .

Right now, in this country, there are more economists than you would suspect who are utterly convinced that the depression *is* coming, and soon; and as desperate as the present administration is to have you believe otherwise, the economic indices from here and abroad support that contention right down the line!

The evidence is overwhelming!

Certainly, the market has not been as sound as it appears. Despite technical rallies and frequent bursts of optimism, great uncertainty still prevails, and the European markets are in substantially worse shape than ours.

We have been forced to devalue the dollar, and at best that is only the beginning . . . only a stop-gap measure! We still have a dangerously unfavorable balance of trade, we owe 50 billions in gold which we are committed to pay off at the rate of $35 per ounce, but we can't begin to meet those obligations because our monetary gold reserves total less than 10 billion dollars!

To make matters worse, we can't compete with the Japanese or Europeans right here at home in our own market-place, let alone overseas, not only because our labor costs are too high, but because our machine tools are obsolete and our manufacturing techniques are outmoded. (Our heavy industry remains virtually unchanged since before World War II, but the German and Japanese tools and techniques are *post* World War II and thus vastly more efficient.) And that, bitter pill though it is, is absolute and incontrovertible fact!

Phase II looks like a bust. Inflation is still with us, and unemployment is still risnig . . . 6% nationally, 7% in sections of California, a staggering 15% in Seattle and, in some areas, higher still!

Think of it! 10,000,000 Americans are currently unemployed, 17 million are on relief and 20 million more are living under poverty conditions! That's 1/5th of the population, 20% of the nation *already* in the throes of depression, and that figure is growing daily!

The symptoms are everywhere. In Dallas, 25% of the office space is vacant. In Detroit, the Bank of the Commonwealth . . . the country's 50th largest . . . is about to close down. . . . In New York and other big cities, landlord's are abandoning once lucrative properties. In the world of high finance, where the goal was diversification and the watch-word was acquisition, the cry is now *divestiture!* Pare down! Lighten the load! Get ready!

Look at the plight of our own cities, if you are not convinced. Municipal governments virtually bankrupt! A shortage of housing, an overabundance of people, a racial problem that is growing worse instead of better! Air and water polluted. Education deteriorating, drug usage and violent crime still on the rise, police, firemen, street cleaners and other civil servants demanding higher and higher wages, but despite ever-increasing taxes (state and local taxes have gone up 100% in the last 10 years!), there is still not enough money to begin to meet their demands! And no end in sight!

And it's the same story all over the world!

In the once prosperous Ruhr Valley, the blast furnaces are growing cold, the steel mills are shutting down, and heavy industries are grinding to a stand-still. Unemployment in Germany, the most prosperous nation in Europe, is increasing rapidly and it's the same story in Britain, Italy, France, the Scandinavian countries and, in fact, throughout the world!

In short, it's all coming to a head! Despite the constant flow of publicity to the contrary, despite Washington's optimistic pronouncements in this election year, despite their intensive efforts to gloss over the obvious signs, the fact remains that the economy *is* shakier now than at any time since World War II, it *is* getting shakier by the minute, and not only is an imminent depression an utter certainty in the minds of many economists, but indeed, in many areas of the nation and the world it has already arrived!

The question is no longer, "Is it going to happen?" The question is, "What are you going to do about it when it does?" Not next month or next year, but right now? What are you going to do to prepare yourself, to keep your holdings intact, and even make money from the opportunities that invariably present themelves during a depression? Are you going to sit back and hope it will go away, or are you going to rear back and do something about it?

You can, you know. *It is possible!* You don't have to be a millionaire to turn the depression to your advantage! In every depression, there have always been men who made money while others were going broke. There have always been businesses that flourished while others were going under. There have always been stocks that were going up while most were going down.

And there have always been men living securely and well while others were scuffling merely to stay alive!

188

There *are* techniques to use, there *are* methods that work! You don't buck the tide, you swim with it. You don't fight the depression. You join it! And you do it with knowledge. With know-how.

By knowing what to do and how and when to do it! It's just as simple as that.

That doesn't mean you can simply apply the techniques that might have worked 30 years ago. This is a new era. It requires new methods tailored for this era. But those methods do exist. They are available, and now you can learn them. Now you can get all of the facts, all of the figures, all of the expert advice and information you must have, to know not merely how to survive during the coming depression, but how to make money from it! This specific, how-to instruction and advice is contained in a brand-new, just-off-the-press volume called

HOW TO BEAT THE DEPRESSION
THAT IS SURELY COMING!
by Dr. Robert Persons, Jr.

This is not just another book. This is a hard-headed, no nonsense, how-to manual . . . 212 large (8½ x 11), beautifully produced pages of the most authoritative information and advise on every aspect of the depression and how to profit from it, by a practical, eminently knowledgeable Ph.D. in Economics who has been Business Analyst Editor of Business Week, Chief Analyst for what was one of the world's largest and most successful investment services . . . and is currently a Professor of Economics and Director of Finance and Banking at the University of Bridgeport.

In this brilliant and far-reaching manual, you learn everything that could conceivably be of interest and of value to you during a depression!

You learn which type of businesses flourish during a depression and which types go under, and why!

You learn which stocks rose during the 1st great depression, which ones declined, which ones are likely to react during this coming depression, and how.

You read actual, step-by-step case-histories of men who made fortunes during the last depression . . . and of a few who lost them!

You learn how to take advantage of the incredible real estate values that invariably present themselves during a depression, and how to avail yourself of those opportunities even if you have virtually no capital to work with!

You get practical, specific, "how-to" advice on every aspect of handling your current affairs. Experts advise you on what to do about the real estate you now own, including the house you live in . . . what to do about your job if your current situation is less than perfect . . . on how to handle your personal and your business banking and much more of extreme value relative to banking.

You learn about incredible investment opportunities you can take advantage of with virtually no capital.

You learn time-tested techniques for building capital during depressed times and you get a wealth of other practical, usable information that ranges from some very interesting advice on short sales, warrants, puts & calls and commodities, to a cool, detached view of the market in general.

This is a thorough compendium of the vital, useful information and advice you need, not only for mere survival, but for money-saving, money-making investment during the depression . . . a wealth of specific information and advice never, ever available from a single source before!

LIKE HAVING YOUR OWN STAFF OF EXPERTS

Having this book at your fingertips is like having your own staff of experts . . . The same as saying to those experts, "Give me all of the vital information I should have. . . . Compile this information. Evaluate it. Then translate it into neat, plain language. Tell me what I have to do to make money in the years ahead. . . . I don't want vague, wishy-washy general information. I want specific facts . . . solid, concrete advice I can put to work to help me beat the coming depression!"

Having this book at your fingertips is just like that! It sorts out the advice of the experts for you. It culls out the good and it throws away the bad. You get the nuggets of solid information you need and the rest is discarded.

Here it is . . . stripped of excess verbiage, stripped of obtuse meanings . . . objectively and expertly analyzed and succinctly presented in plain, unmistakable language for just a fraction of what you would normally expect to pay. It's the solid, money-making information you need and should have, right at your fingertips! Information that can help save—and make—a fortune for you in the difficult years that lie ahead!

NO-RISK TRIAL

To prove our sincerity . . . To demonstrate the tremendous confidence we have in this book . . . To convince you beyond a shadow of a doubt that it will be more valuable to you than any book, service or report that you have ever owned in your life, we make this offer. . . .

Send for HOW TO BEAT THE DEPRESSION THAT IS SURELY COMING now! Read it for 10 days entirely at our risk. Then, if you don't agree it is far and away the most valuable book you have ever owned . . . If it hasn't been worth every penny you paid or, if you are dissatisfied for any reason at all, simply return it and we will refund your full purchase price immediately, no questions asked! You must be completely delighted in every way or HOW TO BEAT THE DEPRESSION THAT IS SURELY COMING has cost you nothing!

Now, surely you will agree that is a fair proposition. We certainly wouldn't make that offer if we weren't sublimely confident you will use this book successfully. The rest is up to you. If you would like to take advantage of the important information in this book, don't hesitate or delay. Right now, while it is still fresh in your mind, fill out the enclosed coupon and mail it at once!

Sincerely,
Ernest J. Miles
Publisher

We made a small test mailing of fourteen thousand names. In order to break even we had to sell approximately eighteen books for every thousand pieces we mailed out, or 1.8 percent, and we failed to do that in two out of the five lists we mailed to.

As soon as it became obvious that direct mail was not going to work to any degree, I put together a space ad, which we tested in the *Wall Street Journal*, where it did pretty well. It was obvious that space advertising was the way to go, as the following figures bear out.

In July we ran a 555-line ad in the Eastern Section of the *Wall Street Journal* (approximately three columns by 13½ inches deep) at a gross cost of $2,500. Actually we had an arrangement with our advertising agency. Since we wrote the ad and prepared it at our expense, they shared their commission with us, so it actually cost us almost $200 less. In any event, we needed 293 orders to break even. The ad pulled 503 orders, so everything over the 293 we needed—210 orders, less printing and mailing costs—was gross profit. Our $2,500 investment made us $1,680 which is good but certainly not sensational in the mail-order business.

When we ran the same ad in the same medium in September, we pulled 612 orders for, a profit of $2,552. Normally ads become less effective the second time they are run. In this case we can conclude that because summer vacation was over more people saw—and responded to—our ad. Perhaps even more important, the economic climate was probably more depressed during September than it had been in July, and our book definitely sold in direct proportion to the degree of concern people had about the economy.

The third time we ran, the ad pulled 530 orders.

Unfortunately, in only a half dozen media in the United States can you reach a concentration of investors. Besides the *Wall Street Journal* (usually the best of all the mail-order media for offers of this nature) and the *New York Times*, there are the *Chicago Tribune* (which has a financial section and pulls fairly well), the *Los Angeles Examiner*, *Barron's* (which is good, but very expensive), the *Capitalist Reporter*, and a few others. Of course, we tested various newspapers that we knew were read by men with the qualifications we required, but none of them actually paid off. For example, we tried, with little or no expectation of success, a newspaper published in White Plains, New York, a very affluent suburban community about forty-five minutes out of New York City and the home of a great many wealthy New York executives. To say we bombed would be the understatement of the year. We even tried *Newsweek*'s Midwestern section, with the same dismal results.

Why did we do so badly in other media? I am not really sure. Very few newspapers pull mail orders, and these were apparently among them. Probably the men who would be interested in our proposition do no more than skim through the paper and therefore didn't actually see our ad.

All things considered, however, the book did very well. It was never really as hot as a good mail-order deal can be, but in the final analysis fifty thousand copies at ten dollars each isn't too bad for a book or anything else.

THE
ADVERTISING BOOK

S OME TIME AGO, perhaps for want of something better to do, I decided to write a book. I had what I thought might be a commodity of interest to a great many people. The product was my advertising know-how— the information I had acquired and used with eminent success over a period of years.

When I was satisfied that I had enough material to make an interesting, informative, and useful book, I wrote chapters on advertising copy, art, research, media, and other topics I consider basic to the subject.

Now, if I hadn't been on an ego trip, I would never have proceeded in that fashion. The first thing I should have done was analyze my market. Before I so much as picked up a pen, I should have asked myself several vital questions and then come up with accurate answers:

Q. Is there a market for book advertising?

A: Yes.

Q: Is it a mass market?

A: No. On the contrary, it is rather specialized.

Q: Who comprises this market?

A: Ad managers, advertising-agency employees, and businessmen who use advertising to sell their goods or services.

G: Have there been other advertising books?

A: Yes.

Q: Have those other books been successful?

A: Not particularly. (A friend of mine at one of the largest and most successful publishing houses—masters at direct-mail selling—told me they had never had any particular success with an advertising book. Knowing that, I should have had enough sense to steer clear of the whole area. But remember, I wasn't evaluating the situation in terms of cold, hard, dispassionate logic, and making money was not my primary objective in this instance.)

Q: Why weren't they successful?

A: Because the market is relatively small and because it is spread out and therefore difficult and expensive to reach.

Q: How could I reach that market?

A: I could advertise in the two or three trade journals directed specifically to advertising men, but space in those journals is quite expensive, and I have no idea whether their readers buy by mail. I could have tried the *Wall Street Journal* or the financial pages of the Sunday *New York Times*, but because the market is sparse I didn't think a large ad would pay off, and I couldn't begin to cram enough copy to sell the book in a small ad.

The only sure way to come up with accurate answers is by testing, but that's a very costly procedure, warranted only if the deal has a sufficient potential, and I didn't think this one did.

After considering the various possibilities, I concluded that even though the book had limited potential, I would take a crack at direct mail. That was the best way to reach specific prospects, and it would enable me to make my story as long as I felt necessary to sell my product. I contacted a mailing-list broker and told him about my project, and I requested as much information as he had concerning that market. After giving the matter his expert consideration, he supplied me with a number of cards on which appeared descriptive material relative to the lists he felt might be relevant.

I went through the cards carefully and decided that there were about three quarters of a million names that might be potential buyers and that about twenty-five thousand names would give me a fair test. If my test lists pulled enough orders to be profitable, I would then plan a large mailing to the remainder of the names, and perhaps test additional categories as well.

Satisfied that I could make a successful mailing, I proceeded to write a direct-mail piece for the ad. To say I worked long and hard would be the understatement of the century. I worked for weeks and weeks. Writing copy—at least for me—is a long, difficult task. As we have discussed, the copy does the selling; it's all you have to tell your story and make customers, so no matter how much effort you expend, it can never be too much.

While I was writing the copy a lot of good sales points for the book presented themselves, and they were later incorporated into the text. For example, it is an accepted fact that a premium always helps to sell a product, particularly a mail-order book. Ideally, a premium should be a very low-cost item of great value to the customer and not generally available elsewhere.

In this instance I thought of the Ad Evaluator, a version of which appears in this book. I said that the Ad Evaluator was an invaluable tool, and I meant it sincerely. It is!

For example, if you are an advertiser, the Ad Evaluator can quite realistically save—or make—you a fortune! Use it successfully on just one occasion, and you know it could be worth a dozen or a hundred or a thousand times the cost of this book!

Of course, my knowing it is one thing; convincing prospects of it is another. But then, that's what copy is really all about, isn't it?

In any case, the copy was eventually completed, and because I wasn't entirely certain which approach would be best—a booklet or just a long letter—I decided to do both! You see, I felt it was better to risk a slightly larger amount of money at the beginning and be sure of the approach than to suffer lingering doubts later on.

Several other problems came to mind as well, of which pricing was the most important. How much should I charge for the book? Since I planned to publish it myself, I could alter the quality and format—and hence the cost—however I saw fit, so it made no sense to be guided by costs that didn't even exist at that point. The logical way to proceed would be to think the matter through as clearly as possible, set the price that seemed the most practical (and made the most sense arithmetically), and proceed from there.

In most instances, the less you charge, the more you sell. The less risk, the more risk takers. On the other hand, when individuals are really sold on something or feel they really need it, price is not an issue. They would just as soon pay ten dollars as five, or twelve dollars at ten, and of course, the more you get for the item, the fewer items you have to sell in order to pay off.

In this instance, I was not interested in building a business. I had no other items to sell, and I didn't plan to have any in the future. Nor was I interested in building a mailing list for subsequent rentals, because I didn't anticipate selling enough books to build a list of sufficient size to make list rental worthwhile.

In view of all this, and also because I really thought the material was extremely important and valuable, I decided to test the book at ten and twenty dollars. Interestingly enough, they did equally well, profitwise. Results were fair but not worth projecting, basically because the lists that worked best—presidents of ad agencies for one—were simply too small to bother following up on.

That's the basic story. Following is the brochure I wrote—in my estimation a good piece of copy for a deal that really wasn't worth getting involved with in the first place.

7 SECRETS GUARANTEED
TO DOUBLE, TRIPLE,
QUADRUPLE THE EFFECTIVENESS
OF YOUR ADVERTISING OR YOU
PAY NOTHING!

How would you like to make a fortune through the incredible power of advertising? . . .

. . . literally double, triple, quadruple the power and the effectiveness of your ads?

. . . literally be able to look at any ad with absolute confidence and say, "Yes this ad has it . . .", or "No, this ad is no good because . . .", and really know what you are talking about?

Believe it or not, it can happen quickly, easily, effortlessly! *You* can know and understand more about advertising than 90% of the so-called experts! *You* can acquire a brilliant insight into just what it takes to sell your goods or services, and you can put this newfound knowledge to work for you immediately to give you a tremendous advantage over your competitors and make you far more successful in any business endeavor!

Be as skeptical as you like, but that's an absolute fact! You don't have to be a creative genius to recognize, to write or to have your agency prepare great, selling advertising! You don't need years of experience!

All you need is a little bit of perspective, a clean-cut conception of what you are trying to accomplish, and 7 time-tested, success-proved advertising principles, (used by a handful of successful businessmen to quietly amass fortunes) . . . 7 simple, basic truths, not well known, but so powerful so impelling, so sure-fire, and so psychologically sound that if you merely know what they are, you can double, triple, quadruple the pulling power of your ads!

A strong statement? Perhaps, but a proved one!

These principles have taken years to compile, years to perfect, but the instant you are exposed to them, you will recognize their incredible potential. The instant you see them, you will understand how and why the small in-group of hard-sell businessmen who use them, operate with such stunning success!

And now an acknowledged expert—not a teacher, not a book-writer, but an *experienced advertising man with an amazing record of success* puts that information right at your fingertips in quick, easy to use folio form which he calls THE CLIENTS HAND-BOOK or 7 SECRETS TO GREAT ADVERTISING!

Not a book

Please don't confuse this publication with any book or manual you have ever seen before! THE CLIENT'S HANDBOOK is new, different, and despite its title, not a book! It is a beautifully produced, limited edition portfolio consisting of 9 sections, each in its-own special folder . . . In all, over 150 pages plus reproductions of over 50 actual ads, illustrations, charts, and so on, all boiled down to their very essence, ingeniously indexed and ready for instant use!

In short, THE CLIENT'S HANDBOOK is a lean, hard-hitting, down-to-earth series of practical, how-to instruction. It doesn't waste your time with wild theories or idle speculations. It contains no padding, no puffery, no excess verbiage. It is direct, it is to the point, it reveals tried, proved advertising concepts . . . the secrets, private records, inside tips, actual examples and advice, used by the author and his associates to literally make millions, and which can put a fortune in your pockets too!

Where advertising books talk in generalities, this privately published, no-holds-barred folio talks in specifics. Where ordinary books say, "An ad for a popular automobile . . .", THE CLIENT'S HANDBOOK says, "This Volkswagon ad illustrated here which ran in the New York Times on January 15th is lousy because . . .", and then it *shows* you why, not sketchily, not vaguely, but point-by-point right down the line! And that's just the beginning!

No existing advertising book goes that far. Most ad books pussy-foot all over the lot, awed and deferential where the advertising profession is concerned, and reluctant to step on toes. Not so THE CLIENT'S HANDBOOK!

This is *your* manual. It is written to show you, the advertiser, how to realize the huge rewards good advertising offers, and when it has to call a spade a spade, it does so!

In THE CLIENT'S HANDBOOK the author says, in plain language, that with few exceptions the average advertising man is incredibly naive about advertising and he tells you how their ineptitude can be costing you a fortune!

He contends that 90% of the ads written today are farcical, and he proves his point with an analysis of over 20 current advertisements from Ford Motors to Schrafft's Ice cream which points up the weaknesses of your own advertising.

He says that a great many advertising clients—and that may include you—are being inadvertently victimized by their agencies misconceptions, and in this book he tells you how to protect yourself.

But most important, he says there are fortunes being made every month of the year by a handful of men who know and understand the basic principles outlined in this manual, and he says there is no reason in the world why you can't do the same thing!

And to help you do precisely that, he reveals the established formulas and techniques, tested, proved, and amazingly easy to utilize, which are making fortunes for others and which can vastly improve your advertising . . . can increase its pull, enhance its effectiveness, make it more impelling, not just occasionally, but time after time! He shows you what those techniques are and just how you can put them to immediate use, whatever you are selling, however much it costs.

And to make it easy for you, everything is broken down into easy-to-follow, step-by-step form so simple, so logical, you'll have an infinitely clearer conception of what advertising is all about the moment you glance at them. For example:

- You get a simple, 3-part Ad-evaluator which accurately *tells you if any ad, large space or small, is good, bad or indifferent.* And why!

- You get a simple check-list which enables you to evaluate the worth of any layout with great accuracy, even if you don't know a thing about art!

- You get 9 essential copy points, logically and sensibly illustrated, which are a step-by-step guide to *great* advertising copy!

- You get an easy-to-use tip which takes less than a moment to read but which enables your copywriter—or you—to write more impelling salesletters than perhaps ever before!

- You get detailed, point-by-point critiques and analysis of over 20 ads Madison Avenue thinks are so hot—including the Volkswagen ads, the ridiculous airline ads and others which the author believes are real horrors which have been fooling clients and most of but not quite all of Madison Avenue for years.

- You get 15 examples of really good ads and a precise analysis of what makes them superior.

- You get 10 examples of the world's best reason-why copy by the world's best reason-why copywriter . . . and obscure mid-western catalog writer whose grammar may be lacking but whose copy is so impelling, it makes the average Madison Ave. effort puny by comparison!

- You get a complete analysis and a detailed case-history of the copy and the concept which shot an idea into the 4th largest investment service in the country (24,500 subscribers at $36 per in just 14 months!)

And this is just the beginning . . . just a smattering of the vital, useable information this book contains.

You learn how to pick your advertising agency, and how to get the most out of it after you do. You learn what to beware of from arty directors and eager copywriters, and how they can hurt your advertising if you don't keep them in check. You learn how large an ad should be, how long the copy should run and how, in many instances, illustrations can ruin the effectiveness of your advertising, and on and on.

And to sum it all up, you get the 7 secrets to great advertising . . . 7 vital advertising truths, the inclusion of which in any ad virtually guarantees that ad must be a winner!

In short, then, you get a crystallization of all this eminently successful advertising man's practical, money making experience . . . the facts, the principles, the concepts which have literally made millions for him and for others in this same fascinating but heretofore limited school of hard-sell advertising.

Examine Without Risk

Because THE CLIENT'S HANDBOOK contains such an incredible wealth of vital information, advice and actual how—to help, most of which has never been revealed in such depth before, we are certain you will find it invaluable . . . certain that once you see it, once you read it, you will recognize that herein lies the essentials which can make a fortune for you . . . can make your advertising so superior to that of your competitors, there can simply be no comparison.

We therefore have no hesitation in offering it to you on an unequivocal money-back guarantee.

Simply send for it now. Read it. Examine it. Put its principles right to work for you. If you are not absolutely certain THE CLIENT'S HANDBOOK is everything we say and more . . . if every word doesn't make great sense to you no matter how dubious, how skeptical you now are, don't keep it! Return it within 10 days for a complete and immediate refund, no questions asked!

You must like THE CLIENT'S HANDBOOK so well that you never want to be without your copy, or it costs you nothing!

Money-Back Guarantee

Send for THE CLIENT'S HANDBOOK now. Read it, examine it, actually use it entirely at our risk. If you aren't convinced THE CLIENT'S HANDBOOK is every bit as valuable as you have been led to believe, don't keep it. Simply return it within 10 days for a complete and immediate refund, no questions asked. You must be completely satisfied or it costs you nothing!

Who Is the Author and What Is His Authority for These Statements?

The author of THE CLIENT'S HANDBOOK is also the writer of this copy. He is therefore placed in the awkward position of having to write his own blurb. Briefly, then, and without embellishment, here are some of the most significant facts.

His name is Joe Bart and he is a highly regarded copy-writer with an imposing list of outstandingly successful ads, radio and T.V. commercials to his credit.

He has a solid advertising background, has worked for a number of the top hard-sell agencies, and was fortunate enough to learn, early in his career, the incredible power of good copy.

He subsequently became a principal in and wrote the copy for a number of extremely successful operations, the most recent of which was investor's intelligence which zoomed to the fourth largest investment service in the United States in fourteen months (at its peak, 25,500 subscribers at $36 per)! In 1960, at the age of 35, he was able to retire from business, forever grateful that he had an opportunity to learn and to use so profitably, the advertising principles set forth in THE CLIENT'S HANDBOOK.

Who Can Profit From the Client's Handbook?

ANY ADVERTISER large or small, national or retail, industrial,

205

institutional, or mail order, in space, on radio, T.V., car-cards, by direct-mail or whatever, can profit from THE CLIENT'S HAND-BOOK.

Why?

Because THE CLIENT'S HANDBOOK reveals the guarded secrets of great advertising which can make a fortune for you! . . . Unassailable advertising truths so vital, so logical, so sure-fire that if you are alert enough to grasp this opportunity and put these principles to work for you, your advertising will be vastly superior to anything your competitors are now running.

RETAILER/Whether you are running large ads or small, this manual points out the mistakes you are now making. It shows how you can use advertising to increase traffic and build sales. It shows how you can substantially reduce the size of your ads and their frequency, and still make them more potent, more effective, more profitable, than ever before!

NATIONAL ADVERTISER/No matter who your agency is, no matter how experienced you are, this manual gives you the perspective you need! It points up the mistakes you are now making. It shows you how widely accepted Madison Ave. misconceptions are wasting your advertising dollars! It makes you expert enough to judge ads with confidence, and it guarantees to show you just how to make your advertising far more impelling and persuasive than it now is!

INDUSTRIAL ADVERTISER/You learn why most industrial ads perhaps including yours—are so effective. You learn how easy it is to get your sales-point across to the information-hungry readers of trade magazines, you learn how to stop throwing away advertising dollars on wasted space and meaningless copy, and how to get the most out of every ad you run. You also get much vital information on direct-mail, sales-letters, printing, mailing-list selection and so on.

MAIL-ORDER MAN/Here are the *real* secrets of mail-order success—not the innumerable details of testing, postal regulations and so on, but the very essence . . . the proved principles of hard-sell, reason-why copy which have accounted for virtually all of the great mail-order hits of the last 25 years! Here are analyses of highly successful mail-order deals, actual day-by-day mail-order results, important insights into direct-mail and other features pertinent to mail-order men.

ADVERTISING MEN/Since THE CLIENT'S HANDBOOK is devoted to passing on information and advice proved to increase the effectiveness of advertising, and since this information is relayed in complete, how-to detail, it would certainly seem of interest to any advertising man genuinely concerned with doing a better job for his clients.

FREE *ad-evaluator kit*

Use this ingenious, handsomely constructed plotting-board to accurately evaluate any ad, large or small, quickly, easily, expertly! Use it to tell whether that ad is good, bad or indifferent and why!

Check off 7 easy questions and you know whether the headline is right, whether the layout is satisfactory, whether the copy is doing its job, whether the overall ad effectively sells your product or service!

This simple device can't write an ad for you, but it can save—and help you make—a fortune by showing you how to cull out the weak ads, how to increase the power and the effectiveness of the good ones! And now this handsome evaluator in handy container with special marking pencil is yours FREE with your copy of THE CLIENT'S HANDBOOK!

THE PITCH

THE OLD-FASHIONED pitch was one of the most powerful selling media ever developed. You've probably seen one somewhere along the line. The pitchman, an adroit and persuasive speaker, attracts a crowd and then delivers a prepared pitch from memory. At the end, which may be anywhere from fifteen minutes to an hour and a half later, depending on the product, the crowd, the weather, and in certain instances, the imminence of the law, he sells the item whose virtues he has been extolling. Then, after the crowd disperses, a new group is gathered, and the process begins all over again.

The pitch started a long time ago, and although its origins are obscure, its efficacy as a powerful selling medium is not. And small wonder. After all, it wasn't dreamed up overnight. The original pitches were perfected over long periods of time. They were tried and changed and rearranged until, like a good Vaudeville act, all the patter and all the little bits of business were polished to gleaming perfection. Like their counterparts in show business, the ineffective pitches soon fell by the wayside, but the good ones persisted. They survived; they flourished; they made money.

Since items of broad general appeal were usually sold, one of the determinants of the success of the pitch was the size of the audience to which it was delivered. The larger the group that could be induced to listen, the more prospects and the greater the ultimate sales. For that reason, the pitchman was ever alert for new and larger audiences. Then in the late forties, one pitchman got the idea of a lifetime—television. A new bonanza was uncovered, a new era born.

Several products were tested with spectacular results. One was a lanolin hair dressing, and another was a reducing product, which was equally successful. The hair product, a respected national brand, is now firmly entrenched on druggists' shelves throughout the nation, but the reducer and the vitamin product have gone the way of many promotional items.

That was hard-sell advertising at its most potent—rough, tough, and sell, sell, sell all the way. There were no illusions, no pretenses. The objective was to sell merchandise with a vengeance. It was just one more example of the incredible power of good advertising.

That enormous success was of course widely imitated by any number of products of various types—reducers, weight additives, travel books, insecticides, rosebushes, weed killers, and whatever other high-margin items promoters could dream up.

It is interesting to note that even though today's audiences are somewhat more sophisticated than those in the fifties, and although the mail-order business isn't what it used to be, the prime factor militating against the more frequent use of the pitch is not that it no longer works. Pitches are rarely heard today because most stations are flourishing and have no time available for fifteen-minute pitches.

Let the stations fall upon meager times, however, and look out!

WHY THE PITCH WORKS SO WELL

The pitch is frequently humorous, always earthy and personal, often controversial in content and sarcastic in tone. It generally starts with a hook—a device used to attract a crowd and pique their interest long enough to give the pitchman a chance to go to work on them. The hook can be any of a number of devices from a trumpet solo to the promise of a strongman act that may not materialize until the pitch is almost over. (Don't confuse the hook with the headline. The two appear comparable on the surface, and some of their functions may be similar, but they are actually different. The hook precedes a pitch that generally sells a product of very broad appeal. Hence, it doesn't have to select or qualify specific prospects; it merely has to stop people, any people, and then only for a moment, somewhat the way a curiosity headline does. The pitchman does the rest. A good headline, on the other hand, has no live pitchman standing by to pound home the copy message. It must stop qualified prospects and induce them to read on, and therein lies the essential difference.)

If the pitch is good, it has a hypnotic effect. As you may have discovered from personal experience that once you become engrossed in a pitch, it is difficult to turn away. One seems to be compelled—perhaps by the sound of the pitchman's voice, by the rapid flow of language, by the content of the pitch itself, or by a combination of all three—to listen right through to the bitter end. Or again, perhaps one's reluctance to leave is reinforced because, having lingered awhile, one has an investment in time that would be lost by leaving prematurely.

Whatever the reason, the result is that a substantial percentage of the audience listens in rapt attention to the very end. The pitchman pokes fun at our foibles and gets us laughing at ourselves, and while this is going on, he fills us with pseudo-facts and fancies, all of which have a bearing on the product he is eventually going to sell us.

One interesting and important fact that tends to bear out the conclusions reached in these pages in respect to long copy is this—when working in the field, the pitchman quickly discovered that the longer he could keep his audience listening to him, the more merchandise he could expect to sell. That was axiomatic. At the big annual fair in Toronto each summer—in past years a Mecca for pitchmen—it was common to keep audiences standing in the hot sun for an hour and a half or longer! True, a lot drifted away, but those who remained were enthusiastic prospects who usually ended up buying.

Of course, an hour and a half in the sun is a far cry from the half hour on radio that the following vitamin pitch took, but even a half hour is rather considerable, particularly when you stop to think that it is virtually all commercial. Remember that, next time someone tells you your copy is too long.

Probably the most important aspect of the pitch, from the point of view of what can be learned from them, is the closing. Note that the pitchman closes strong! He needs results. That is his only excuse for being. If he doesn't make sales, he doesn't eat, and if he doesn't eat, he can't pitch. It's as simple as that!

He doesn't terminate his pitch and stand around waiting for sales to come to him. On the contrary, he pitches and pitches hard. He uses every device at his command. His language is strong, persuasive, hard hitting. He sells and keeps on selling right down to the wire.

Bear in mind that the examples you read here are subject to the time and copy limitations imposed by radio. Imagine how much stronger the closing is when there are no restrictions except those imposed by the pitchman's own ability! He sums up his claims, he makes a strong guarantee, and he appeals to the good sense of his audience. "I don't care what you have tried, what you have used, or what you have done. If what I have told you has sounded sensible to you, and if you honestly and sincerely want to bring your weight down to normal, to improve your appearance, your health, your potential span of life, here is all I ask you to do. . . ." Finally, specific buying instructions are spelled out. On radio or TV, the command is, "Call this number *now*!"

The following pitches appear precisely as they were transcribed, which explains the various errors in tense and so on. Here, again, incorrect grammar is of no major consequence if sound, selling ideas are presented.

LIFE CAN BE RIDICULOUS

Thirty-minute radio script

Listen and laugh at "Life Can Be Ridiculous," a program of transcribed fun.

A friend of mine came rushing up to me the other day all pale, trembling, nervous. He said, "George, I've just had the most terrible news."

I said, "What happened, Joe?"

He said, "Well, I just came from my doctor. My doctor tells me I'm very sick, very sick."

I said, "What's the matter with you?"

He says, "Well I don't exactly know the name of the disease, but it sounded something like Australian maldusian freakus, or something like that."

I said, "Well, it sounds terrible. What are you supposed to do about it?"

"Oh," he said, "the doctor gave me a big long list of things to do.

I've got to watch my diet, stop drinking, stop running around, cut down on my smoking, all kinds of things."

"Well, what are you going to do?"

"What am I going to do about it? I'm gonna change doctors, naturally."

And I really don't blame the guy. After all, if he did what the doctor told him, took care of himself, what would he have to talk about? What would he have to complain about? He would lose a very important topic of conversation. I don't know, people always love to talk about their ailments. Have you ever known anyone who had an operation?

You know and I know that every operation in the world is the longest, the hardest, the toughest, and the most dangerous. Nobody ever has a trivial operation. Everybody's is a trick. They want to tell you about it. They drive you crazy. Sometimes they are not as sick as they think they are, too. For example, I knew a fellow once, every second time you met him he had one thing he talked about. He had a terrible buzzing and ringing in his ear. He did everything for it, according to him. He took long vacations, quit working, took massages, took exercises, horseback riding, even underwent psychoanalysis. Nothing seemed to help, until one day in a haberdashery he learned that he was wearing a shirt a half size too small. As soon as he changed the size of his shirt, the buzzing and ringing went away. Since then he's never opened his mouth. He hasn't got a thing to talk about. He claims that he appreciates what the haberdasher did for him, but the fact of the matter is, he stopped going to that shop and now buys all his shirts from the guy's competitor. So, I guess he wasn't so appreciative after all.

If you took away the weather and ailments from most people they would never have anything to say except "Hello" and "Goodbye."

Then there is another class of people. I call them the pill bearers. Whatever is wrong with you, they understand. They've got a pill for it. You can't sleep, here's a pill. You got a headache? Here's a pill. Anything that's wrong with you, they've got a pill for it. I call them the pill bearers, and if you do business with them long enough, you'll soon be doing business with some pallbearers. Take my word for it.

Then there is another class of amateur physicians that it is a good idea for you to keep away from. These are the ones who have never been to a medical college, never read a book on the subject, but they know all about diet. You're too fat? They will tell you what to eat. You're too thin? They'll tell you what to eat. You catch cold? They'll tell you what to eat. They know everything in the world there is to know about it, but just follow them around and see what they eat themselves. They are pretty remarkable. He knows it is healthy for you, he certainly ought to know what's healthy for him, and he does. Look what he has for lunch. Here's a real diet, to build a good sound healthy body. A couple of hamburgers, there's not enough vitamins in just plain old hamburgers. I'll tell you how to fix it. Smother 'em in catchup, souse 'em in relish, douse 'em in mustard, use a little salt and pepper, dash of horseradish. You need plenty of green vegetables, so he says, "I guess I'll have an extra dill pickle, please." Then he says, "I love hamburgers!" How does he know whether he loves hamburgers or not? He never tasted one. By the time he gets finished putting all that stuff on it, he hasn't the vaguest idea what they taste like.

And he doesn't bother to chew, either. He's in a hurry. There's not much time for lunch, swallow 'em down fast, wash 'em down with a bottle of pop, and he's ready to go. He sure is. Ready to go right back to the office and sit there and suffer for the rest of the day.

Comes midnight, Joe has repeated this performance two or three times, and he's in great shape. Now he's going to bed. Comes midnight, Joe's wrestling with his blanket and begging that strange animal on his bedpost to go away.

Comes morning, he's in great shape again. A little toothpaste to kill the taste in his mouth, a cup of coffee to kill the taste of the toothpaste, a cigarette to kill the taste of the coffee.

He doesn't read the paper; he wrestles with it. He sees a headline about new taxes, he sits there and grinds his teeth. He reads the stock-market quotations, sees that International Steel fell two points, his blood pressure goes up four, his stomach is doing a two-step, his heart is racing like a politician chasing a vote, he staggers into the office, screams at his secretary until noon.

The lunch whistle blows, Joe isn't hungry, but the clock says to eat, so he eats. You know what he eats. I just told you.

Comes six o'clock, Joe isn't feeling so good. So, what's he going to do? Change his diet? Of course not. He's going to go home and argue with his wife. Not that she deserves it. Of course not. Why the poor thing, she's been sweating over a hot bridge game all day, having to listen to all that gossip. Before she knows it, it is almost time for Joe's supper. So she rushes home, boils up a couple of potatoes, otherwise known as concentrated diabetes, warms over yesterday's meat, rips open a couple of cans, ten minutes after she steps into the kitchen, a meal fit for our hero.

As soon as Joe drags his weary body through the door and starts to the supper table, she says, "Darling, you'll have to hurry, I've got a beautiful four-course meal for you. We will have to be at the show in eight minutes." Eight minutes later they are in the show. The lights go out, and so does Joe. And it is a good thing, too, because if he didn't collapse, he would throw all kinds of people out of work. What kind of people? Why, the so-called health experts. The food faddists.

And where does the most of our food fads come from nowadays? From the greatest health center in the world. Hollywood. Why, there are more health experts in Hollywood today than you can shake a testimonial at. If a movie actress tells us she eats yeast for her complexion, overnight ten million people try to turn their stomachs into a brewery. And if it isn't yeast, it could be a grapefruit diet, or a grape-juice diet, or a fruit-nut diet, or a vegetable diet, or the latest fad of protein diet. It's wonderful. It only costs you thirty or forty dollars a day for a nice lean steak or chop. But in a clinical test they have just discovered that if you follow a straight protein diet you'll have nausea, you'll suffer from headaches and diarrhea.

Of course, they don't tell you that. Why should they? Three months later they'll be using your stomach for a guinea pig for another kind of diet. Excuse me. I said the latest diet is the protein diet, but I'm behind the time, because already we have the latest, latest diet. What is it? Blackstrap molasses. Would you like a bit of advice? Never take blackstrap molasses without a bottle of cola. Why? Because if you look up blackstrap molasses in any encyclopedia it will tell you that the best dietary use for blackstrap molasses is in the manufacture of rum. And who ever heard of rum without cola?

I know what you're thinking. You're thinking, He doesn't mean me. Why, I don't eat like that. I don't follow the food-fad fanatics. Why, I have a balanced diet.

The Pitch

You know what that means don't you? If you have a great big piece of meat on one side of your plate, but a great big gob of mashed potatoes on the other side to balance it. That's a balanced diet. Then, when you're sick, you say there ain't no justice. And speaking of justice, how many of you can say, like the great Chief Justice of the Supreme Court, Oliver Wendell Holmes, who was not only famous as a judge of the laws of men, but who was equally famous as the judge of the laws of nature. At the age of 94 he said, "What wouldn't I give to be 70 again."

As a matter of fact, how many of us will ever live to see 70, much less 94, yet by all the laws of nature, mankind should reach the age of 100 to 140 without even half trying. Why? Because scientists tell us that animals like sheep, a dog, a cat, a horse, normally live five to seven times the length of time that it takes for them to reach maturity. A man or woman reaches maturity at about twenty, therefore should live from 100 to 140 easy. These are not my figures. These are the figures of Baranough and Bougamiller, two of the most famous scientists and doctors the world has ever known.

Now, I'm not suggesting that we could live to be 100 to 140 by living like a sheep or a cow, although many of us when we reach 40 feel like 140. I'm only suggesting that maybe our so-called dumb animal friends aren't so dumb after all. Why, ladies and gentlemen, if the average adult in our country had the natural instinct of a pet dog or an infant, half the hospitals in this country would have "Vacant" signs on them. Why, children and animals know more about eating by instinct than we are able to figure out with our famous intelligence.

Sounds silly, doesn't it? But let me give you an idea. Pick up an orange, hand it to a little boy two years of age, and watch what he does. Before he even looks at the orange, he starts to eat the peel. But mama wants him to throw it away. She thinks it's garbage. But it isn't. It's a food, rich in iodine; it has calcium and other valuable food essentials.

Here's another thing. If you have ever been in a house where there is abject poverty, a baby crawling around on all fours on the floor will crawl over to a plastered wall and try to lick the plaster from the wall because that plaster is rich in lime, which is calcium, and its body, bones, and teeth are literally starving for that calcium. Take a dog, a dumb animal. When a dog is sick and you try to give him medicine, he will try to bite your arm. But if you turn him loose, he goes to the woods and looks for grasses and roots and herbs from the garden of nature, which is the laboratory of God.

But we, we're smarter than a dog. We never change our diet. Of course not. A little gas, a little heartburn, we know what to do. The great American after-dinner food, bicarbonate of soda. Fine. Eliminates the heartburn, but also alkalizes the normal stomach digestive acids so that you can't digest food properly; then you wonder why you feel weak, tired, nervous. So you take another pill, and eventually you become a pill bearer. But never, never change your diet. The fact of the matter is, it's not enough that we have to ruin our own health, but we also ruin the health of our children. Can you stand a bit of a shock? A recent survey by nutritionists has just revealed four out of five children are undernourished. Think. Four out of five of our own children are undernourished, and this is the greatest, the most powerful nation in the world. The result. In a time of a national crisis, just as the one we are now going through, and through which we have been drastically forced to lower the physical standards, we find the draft boards rejecting 17 percent in one district, 36 in another, and as high as 50 percent in still another, and this is the flower of our nation I'm talking about, our youth.

Surely these figures must reveal how many of us are ruining our health, shortening our lives, by neglecting the only body we will ever own, by not putting back into our bodies the vitamins and minerals we burn up in everyday living. Oh, I know, I've heard that wives and mothers get insulted when I talk about this. They say, "Why I give my children and family the best of everything. You ought to see the fancy prices I pay."

Of course you buy the best of everything. Of course you pay the top prices. But like the boys used to say in the army, "It's not the food you buy, it's the way you prepare it."

Take orange juice, for example. As fine a health food as nature can grow or money can buy. Do you know that if you prepare orange juice in advance and leave it in your refrigerator the vitamins have a chance to escape, and they do. In other words, you are paying for the orange juice, but you are drinking water. Think it over.

And this fatal disregard for our health is typical, it seems to affect all of us from the housewives to the butcher, the baker, the advertising man, even the Congress. Not too many years ago, I was shocked by what took place in Congress. It seems that session after session the courageous congressman was trying to get a bill passed that would not only help the people in his district who had tuberculosis, but would help tuberculars all over the country. Year after year he presented his bill, year after year Congress voted it down.

One day a Midwestern Congressman reported a serious outbreak of the disease in many pig herds throughout his district. Almost without debate Congress passed a bill for millions of dollars to save the pigs. When the courageous Congressman stood up in the halls of Congress, he said in effect, "For years I've been trying to pass a bill to help sick people. Gentlemen, my question to you is this. Is the life of a pig worth more than that of a human being?"

Do you want more? If your car starts to weave a little, right down to the mechanic to see what's wrong. Your pet dog is sick, right down to the veterinarian to find out what's wrong. But if you're feeling a little sick, a little tired, a little headachy, don't go to the doctor to find out what's wrong, to remove the cause of the pain. Oh, no. Take a pain killer instead. Fine. Drown out the warning signal that nature is trying to send you. We don't want to hear it, we don't want to know about it. We haven't any time. We're always in a hurry. Nowadays many of us act like we are trying to beat everyone else to the graveyard.

Meet a man on the street. "Hi Ed, where you going? What's your hurry?"

He says, "I don't know, but I got to be there."

"What are you going to do when you get there?"

He says, "I don't know, but I better not be late."

That's why we eat in a hurry, sleep in a hurry, live in a hurry, die in a hurry, buried in a hurry, and forgotten in a hurry. Let's face it, ladies and gentlemen. We all have a body, but we don't know how to feed it. Your stomach for example is a little larger than your fist, yet into this little organ, you put an appetizer like shrimp cocktail, fruit juice, half a grapefruit, tomato soup, a meat course, catchup, spices, potatoes, either fried or mashed or starched or boiled, and a vegetable or two, some salad with vinegar and plenty of dressing, a few slices of white bread, a couple glasses of ice water, to freeze the stomach and dilute the digestive juices. Then, oh boy, here comes the dessert. Pie or cake maybe with ice cream and wash it down with some scalding tea or hot coffee, and then you wonder why you suffer. You wonder why you feel heavy, loaded, bloated.

Now, would you like to improve your diet? Would you like to eat so that you get all the elements your body needs for proper nutrition? Unfortunately, this is just about impossible. You see, our diet must be deficient because of forces beyond our control. When our grandfathers tilled the soil, they returned to it all the organic elements that it needed. They let the land lie fallow between the plowing and seeding, and the soil had a chance to replenish itself. Today a farmer cannot take the time to do this. He wants to get everything he can out of the soil. He can't wait. As a result, the soil is getting poorer and the farmers are getting richer.

The land in this country has lost much of its fertility in the last sixty years. It is simply being worn out. Our crops, although they appear sound and healthy, lack many of the life- and health-giving elements they should have. When you eat these crops, ladies and gentlemen, when you drink the milk or eat the meat of the animal that feeds on the grass grown on the soil, you may not be getting enough of the vital food elements, and if you don't you are going to suffer.

Now, perhaps you are hungry. Perhaps you are saying, "What can I do? Not only am I eating the wrong foods and preparing them incorrectly, but now I find that even the earth is against me."

This is where modern science comes to the rescue. Most of you know something about this under the general heading of vitamins. But vitamins are only a small part of it, although a very important part. I claim if you could learn to feed yourself exactly as you should be fed, then and then only is it possible for you to enjoy better health.

Now, ladies and gentlemen, I do not expect you to believe these things simply because I say them. I expect only one thing. I personally like to talk to skeptical people because skeptical people are usually logical people. But people I can do nothing with are the ones that sit down and listen for a minute and then say, "Well, I don't know what he is going to talk about, but I know it is not the truth." And even worse than that are the ones that sit and listen to me and every time I say something they say yes. They agree with me. That's right. When I get all through they say every word he said was the truth, but I don't believe him anyhow. They remind me of the spectator at the zoo who watches the kangaroo for thirty minutes and says, nope, there is no such animal.

Ladies and gentlemen, listen to me. We eat to put into our bodies what our bodies and blood are made of. What are we made of. The Bible, for example, says we are made of the dust of the earth. Do you doubt that? Pick up a handful of earth and carry it into a laboratory and say, "Mr. Chemist, what is in this earth?"

Under analysis he will tell you that it contains certain minerals. Then take a drop of your blood or a bit of your flesh and have it analyzed. It contains the same minerals. You are literally the dust of the earth. And when you die, these minerals go back to the earth. You return to the dust of the earth exactly as the Bible says. Yes, ladies and gentlemen, the vitamins you hear so much about bear the same relation to those minerals that the spark in your automobile does to the gasoline on which it runs, and one without the other is no good. It is like a wedding without a bride.

But you say a machine is different than the human body, and you're right. Why? Very simple. In a machine if a spark burns out, you can replace it. If you have abused your body, you can't ask Mother Nature to send you down a new heart or new kidneys, or a new liver, size nine. It doesn't work that way.

Ladies and gentlemen, in this day and age, do I have to tell you that without these essential substances you cannot enjoy health? Without calcium you cannot have good bones and teeth. You also need phosphorous and vitamin D for them. You know these things. Do I have to tell you that without iodine and other essential substances, the glands of the body cannot function properly, and if your glands cannot function properly, you will lack pep and vitality? You will be old before your time. Ladies and gentlemen, do I have to tell you that if you don't have enough iron you won't have enough energy? You know these things.

What's wrong? Nowadays it seems that everyone wants to live a long time, but nobody wants to grow old. Nowadays when people do get a little tired, a little worn out because they have neglected their bodies, neglected to rebuild and vitalize their bloodstream, why the first thing they do is reach for a pill. It is nice and simple.

The Pitch

Somewhere they read an advertisement for a new wonder pill. The advertisement said take our pill for seven days and feel like sixteen again. So they start the pill habit, the tonic habit, then it's salts, seltzers, herbs, chemicals, drugs, laxatives, nerve tonics, those powders that come in little boxes, and if you take enough of them, they will put you in a little box of your own. And they will put a lily in your hand, and they will say, "Doesn't he look natural?"

Because if there is anyone listening to me who has started this habit, I'm sure you know that the more pills, salts, powders, medicines, drugs you take, the worse you get. Why? Because nature is wise. Nature says to you, "If it has taken ten years to make yourself sick, don't expect me to get you well in ten days. Why, ladies and gentlemen, it takes nature 90 to 120 days to rebuild your entire bloodstream. How can you possibly hope to do this in ten days? What do I mean? Simply this. Not one drop of blood that is circulating through your body at this moment will be there in 90 to 120 days.

That is because we are mammals. We have a bloodstream, and in that bloodstream we have cells. Like all things that live and grow, these blood cells are born, they live, they die. Their average life is from 90 to 120 days, which means that two months from now half of your blood stream will be entirely new. In 120 days not one drop of blood now circulating through your body will be there. Nature will have given you an entirely new bloodstream. But if you feel tired and worn out now because your bloodstream is tired and worn out, because you have starved it for years with a diet that has been deficient in vitamins and minerals, and you continue the same eating habit, 90 days from now, you will feel just as tired, just as worn out, as you do now, because you have replaced this tired blood with more tired blood cells.

And if you have been living on the kind of deficient diet that I have been talking about, and if you will give nature a chance, if you will nourish this new blood stream with vitamins and minerals that it cries for, I promise you that ninety days from now, you may look forward to more pep, more energy, more vitality than you've felt in years. You will not only look better, but feel better. You'll find joy in life; you'll replace tiredness with buoyancy and energy because you will have built back healthy, normal blood cells in place of the tired and worn out ones you now have. Now, you say,

223

The Pitch

"That's fine, Mr. _____, but how can I get all these vitamins and minerals I need? If vitamins alone aren't enough, if minerals aren't enough, if food accessories by themselves aren't enough, doesn't that mean that I will have to go out and buy myself a bottle of Vitamin D, and another of Vitamin D_1 and another of D_2, another bottle of vitamin C and E and some niacin, calcium, and some phosphorus? Why, I would need some thirty bottles in all. Why, it would cost me a month's wages. I would need a shovel to get all these pills and tablets down."

No, it doesn't mean that at all. Why? There are a number of ways in which you can be sure of getting the proper diet. There is, for example, the way of the nutritionist. If you went to a nutritionist, he would say to you to eat 80 percent raw foods and vegetables that have been raised in fertile soil, very, very little meat, practically no alcohol, lots of raw and uncooked foods. He would tell you not to use tobacco; he would tell you not to use this and that and other things, and if you would follow his advice, you may live to be a hundred.

But who wants to be a hundred if they have to live that way? That may be a way of doing it, but I'll tell you this, it is not a way that I have been able to do in this civilized world, but there is another way. You could go to a primitive country where people are noted for their perfect health, and if you ate like them, and lived like them, probably you could develop perfect health too. That's fine if you like to climb trees and fish through a hole in the ice. But I know that I wouldn't personally give up the benefits of civilization for anything.

Now, there is a third way. There are fancy sanitariums for $500 a week. They'll put you on a very, very complicated diet of milk three times a day or something of that nature.

Now, the last way that I am going to mention I call my way. It's my way because I've used it. It's my way because I have taught it for well over twenty years. Ladies and gentlemen, with your permission, I'm going to show you the most complete, perfect vitamin-and-mineral accessory that can be bought or sold anywhere on this earth. In other words, here comes the commercial. The name of it, please remember the name, _____ complex which stands for _____ complex, the vitamins, minerals, proteins, and vitamin B_{12}. It fills every gap and every deficiency in your daily diet.

224

The Pitch

One bottle of _____ complex contains enough tablets to last you for forty-five days. It is the equivalent of a hundred pounds of life-giving health food from which both bulk, roughage have been removed, leaving a combination and concentration of every vitamin, every mineral known to be essential to human nutrition.

Now, I know that some of you are going to say, "Well, all of this sounds very good! I'm going to try some of that. If I know human nature, it will come to your home, you will use it three or four days, then it will wind up in the medicine cabinet. And if you are that kind of a person, I say forget all about _____ complex. If you ever decide that you want to try to vitaminize and mineralize your body, I want you to do it my way, and that means at least ninety consecutive days. In other words, I want you to use two containers of _____ complex, and that is the amount it takes to last you for ninety days.

Now, I am not inferring that one container wouldn't make a difference. As a matter of fact, if your diet isn't sufficient in iron, two tablets of _____ complex contain enough iron to make you feel a little bit better. Have just a little bit more energy, thirty minutes after it has been absorbed in your blood stream. If you use it for thirty days you may feel better than you have in thirty years. But if you stop at the end of thirty days, thirty days after that you could be right back where you started from, and if all you are looking for is relief, I don't recommend _____ complex. _____ is for those of you who are tired, those of you who are looking for results, permanent results, and are willing to let nature and your own blood stream give you those results.

Now, how do you use _____ complex? Two of these food tablets twice a day, and you have taken what modern science has decided to be the full basic requirement of every vitamin known to be essential to the diet, plus substantial quantities of every mineral known to be essential to the diet and every one of the essential eleven proteins.

You do not need more than four tablets. You take more, your body will discard the excess. You will have wasted it, and this food supplement is not to be wasted.

Now you say, "Well, how much is it?"

Ladies and gentlemen, a bottle of _____ complex, enough to last you for forty-five days, costs five dollars. A fraction over a dime a day. But I said I want you to use two bottles. That's right, ten dollars.

Some of you men sitting out there right now, saying it's expensive. Expensive? They think nothing of going out and spending twice as much to see how sick they can make themselves the following day. They hesitate to invest ten dollars in the only body they will ever have.

Remember, ladies and gentlemen, you cannot go to the corner store and buy a new body when you destroy the one you have now.

Now, ladies and gentlemen, I want you to start using _____ complex right now, and I'm going to make it impossible for you to delay. I'm going to make _____ complex available to you at the lowest possible price that I could ask any self-respecting human being to invest in the only body he will ever possess. And since you must use it for ninety days, here is what I will do. I will take two bottles of _____ complex, enough to last you for ninety days, and I will make them available to you immediately after this broadcast for the price of a single bottle, or five dollars. Why, ladies and gentlemen, that's gotten it down to pennies a day, less than it costs to read your daily newspaper, to help you build back a healthy body.

Now, don't say, "Fine, I'll send for two bottles and take one for myself and give one to my husband. Two bottles are for one person. If another member of your family needs it, don't give him one of yours. Order two bottles for him. And if you will order two for yourself for five dollars, two for another member of your family for another five dollars, that's ten dollars' worth, then here is what I will do for you. I will give you at no extra cost, a fifth bottle, which is enough for a child under the age of twelve.

In other words, you can get two of them for five dollars, you can get five of 'em for ten dollars, and whether you get two for five or five for ten, you get them with this understanding:
Take _____ complex into your home. Use it. Use it for the next thirty days. At the end of that time, get in front of the mirror and take inventory like a businessman. Ask yourself these questions. Do you eat better, sleep better, do you have more vitality, more energy, is it everything I've led you to believe? It is? Fine. Tell your friends and neighbors about it. It isn't? Don't waste your time. Take what you haven't used, mail it back to us, no questions

asked, full purchase price refunded immediately. It is not a question of will it work. It *must* work or it costs you nothing.

Ladies and gentlemen, the average person does not realize the value of health until it's gone. Then, flat on their back, they say, "Doctor, take my money, take everything I have, but save me." A fool waits until it is too late, a wise man knows that an ounce of prevention is worth a million pounds of cure.

So all I can say to you, ladies and gentlemen, is this. If what I have told you has sounded sensible and logical to you, go to your telephone and order _____ complex now, because at this moment you may be no further from better health than your own telephone.

So call this number *now*.

A HAIR-RAISING TALE

"A Hair-raising Tale" was one of the classic hair pitches reduced in length but otherwise delivered in pretty much the same manner on TV and radio as it had been on platforms at county fairs, at farmers' markets, and wherever else crowds could be induced to gather.

In this pitch, as in all the hair pitches, directions for use are given as though the audience already had the product in their hands. This gives the audience a vicarious sense of participation, in effect puts them right into the action so that they can better appreciate the virtues of the items being pitched. Note also the rationale behind the selling points.

The lanolin story is really quite ingenious, and convincing as well. On the platform or on TV the pitchman would take a small pad of paper, smear lanolin on the top surface, tear off the sheet, and immerse it in a pan of water. It would immediately curl up into a tight little roll. Ostensibly the same thing would occur to your lanolin-treated hair on a damp day or after you applied water. This was a most convincing sales point. Actually, the lanolin contributed nothing to the curling effect. Its application to one side of the paper merely waterproofed that side. The water, free to enter only the other surface caused the paper to roll up. Ordinary petroleum jelly works just as well.

The Pitch

This test, at least thirty years old and probably more, anticipated (or perhaps inspired) some of the demonstrations that currently glut TV. American ingenuity to the fore! Who can fault the pitchman in this era of magic floor waxes that wipe miraculously clean with one easy swipe, of cleansers that magically remove deep-down stains to the inane commentary of pseudo-housemaids, of nostrums that blast open nasal passages right before your eyes, dissipate headaches in mere seconds, and keep nervous young ladies smelling fresh as daisies come hell or hot weather?

Fifteen-minute radio script

Dim the light, pull up your chair, and turn up the volume; I'm going to tell you a hair-raising tale.

[Five seconds of music]

_____ presents . . . _____ in "A Hair-raising Tale."

Now, listen to this, because this will kill you. A few days ago I met a girl. She was beautiful, the kind of girl that every man hopes someday he'll meet; so I made a date for last Saturday night. I was so anxious to see the girl that I got to her house a few minutes ahead of time.

You should've seen what I saw. Around her head she was wearing a big napkin, she looked like an immigrant. I asked her what it was.

"This? Oh, this is the latest thing," she said. "It's a babushka. All the girls are wearing them."

Get a load of this—the latest thing. My grandmother looked like that when she got off the boat.

Of course, I knew what had happened—she wasn't fooling me. She wanted to make a good impression, and nowadays when girls try to make an impression on a Saturday night date, they wash their hair on Friday, put it up in rags, ribbons, newspapers, clamps, curlers, rubber bands, bobby pins . . . sleep on the nose all night. When they get up in the morning they look like a plucked chicken . . . can't let anyone see them like that.

No, here's what happens. The new look. On goes the napkin, over the head, under the chin, she can go out shopping— no one knows. Come Saturday night—five minutes before the date, off comes the babushka, out comes the tools, fluff it up a little . . . she's ready for her entrance.

Five minutes later if it starts to rain—stringlets instead of ringlets, noodles all the way down to her nose. You know, forty or fifty years ago our mothers and grandmothers had beautiful, healthy hair. In those days a woman's hair was truly her crowning glory. They washed their hair when it was dirty, brushed it a hundred strokes a day, and never say the inside of a beauty parlor. Today the girls wash their hair because it's Friday, brush it only when they are going to a party, get it dyed, fried, bleached, broiled, roasted, toasted, baked, burned, waved, curled, permanent waving solution, ammonia, shellac, lacquer, glue, embalming fluid, mucilage, sit under upside-down pots, hot machines, cold machines, quick drying machines until they are half-baked, use lemonade, vinegar, peroxide. . . . The result? Six inches of burnt straw!

Don't laugh at me. Turn around and look at each other. The latest thing is beer. What beer has to do with hair, I don't know. It started in Hollywood a few years ago at one of those parties. Today you can walk in any drugstore in the United States and buy a twenty-five cent bottle of beer to wash the hair with for seventy-nine cents.

Girls, I've got news for you. If you must use beer there is a better place to put it. Drink it. It will go to your head anyhow. Look at all the fun you can have. Is it any wonder we have 500,000 bald women in America today? By this time all the men listening are smiling. You guys have a lot to smile about! There are ten million bald men. Ten million! And the funniest thing of all is the fact that when men start to lose their hair they always run down to the corner barbershop and ask a baldheaded barber what they should do about it.

"Sit down in the chair," says the barber. "You've come to the right place." He goes over to the shelf, gets down a couple bottles of perfumed alcohol. He says, "What color do you like?" What color do you like! It comes in eight thousand colors, you can match anything.

Of course, you can't look through all eight thousand bottles—you'd be there for a month. So you chose the biggest one, usually. This time the biggest one is red. You say, "Red is a nice color, I got nothing against red, but tell me something—does this stuff really grow hair?"

"Grow hair!" says the barber. "This? Smell it."

So you smell it. Your brain is supposed to come down to your nose. It smells good, you figure it can't be too bad. "How much is it?"

"Twenty-five cents a sprinkle," says the barber. "It is the best we've got."

You figure, what have you got to lose? You've got no hair, you've got a quarter. You say, "Go ahead, give me the works."

So get this. The baldheaded barber sprinkles the perfumed alcohol on top of the guy's head, and then he rubs it in. If you are a good customer, he rubs a little longer. When he is through rubbing, he combs it real nice. A little pompadiddle down the middle makes it look like you got more this week. Then he says, "Look, this stuff doesn't work overnight."

He's right!

He says, "You better come back next week, get another shot."

You do, and you get your head scratched again. By this time you're starting to like it. It feels good. So you make an appointment. From that day on, the rest of your life you're stuck. Once a week you go to get your head scratched. You wouldn't wake up if the roof fell on you. I mean it. After all, if alcohol could grow hair, most of the men I know would choke to death before they got to the barber shop.

Ladies and gentlemen, I am going to end my tale by showing you a quick, easy, natural way to end your hair trouble. But before I give you that information, I want you to listen carefully to the statement I am about to make. To be healthy, hair—just as everything else that is a live, growing thing—must be fed and nourished. Our hair is supplied with nourishment by our blood stream and our nautral oil supply. And when we remove the natural oil from our hair faster than Mother Nature can replace it, we then are truly on the road to hair trouble.

Excessive washing, too many permanents, alcohol tonics—all these things remove the natural oil. Even spending time outdoors in the summer sun is detrimental. Many people realize these things and try to replace the natural oil with olive oil or other vegetable and mineral oils—but that's ridiculous. We're not vegetables. In the first place, if olive oil could grow hair, olives would have hair on them, wouldn't they?

Ladies and gentlemen, we are animal organic matter, and the oil I recommend is an animal organic oil that comes from an animal that grows hair much like you and I. That animal, believe it or not, is the sheep. Most animals grow hair the way the hair on our eyebrows and eyelashes grows. This hair grows short, sheds by itself . . . always stays the same length. But the sheep grows hair the way you and I do on the top of our heads. The hair grows long, never stops growing. As a result, the sheep takes haircuts the way you and I do.

Many years ago, the oil was called sheep's-wool fat. But when science discovered the marvelous benefits of the oil, they had to give it a highfalutin name. We know it today as lanolin. They use it in hospitals for burns, plastic surgery, skin-grafting operations because of its healing power.

Here is how it is used in the hair and scalp. Listen very carefully. Apply a little lanolin on each of the five fingertips. Liquefy it by rubbing the hands together. The heat of the body will change lanolin from a solid to a liquid. Massage the lanolin directly into the scalp. Do this at least once a day. Now, it's not an overnight cure-all. But dandruff and excessive falling hair caused by neglect, dry scalp due to excessive washing, or infected scalp may be corrected by diligent use.

Here's step two for the men. Liquefy a little more in the palm of the hand. Go over the surface of the hair as you would a pomade or dressing. Use nothing else. Comb it. It will stay in place all day —all the life and luster you want, but no greasy residue to come off on hats and pillows . . . nothing to gather dirt from the air.

Step two for the women. A little lanolin on the fingertips . . . liquefy it. Rub it in the tip ends of the hair, all over the top of the head. Do it every day for at least thirty days. At the end of that time, believe it or not, you will have stopped the tip ends from splitting and cracking. Your hair will get longer, thicker, healthier. You can wear it any style you want, and you won't have to use rats or mice or those other animals you girls go down to the dime store to buy.

Now, because lanolin has nothing to do with color, you can use it on any color hair. But it will add life and luster. Show me a blond-haired person . . . I'll show you a golden blond. White hair . . . silver white. Black hair . . . jet or blue-black. Brown hair . . . rich chestnut brown, plenty of golden highlights.

Here's step three. Men and women alike—once a day, grab a handful of hair in each hand. Your own preferably. If you don't have any of your own, forget the whole thing. If you have some, wonderful! Grab a handful. If there are a few men listening to me who won't be able to get a whole handful, get whatever you can. Give it a pull. Pull it, tug it, yank it . . . all over the top of the head. This doesn't hurt, it doesn't cause hair to fall out.

By doing this, you stretch the hair, strengthen the follicle, and above anything else, you loosen the scalp. That's the important thing. Show me a man or a woman who has lost his hair—or even part of it—I'll show you a man or woman whose skin on top has shrunk down as tight as a drum. It's shiny, polished, it's bald. Show me a man or a woman with a loose, flexible scalp—I'll show you better flow of natural oils and, by the same token, better hair.

Here's the fourth and last step. It will interest the women more than the men, because this is how to have the waves and curls. Men aren't interested in waves and curls, but you guys are interested in saving money. And you know, nowadays, in the beauty parlor, a good permanent wave costs fifteen or twenty dollars. It's a lot of money. 'Course, they have a new gimmick for the thrifty girl. They can run down to the drugstore now and buy a whole chemistry set for a dollar and a half. It's got it all there. They do it to themselves.

Then they run around to their girlfriends' house. "See, I did it myself."

You don't have to tell them—they're looking. Start the way you always do . . . by making those little divisions you're so proud of. When your hair is divided, rub the liquefied lanolin in the tip ends. Put your hair up the way you always do—rags, ribbons, newspapers, clamps, curlers, rubber bands, bobby pins—the whole business. Before you go to sleep, dampen the hair around each curler. When the hair is damp, go to sleep.

When you get up in the morning, the hair will be dry. Take out all the tools. Count them—don't leave any up there in case it should rain. They might rust. Get 'em all out. Then give your hair a vigorous brushing.

The Pitch

You'll see the results the first day. And if it should rain that day, instead of looking like the seahag, all that will happen is the waves will wave and curl just a little bit more. I know you find it hard to believe, but stop and think. On a damp day, the wool of a sheep starts to curl. The wetter it gets, the tighter it curls. People with naturally wavy or curly hair find the same thing happens to them when it rains. Why? Because animal organic oil absorbs moisture, and when it does, a natural contraction takes place.

Lanolin absorbs 40 percent of its weight in water. Now as I said earlier, this isn't an overnight cure-all. But if you use lanolin the way I've told you for the next month or so, you women will never again take a permanent. And you know as well as I do that the only thing permanent about a permanent wave is the permanent trip back to the beauty parlor.

And now, you lucky people, here comes the commercial. If any of you cowards turn to another station, I'll never talk to you again. Seriously, I know that many of you have already decided to use the pure lanolin compound on your hair. I hope the one you decide to use will be the one manufactured by my sponsor, _____. Why? Because it is the one I use, and in my opinion, it is the finest product for its purpose that your money can buy.

_____ comes in two sizes. The regular size, which is enough for two people for ninety days, normally sells for $3.98. The family-size jar, enough for a whole family for a year, normally sells for $5.95. But in order to get you to pick up your phone and order it right now—not tomorrow or next week, or when you get around to it, but right now—we're not only going to cut the price of the regular jar to $2.00, and the family-size jar to $3.00, which is about half the regular price, but to make sure that you don't use anything else to wash your hair while you're using _____, we're going to give you, absolutely free, a dollar-size bottle of our new shampoo with the regular treatment, and twice as much with the family size. In other words, you get the $4.98 value for $2.00, the $7.95 value for $3.00.

And for once in your life, you're not buying a pig in a poke, because it's sold to you with this understanding. When you call us, we send you the treatment C.O.D. You pay the postman. Use it the way I've shown you for at least thirty days. At the end of that time, when this has done for you the things I've led you to believe it will, tell your friends about it. Get us some new customers. That's what _____ is interested in.

If, on the other hand, you're not absolutely satisfied with the results, you have tried the treatment at my company's expense. Return the treatment to _____, and your money will be sent to you by return mail.

Ladies and gentlemen, I have done everything but go to your home and put it in your hair every day for thirty days. Now it's up to you. If you're tired of hair trouble and you believe, as I do, that _____ has the answer, step to your telephone now. Call the number you are about to hear. And if you don't believe, or aren't convinced, call the number anyhow. Because if it works, and it will, it's certainly worth the price. If it doesn't, it has cost you absolutely nothing!

THE FATTEST MAN IN TOWN

This is a new pitch, one of a dozen or so written specifically for mail-order sales via radio. It was quickly discovered that the same pitch in the same time slot night after night soon wore out its welcome, as demonstrated by a decreasing number of orders. Varying the pitch remedied this situation to a great extent, hence this new one and others like it. While they didn't really have that old-time flavor, they were exceedingly successful.

THE FATTEST MAN IN TOWN
[Fifteen-minute radio script]
PITCHMAN: *What is it that . . .*
VOICE: waddles like a duck?
VOICE: wheezes like a water buffalo?
VOICE: eats like a pig?
VOICE: and looks like a hippopotamus?
ANOUNCER: *Listen and laugh as* _____ *presents* _____, *transcribed.*
PITCHMAN: What is it that . . .
waddles like a duck?
wheezes like a water buffalo?
eats like a pig?
and looks like a hippopotamus?

234

The Pitch

Why, its a man—the most unusual man in the world! He isn't famous, but people point him out. He isn't a comedian, but folks chuckle when he passes. He's your neighbor and mine . . . *the fattest man in town!*

Oh, I know what you're thinking. What a terrible thing to say. Why, you shouldn't poke fun at the poor fat man. The poor soul, he can't help himself.

And I say to you, oh yes he can! I claim that practically every overweight person with few exceptions has no right to be fat, and if you'll listen to me, I'll prove it! Nineteen of every twenty overweight people tuned in to this station right now have no excuse for weighing one single pound more than they should. And if you doubt me for a moment, ask your own family doctor.

But—you ladies who mourn for your girlish figures, you men who are running out of notches on your belts—you positively can and you positively should weigh less. Oh, I know what you're thinking. I've heard all the standard excuses. Not too long ago, a heavy man in my audience came up to see me after one of my lectures. He said, "Mr. _____, it's all very well for you to talk about overweight, but what about fellows like me?"

I said, "What about you?" and he said, "Well my fat is hereditary. Everybody in my family is fat."

Now, that's one of the more familiar excuses. The fat man looks at you, he sighs, then he has another helping of strawberry shortcake. Or the fat lady passes the soda fountain, shrugs, and says, "I was born fat." Then she dashes in and orders a double banana split. She gets home that night, she sets her bathroom scale back a couple of pounds, and she's happy . . . The soda jerk is happy . . . The girdle manufacturers are happy . . . Everybody is happy but her husband. So to drown his sorrow, he has a couple of quarts of beer, and before you know it, it's a contest between him and his wife to see who can develop the biggest paunch. Then they wonder why they are overweight.

But there is nothing to wonder about. The answer is simple. They eat three or four times as much as they should! Eating is their hobby. Papa gets home, the first thing he says is, "What's for supper?" Or, if he's in a very good mood, maybe he says, "It's time we had a change. Tonight let's eat in a restaurant."

They get the menu, it says, "Home Cooking." They go to a nice

The Pitch

place, a combination restaurant and filling station. You eat there and get gas. But it's very clean. The food is untouched by human hands. I guess the chef is a monkey.

Mama looks at the menu, her mouth starts to water. Papa looks at the prices, his mouth starts to foam. So for economy, they decide on the special dinner. It only has six courses—appetizer, soup, entree, dessert, coffee, and bicarbonate of soda.

In between courses, they eat half a dozen rolls and a pound of butter. Then when the waiter asks what they'll have for dessert, mama says, "I'll have a pie à la mode, but no whipped cream. I have to watch my figure."

It's just as well she watches it. Papa hasn't looked at it in years.

When they get home, papa says he's so full he doesn't care if he never sees food again. An hour later, where's papa? He's in the kitchen raiding the icebox. And mama smiles. "Always eating. Just like a growing boy."

The only difference, papa is growing sideways. Sounds amusing, eh? Believe me, it's not. The latest medical statistics prove that overweight people are more apt to suffer from heart disease, high blood pressure, diabetes, and diseases of the gall bladder, kidneys, and other vital organs than thin folks. That's right! Every extra pound you carry, carries you one step closer to an untimely end. And if you think I'm exaggerating, then why do fat people pay higher insurance premiums than normal people? I'll tell you why. Because the insurance companies know their business. They know that for every extra pound you carry, you may be cutting off 1 percent from your life potential. So if you are twenty to 30 pounds overweight, figure it out for yourself. You are taking years off your life potential. And I'm not even talking about appearance.

Pity poor mama! She wants so much to be stylish. She's always reading the fashion magazines. Every month they show a new silhouette. One month it's the padded-shoulder silhouette. The next month, it's the padded-hip silhouette. The month after that, it's the padded-back silhouette. Mama is waiting for them to combine them all. Then she'll be in style. Only trouble is, while she's waiting for that to happen, she keeps getting heavier. She's a padded silhouette, all right, only on her, it's from the top of her head to the tip of her toes.

Then one day, she decides enough is enough. She's going to do

236

something about it. She's going to surprise papa. She'll exercise and lose weight. So she buys a book that tells how. Only one trouble. Who ever heard of anyone who lost weight by reading? But mama doesn't worry about that. She buys the book anyway. On the way home, she's so exhausted from carrying it, she stops off for a chocolate malted. What does she care? The book will tell her how to work it off.

And what does the book say? To work off one chocolate malted, run seventeen miles. Can't you just see mama jogging along the highway in tights?

When papa gets home, instead of supper, he finds mama bumping herself against the wall. Papa says, "Where's supper?"

Mama says ,"Just a minute. I'm breaking down fatty tissue."

Papa's hungry—mama's breaking down fatty tissue. But it's not as amusing as it sounds. For the facts of the matter are these. If mama wants to exercise off just one single pound of fat, she'll have to run thirty-six miles. Or if she thinks running is undignified at her age, all she has to do is climb to the top of the Washington Monument forty-eight times. That's how much exercise you actually have to do to exercise off one single pound. But mama thinks she can wiggle a little bit and lose thirty pounds of excess weight.

It's like the man who works in an office. His paunch is getting so big he can't reach his desk from a sitting position. So what does he decide to do? Every night he'll exercise for fifteen minutes. Get him! For eight hours a day he sits at a desk. For eight hours he sleeps. For two hours a day he's traveling to and from work, and for another two hours he's having breakfast, lunch, and supper. In the evening he reads the papers for an hour, listens to the radio for two hours, and raids the icebox for about forty-five minutes. That's 23¾ hours he's been sitting, sleeping, or eating. In the *other* fifteen minutes he's going to exercise and lose weight.

But for every pound he wants to lose, he'll have to do 16,200 pushups. There's really nothing to it! Do you want more? Many people think that when they perspire after hard work or exercise, they are reducing fatty tissue. But that's ridiculous. That perspiration dripping off your brow isn't fat. It is simply water, and all you are doing is dehydrating yourself. One glass of water and you are right back where you started from.

Actually, there is only one exercise which takes off pounds. You can try it tonight at dinner. About halfway through your meal, place your hands firmly at the edge of the table and push hard. That's right. Push yourself away from the table. Do that exercise frequently, and I'll guarantee that you'll lose weight.

I'll also guarantee that you'll be half-famished, unless you know one little secret that I'll let you in on in a moment. It's like the girl who is always dieting—there's one in every family. Maybe she is a sister, a cousin or an aunt. But somewhere you'll find her. She's always on a diet. A milk diet, a fruit diet, an egg diet, a protein diet. For breakfast she has a small glass of juice, for lunch some dried toast, for dinner, half an apple. And at the end of the week, she always weighs two pounds more than at the beginning. Why? Very simple. In order to keep strength up, she stuffs herself between meals.

Ladies and gentlemen, if you are going to diet, you must keep it up! You must be prepared to be hungry and stay hungry for great periods of time. When you let up, your weight goes up. There is no use kidding about it, friends. Diet is a case of mind over platter. It takes an iron will and a cast-iron constitution to keep a diet.

Take papa. Exercise hasn't helped, so he decides to go on a diet. Finally one night he comes home and he says, "This is it. Tonight starts my diet." His mouth hasn't stopped moving since he was born, but he's going to diet. If supper is five minutes late, the neighbors two blocks away hear him screaming. But tonight starts his diet. First thing he does, he starts issuing ultimatums.

No more bread on the table. He's going on a diet, everybody else has to suffer. Three days later, he says, "My, I feel wonderful! I haven't had a bite of bread for three days."

Of course, he's eaten twice as many mashed potatoes, but they don't count. Then, he gets on the scale—he weighs just as much as he ever did, so he shrugs and says, "Well, diets are not for me. I'm not the type."

"All right," you say. "I'm not fat because of heredity. I'm not fat because of my glands. I'm fat because I overeat. But what can I do about it?"

And I say to you, "Eat less and you'll weigh less."

You see, your body acts like a reservoir. Put in too much food and some of it is used, some of it is discarded, and some of it is stored away. But how does your body store up extra food? Do you have little cupboards marked apple pie, mashed potatoes, or pork chops? Of course not. Your body converts that extra food you eat into fat.

Now, if you should stop eating, your body would absorb that fat and burn it up as energy. Why, during the last war, shipwrecked sailors floated around on little rafts for amazing lengths of time without food. When they were rescued, doctors found they were still in good health. The only change was a marked loss in weight. Their bodies had absorbed and burned up their fatty tissue.

Now, I'm not about to suggest that to lose weight you should lose yourself on a raft. There is an easier way to lose weight—a perfectly safe and sensible method which accomplishes amazing results without hunger, without dangerous drugs, diets, machines, massages, and steam baths.

Impossible, is it? Listen carefully. During the last war, nutritionists working with the United States army and navy created many highly concentrated foods rich in vitamins, minerals, and proteins that were fed to the boys in the field. These were known as K rations, and so on. These foods gave the boys everything they needed to give them plenty of energy and keep them in good health. There are only one thing wrong with them. Because they were so highly concentrated, the boys suffered constantly from a feeling of hunger. So the top scientific brains of the country got together and created vegetable cellulose, a food tablet no bigger than a pea which was as satisfying to hunger as a full turkey dinner at Christmas. Why does it have this wonderful quality? Very simple. It expands when it absorbs water, partly filling the stomach. So when you take this wonderful little food tablet a half hour before a meal with a glass of water, you enjoy your meal as much as ever, *but you just can't overeat.*

And here's another amazing thing that the scientists discovered while making their clinical tests: Not only did this gel prevent the pangs of hunger, but it promoted the regularity of the entire digestive system, thereby improving the general health of the boys who used it. Now, ladies and gentlemen, do you realize what this discovery means to *you*, if you are a person who wants to lose weight? Now, for the first time, a food accessory has been created that not only gives you the proteins that are essential to reduction, the vitamins and minerals that are essential to health and energy while

239

reducing, but also that contains this wonderful new substance discovered for the army which eliminates hunger pangs and makes it impossible for you to overeat.

And now, ladies and gentlemen, I want you to listen and remember the name of this product, how you can get it, how much it will cost, and how you can try it without a penny's risk or obligation! The name of this new way to slenderize is _____s spelled _____, and _____s must help you reduce *safely*, because they mean no dieting, no drugs, no exercise, no hunger pangs, no massages, no machines.

What can you eat? You can eat anything you want to. Because when you use _____s you just won't want to eat too much. Drugs _____ forget about them, because _____s do everything for you that the drugs could do, *but* _____ are absolutely beneficial to your health. How fast can you reduce? Just about as fast as you want to because the more _____s you use, the less you will be able to eat.

Why, ladies and gentlemen, in test after test conducted with this wonderful reducing aid, people lost up to eleven pounds the first week, up to thirty-eight pounds the first month, without ever suffering one pang of hunger, without ever taking a single drug, without exercise, without doing anything difficult, dangerous, or expensive. Simply because _____s made it impossible for them to eat too much.

Now, I don't care what you've tried, what you've used, or what you've done. If what I have told you has sounded sensible to you, and if you honestly and sincerely want to bring your weight down to normal, to improve your appearance, your health, your potential span of life, here is all I ask you to do. When you call the number you are about to hear, your postman will bring you a three-week supply of _____s for only 2.98. That means it costs you only a little over a dime a day to get rid of excess, ugly fat—a dime a day to chase your fat away.

Now, I said that I would allow you to try _____s at no risk, no obligation. Here is what I mean. When you order your three weeks' supply of _____s for only 2.98, we will also send you in a separate package, *free, an extra ten-day supply.* Use this supply that we give you for the ten days. At the end of that time, if you have not gotten rid of ugly pounds of weight, if you do not in every way look better, feel better, have more energy . . . If _____s

240

are not everything I've led you to believe thy are . . . If people don't walk up to you and say that you look better than you have looked in years—simply send back the package that you have paid for, and your full purchase price of 2.98 will be refunded to you immediately, no questions asked. It's not a question of *will it work?* _____s *must* work or they cost you absolutely nothing. The only thing you have to lose is your extra weight. Don't put off until tomorrow what you can take off today. Call this number. . . .

FRANCHISES— SHOULD YOU or SHOULDN'T YOU?

IN RECENT YEARS the franchise business has grown to extraordinary proportions. In the event you are not sure, a franchise is simply an agreement between a manufacturer or a supplier and an individual or company who contracts to handle that manufacturer's or supplier's product or service under its advertised name in the manner prescribed.

The classic examples are the quick-food operations that are individually owned but operated under a strict set of rules covering every aspect of the operation and usually including a sales quota. In return for a franchise, the individual pays a fee or a royalty and buys the necessary merchandise from the franchiser.

There are a number of fairly obvious advantages to this setup. If the deal is sound, the company offers you a pretested, advertised product or service for which a need has been demonstrated. The company will train you in the techniques necessary to sell or prepare their merchandise, may help you to get the financing required, and may even set up a bookkeeping system for you.

Ideally, they have worked out all the details of the business as scientifically as possible, and they turn that know-how over to you so that the full advantage of their expertise is working for you. The more successful you are, the more money they make and the easier it is for them to sell their next franchise.

Bear in mind that some of the larger and more successful franchisers are often quite dictatorial and extremely independent. They may charge a great deal in the way of initial fees and other charges, they may be unduly restrictive, they probably will require you to meet minimum sales quotas or lose your franchise, and so on; but if they are efficiently run, your chances of success are fairly good.

On the other hand, franchise operations have long been a haven for sharp operators who are interested only in grabbing a fee or dumping a load of virtually worthless merchandise on you at exorbitant prices.

Don't, under any circumstances, get involved in any franchise deal until you personally check it out. Consult your local chamber of commerce and see if they have any information on it. Check the Better Business Bureau as well. If there isn't a local branch handy, contact the national office.

Don't get involved in some hairbrained scheme just because the nice man told you how much money you are going to make. If his franchises were that good, he'd probably be back home operating one himself instead of being out on the road hustling. The really hot franchises are generally sought after to such an extent that they don't have to be sold with the high-pressure tactics frequently utilized by some of the smaller or newer franchise operators.

Some years ago there was a racket—and for all I know, it still exists— called the peanut-machine game, which preyed on hapless individuals all across the country who wanted nothing more than to be their own bosses. It wasn't a franchise deal by any means, although it was usually presented as such. In essence, a con-man-type salesman sold a nut-machine "route" for the generally standard price of six hundred dollars. All you did was invest six hundred dollars, for which you became the proud owner of a string of peanut machines. From that point on you made your living—or supplemented your regular income—simply by taking money out of your machines and putting peanuts in.

In actual operation the company would run high-powered ads touting their sure-fire, moneymaking deal in local papers throughout the territory they were exploiting. The salesman would check into the best hotel in town at the time the ad was due to run and wait for the phone to start ringing.

When a prospect called, the salesman would go into his routine, a pitch so polished and powerful and cleverly worked out down through the years that unless the caller was a strong-willed individual, he had a tough time resisting the temptation to plunge right in, and frequently did despite himself. For example, when the individual called, the salesman would insist that if he was married he bring along his wife. Why? Because the salesman was not about to go to all the trouble of making a long and involved pitch, only to have his mark slip off the hook by saying, "Sounds good, but I think I'd better ask my wife first."

There was a pat answer, whether true or not, for every possible objection the prospect could possibly raise. If he and his wife agreed that the deal sounded attractive, the salesman would hustle them right down to the bank, where they were urged to withdraw cash or a certified check for the full amount. Before they had a chance to think the deal over and possibly change their minds, the salesman was gone, and they ended up with six peanut machines worth a hundred dollars or so and a sack of nuts. They got no further help. Placing the machines was their problem, and the salesman—two hundred dollars richer for his trouble—was on to the next town.

The peanut-machine racket is an extreme example, but bear it in mind. If franchises intrigue you, be careful. Those salesmen are pretty smooth operators. They have to be in order to survive. They receive a very substantial commission (no salary), and they frequently operate at their own expense, so they are anxious—perhaps desperate—to sell the deal. Ask for proof of the earnings the franchiser claims are being made. Get the names and addresses of other franchise holders and contact those people yourself. It will certainly be worth a trip—even if it's a few hundred miles—to find out firsthand whether they are happy and prospering.

Check out the parent company. If you can, pull a credit report on it. If you can't do that, in all probability your bank can do it for you. Don't take anybody's word for anything when it comes to your hard-earned dollars.

Check out the market, as well, and see what your competition is. Find out how much they charge for the same product or service and try to find out how well they are doing and whether the product or service under consideration really does have sales potential. You should also ascertain whether you will have an exclusive territory in which to operate or whether the company plans to franchise other individuals in your area. If they do, is the market big enough to sustain both of you, or are you going to compete with each other and hurt your chances for success?

Never, under any circumstances, sign anything until you have an attorney check it all out for you. Don't be too hasty. Don't let the salesman panic you into anything you might regret later. Remember, they're pretty slick, and most of them have learned their trade well. Don't ever underestimate them.

Remember, too, that your chances of getting rich as the operator of a franchise operation are probably remote. I am sure you can earn a comfortable living if you make the right choice, but the men who really make it are the franchisers—the guys who get the idea, develop the apparatus or machines required, perfect the details, develop a workable, profitable format, and then sell franchises for that operation to others.

Perhaps you can do the same thing. Invent a new novelty food, for example, or possibly resurrect an old one. Think about it for a moment. There have been numerous novelty foods that have enjoyed various degrees of success . . . hot-dogs baked in batter; puffy hot waffles with ice cream and sauce; revolving hot-dog roller grills; hamburgers, cheeseburgers, California burgers, pizza burgers and chili burgers; glazed doughnuts and stuffed doughnuts and jelly doughnuts; soft ice cream, hard ice cream; and so on. Ethnic foods are extremely popular and becoming more so.

Greek foodstands are springing up all over New York. They feature, among other things, souvlaki, which is a type of chopped meat shaved from a huge, spitted slab and placed inside a piece of pita (a Middle Eastern bread) along with slices of tomato, eggplant, and onion.

Mexican food presents a lot of potential. Tacos have always been fairly popular, and I have always had the feeling that if someone devised a simple, practical gadget for frying tacos with the ingredients sealed inside, a successful operation could be put together. Speak to franchise holders and get their point of view.

The following will give you some idea of the scope of the franchise setups available. Don't construe them as recommendations, however. If franchising intrigues you, read franchise magazines, send for literature, call companies, and so on, but don't become involved until you have investigated thoroughly and are absolutely certain of what you are doing.

RETAILING

Retail businesses of various types account for more than 40 percent of the dollar volume done in the United States, and this is certainly the easiest area in which to become involved. A great many franchises are retail operations. A large number of these are in the fast-food field—doughnuts, hamburgers, ice cream, fried chicken, fish and chips, frozen custard, hero sandwiches, and so on. Other popular franchise operations sell merchandise of various types or perform services and repairs on a retail level.

RENTAL SERVICE

The rental business has shown a fairly steady growth. The idea of being able to rent equipment for short-term use, as opposed to buying it, is becoming increasingly popular, and the scope of the items available is vast. You name it—chain saws, power mowers, punchbowls, tables and chairs, welding machines, electric drills, silverware, or whatever—and chances are it is available for rental by day, week, or month for a relatively modest fee.

Rental-business franchises are available, and since most of your investment goes into rental equipment, bank financing is a distinct possibility. Sometimes it is even possible to rent your rental equipment from the franchiser.

DRY-CLEANING ESTABLISHMENTS

Discount dry-cleaning stores in which the public can effect substantial savings make this appear to be a fairly attractive franchise. The cleaning is done by machine automatically and requires little help from you, or so the company claims.

AUTOMOTIVE FRANCHISES

The automotive field has always been ripe territory for franchising. Muffler shops that sell and install new mufflers, paint shops that repaint your car, wheel-alignment and front-end work shops, transmission-repair establishments, and so on, are among the best known.

Some years ago an outfit that claimed to have chrome-restoring-and-reconditioning equipment attempted to become involved in franchising. Perhaps they did so. I don't really know, but that is typical of the type of specialized services available.

HOUSE AND OFFICE CLEANING

Cleaning and maintenance setups of various types have always been popular. They require a small investment and little skill or education, and they afford the franchisee an opportunity to be his own boss. Normally, making a living by the sweat of your brow won't make you rich. Of course, it is always possible that eventually you may reach the point where you have others working for you, and ultimately you may enjoy the fruits of a fairly substantial business. Among the various types of cleaning for such operations have been rug and carpet cleaning and shampooing, and general house and office cleaning.

Actually, you don't have to own a franchise. You can buy your own carpet-cleaning equipment for far less, pay no royalties, and do your own advertising and promotion. Or, if this idea appeals to you, you can start out by doing general housecleaning and office maintenance, then get into carpet cleaning and such.

HAIR PIECES

Toupees and hairpieces are becoming increasingly popular, and franchise setups are available to sell these wanted commodities.

SCHOOLS

School franchises apparently work pretty well too. One outfit sets up franchises to train supermarket checkers. They help you to train instructors, and so on, and claim that the operation is very profitable.

FOAM RUBBER

Foam-rubber-furniture store franchises, which sell foam mattresses and pillows and furniture utilizing them, are being offered.

Once again, investigate carefully and thoroughly, think twice, and realize that although a good franchise will probably help you to earn a fine living, this is probably not the way to get rich.

HOW to SET UP.......
a BUSINESS
on SMALL CAPITAL

PERHAPS THE GREATEST single cause of business failure is undercapitalization. Sometimes a business takes longer to get off the ground than anticipated. Some times it takes more capital to set up properly or more merchandise to keep it going than you can afford to buy. Think carefully before you invest your capital in any venture, and make sure you have enough to keep you going.

The following guides are not intended to replace your lawyer or accountant or friendly neighborhood banker or whatever, but they are calculated to give you a firmer grasp of the realities of setting up a small business with limited capital.

Rule Number 1

Don't plunge into a deal until you have investigated it thoroughly. Be suspicious. Be skeptical. Don't accept anyone's word for anything unless you know that person extremely well, and even then, be careful. People—even the best of them—sometimes do strange things when money is involved. Then, too, even though their motives may be as pure as the driven snow, their judgment may be suspect or their evaluation of a given situation may be faulty and hence misleading.

Rule Number 2

Don't get involved in a business you are not going to enjoy. If you don't like it and you aren't completely confident that you can handle it, don't get into it.

If the business requires special talents or abilities, be sure you have those talents and abilities *before* you get involved. Don't hope to develop them later. It may not happen. Be practical and sensible and don't sign on the dotted line, or anywhere else, until you are sure you understand precisely what you are going to be required to do and know you are going to enjoy doing it.

Rule Number 3

Be sure the arithmetic makes sense before you get involved. A business is supposed to make money. If you aren't sure your business is going to throw off a profit—and enough of a profit to make your effort and investment worthwhile—forget it. You're better off putting your surplus funds in a bank and collecting interest than you are in knocking yourself out to break even. Nobody ever got rich that way!

Guys who really know look at money coldly and dispassionately. They don't take risks unless they are sure those risks are going to pay off.

Rule Number 4

If you are buying an existing business, *be sure to check everything out.* Again, don't take anybody's word for anything. Examine the books. Get certified statements from accountants. Poke around. Be sure that the business is producing the way the seller claims it is.

Check the running expenses as well. How much are rent, heat, power, insurance? Are any special license fees required? Have you been told everything? Are you sure?

Why is the Business Being Sold?

Are any hidden pitfalls going to show up after you buy? Is the building that houses the business about to be torn down? Will a soon-to-be-built highway divert business traffic away from your area? Is a giant competitor, or any competitor, for that matter, moving in across the street? Investigate as thoroughly as you can *before* you sign contracts. It's too late after.

Are You Paying too Much for the Business?

This, of course, is a prime question. If you are buying a retail operation you generally pay for actual inventory on hand plus the fixtures—cabinets, lighting, furniture, etc.—plus what is sometimes optimistically called "goodwill." (If the business is well established and has steady customers, goodwill is an important asset. In many instances, however, it is overstated.)

256

In the final analysis, all that really counts is the overall price you pay. It doesn't matter how it is broken down. The paramount question is simply, *Will the amount you pay for the business return a fair profit?* The opinion of a trusted accountant—or perhaps a good lawyer—will surely be worthwhile.

A good lawyer will see that you don't get taken. He will write legal safeguards into your contract to prohibit the seller from going right back into business and competing with you in the immediate area. He will see that the seller doesn't misrepresent, and he may be able to spot pitfalls that have escaped your scrutiny.

Buying an existing business is fine, but it is not going to make you any richer than the man who sold it to you unless you can use it as the basis for building a much more profitable enterprise. Ideally a going business can serve as an established, working base from which to operate and provide you with the know-how you may not already possess (sources of merchandise, etc.) and thus allow you to concentrate on improving the existing situation.

In some instances there are important tax advantages to be gained as well, but that is something you will have to discuss with your accountant.

HOW TO RAISE CAPITAL

If you are planning to get involved in a business—either by buying an existing one or by starting your own from scratch—you should have some money of your own to begin with. Lenders like to think that you have enough confidence in your project to invest your own money in it as well as theirs. But whether you do or not, capital is still hard to raise.

Banks, for all their propaganda to the contrary, are tough nuts to crack. If you are wealthy, if you have valuable assets—securities or other collateral—then they'll be more than happy to lend you money. If you don't, forget it. Even if you have a sterling reputation and know your banker particularly well, he may want the note co-signed by someone with assets and, at best, will probably be willing to grant a loan only on a short-term basis.

Banks are getting particularly cautious about lending money. Real estate is no longer intriguing to them, so mortgages are becoming increasingly difficult to obtain, and unless securities are blue chip, banks may not be interested in holding them.

LIFE INSURANCE

If you have a reasonably substantial life-insurance policy and have carried it for a number of years, you have probably built up cash value that you can borrow (at a reasonable rate of interest) any time you wish. Life-insurance loans don't have to be repaid at any specific time, which is a mixed blessing. On the one hand, you aren't pressured into making repayment. On the other, however, the value of your policy is reduced by the amount of money you have borrowed, and should you die before the loan is repaid, your beneficiaries will collect your insurance less the amount you have borrowed.

HOME MORTGAGE

The property you own is a traditional source of money and generally the first one considered. If there is a substantial difference between the real value of your home and the amount of money you still owe on your mortgage, that mortgage can be renegotiated. Normally banks are willing—often eager—to renegotiate, because this gives them an opportunity to raise the interest rate, and hence their income. From your point of view, this may be a bad deal. If you have had your mortgage for a long time, chances are you have been enjoying a very low rate of interest, and renegotiating raises your payments substantially and makes you subject to some fairly heavy legal fees besides.

HOW to SELL THINGS
YOU or OTHERS MAKE

IN RECENT YEARS there has been a tremendous upsurge in interest in craft-type products. More people than ever are into crafts of every type and description—leather work, jewelry, candles, macramé, découpage, casting, woodworking, ceramics, and so on. Even more significant from your point of view, people are not only making craft items, but they are buying them as well.

In New York City, for example, street peddlers—young hippie types—are selling a wide variety of craft items. Leather belts, buckles, earrings, necklaces, finger rings and other jewelry, etc. Contrary to appearances, most of these purveyors of crafts don't actually make the objects they are selling. For the most part they work on commissions, and the craft-looking objects they sell are actually made in factories. However, the point is that they are finding a ready market for their wares. People are craft conscious, and perhaps therein lies an opportunity for you.

Obviously you are not going to get rich by peddling earrings on the street corner of your hometown, but suppose you had ten peddlers doing it for you? Or suppose you had a batch of competent craftspeople turning out wares that you sold for them in stores or on street corners, via peddlers, etc.?

Whether you are trying to get rich or just supplement your income, there are definite possibilities here. Selling things that you or members of your family make, or that a whole string of craftsmen that you represent make, could be the start of something interesting.

Following is basic information on various procedures you can use to sell anything from pinky rings to candles to birdhouses. Incidentally, birdhouses must really be hot items right now. Full-page ads for them plus the great current interest in bird watching (see the piles of bird seed being sold in supermarkets) indicates that the world may be ready for the birdhouses that *you* can make—or have made—and sell!

HOW TO SELL TO SMALL RETAIL OUTLETS

Merchandise of the kind we have been discussing can be sold to card shops, boutiques, craft shops, art galleries, and sometimes even restaurants and diners.

The best way to proceed is to call the owner or buyer for an appointment. Explain that you have some unique merchandise you feel he can handle well, that it is a profitable line and easy to sell, that all you want is five minutes of his time to show him your wares, and that you will be glad to stop by any time at his convenience. If calling first is not practical, stop by and ask to speak to the manager, the owner, or whoever does the buying. Then show your line. If it is being handled successfully by anyone else in a similar outlet, be sure to mention the fact. Don't be bashful. The storekeeper makes his money by selling profitable items. If you have something that fits the bill, say so! Tell him what your hottest item is. Storekeepers know that certain items always do better than others.

Try not to sell right from your sample case. If you have some stock right in your car or van, fine, but generally the most professional way to proceed is to take the order and make delivery at a later date, generally in two weeks or so.

The storekeeper may ask you to leave things on consignment. When he sells the item you will receive from 50 to 75 percent of the selling price, depending on the deal you make. This isn't a particularly good idea. If your merchandise is valuable, you don't want to leave it scattered all over town. If the storekeeper is adamant—if it's consignment or nothing—and you are confident your merchandise will sell, it may pay you to leave it with the understanding that if it does sell the way you are sure it will, the next order will be on a regular basis.

When you leave your merchandise present a bill that plainly describes it, indicates the quantity you are leaving, and spells out the details of your deal. Have him sign a copy, which you take with you.

SELLING TO DEPARTMENT STORES

Don't be overwhelmed just because it is a large store. A department store is really nothing but a lot of small departments lumped together, and all you have to do is sell to one of them. Each department is usually headed up by a buyer, and he or she is the person you have to see.

If you don't know his or her name, call the store and ask the operator who the buyer for the boutique or craft or whatever department is. She will tell you or put you in touch with someone who can.

Then call the buyer. Explain what you have to offer and request an appointment. If you are not particularly good on the phone, it might be a good idea to jot down exactly what you want to say, as though you were writing a piece of advertising copy. Chances are he is busy, perhaps even frantic, and since he has never heard of you or your company, try to hook him right away, by starting with something that will arouse his interest immediately.

Maybe something like this:

> Mr. _____,
>
> I have a new and very profitable item that is selling very well and making a lot of money for all the stores that are handling it. . . .

You are using his name so he thinks he may have met you or, in any case, that you know him, so that establishes some kind of rapport, flimsy though it may be. You immediately mention "new," which is something buyers are always looking for, and you mention profit, which is the kind of language he's interested in. You say, "selling very well," and that, too, is the kind of language he wants to hear, and you reinforce that idea by telling him that your items are "making a lot of money" for other stores (his competitors). If that doesn't pique his interest, then he's not even alive.

At this point he asks you what you are selling, but don't go into any descriptive language unless your items are absolutely unique and easily describable as such, because you don't want to risk a rejection at this point. You want to get to see him and show him your merchandise in person. When he asks, you simply say, "Very unique earrings that will

263

only take me three minutes to show you." (Don't say two minutes, because two minutes is just a figure of speech that can mean anything, but three minutes is a short, specific time period.)

In any case, set up your appointment, and when you get in to see him, sell hard. Plan your pitch in advance and utilize the principles of hard-sell copy in this book. Of course, if your items are so attractive that they are obviously selling themselves, fine. Keep cool and keep quiet. But if they aren't or if his interest seems to be less than intense, talk . . . politely but firmly!

When a department store buys, they will give you a purchase order with all the necessary information on it. It will contain shipping instructions, agreed-upon price, terms, etc. If you are not familiar with procedures of this type and don't know anyone who can give you the information you need, there are several very helpful books on the subject (listed at the end of this section) that will fill you in on the specifics.

SELLING TO WHOLESALERS

Wholesalers specialize in selling a particular type of merchandise to appropriate retail outlets. For example, an automotive wholesaler sells related merchandise to automotive-supply stores. A ready-to-wear wholesaler sells to retail clothing stores. A grocery wholesaler sells to food stores, and so on. Wholesalers maintain their own staffs of salesmen and handle a wide variety of products produced by various manufacturers within their field of interest.

Working through a wholesaler has both advantages and disadvantages. For one thing, a wholesaler works on a commission basis. In addition to the customary 40 percent markup the retail outlet takes, you have to add another 15 or 20 percent for the wholesaler. Wholesalers perform a valuable service. They can move a lot more merchandise than you can, but you pay well for it.

Some wholesalers will warehouse your stock, ship it themselves, collect for it, and pay you directly. This is a convenient way for you to operate because you ship your merchandise in bulk to one location.

Other wholesalers sell your goods to stores throughout the country but leave the shipping and the billing to you, and this can pose a headache of considerable proportions, particularly if your business is small or is just getting started. If you have a product and you think working through a wholesaler can be advantageous, think twice before you consent to do your own shipping and billing. The extra effort and expense could eat up all your profits.

FLEA MARKETS

These are generally outlets of very limited scope. The type of merchandise sold is usually in the realm of antiques, used housewares, old clothing, and oddments of various sorts.

The mechanics of the operation are simple enough. A promoter rents an area in a reasonably convenient and accessible location. He divides the space into small segments and rents them to individuals who set up their own little stalls and sell whatever they think people will buy. Sometimes the sellers keep all the profit, and sometimes they must pay the promoter a commission of anywhere from 10 to 30 percent on whatever they sell, in addition to the rental or registration fee they originally paid.

ART FAIRS

Art fairs function pretty much the way flea markets do. In this instance, however, the merchandise is restricted to arts and crafts— paintings, sculpture, ceramics, jewelry, etc.

In either case, selling merchandise under these circumstances is extremely limited. If anyone makes any real money at a flea market or art fair, it is generally the operator, and perhaps that's the angle you should be thinking about. The success of that type of operation is directly proportional to the number of exhibitors and the size of the crowds that come to browse and buy, and both of these elements can be attracted by the proper promotion.

Check it out. If there are no flea markets in your area, perhaps there should be. All it takes is a large space, indoors or out, a method of attracting exhibitors to rent from you, and an audience to buy. You attract both exhibitors and buyers by advertising in local newspapers and by posting signs that announce the time and place of your coming flea market and request exhibitors to call or write for information. Here again, your ingenuity and promotional ability will spell the difference between successful or so-so results.

I have heard of one flea market so incredibly successful that space is sold on a first-come, first-served basis. Exhibitors start to line up at six in the morning and anyone who comes much later than that is usually out of luck. If that isn't enough, the crowds that throng this market are actually charged two dollars a head just to get in to spend their money!

Think about that for a while. Imagine a whole string of flea markets right across the country. Some smart operator will be doing it soon.

COLLEGE DORMITORIES

Some craftsmen have discovered that college students are good customers for craft items, and they have been wise enough to sell their wares in dormitories—evenings are the only practical time—or to set up shop in busy areas on campus. They report that the best time for campus sales is during the hours between ten and three or thereabouts.

MAIL ORDER

For most people, mail order looms as a superattractive way to sell things. No hustling, no selling, no irksome visits to surly buyers or pompous little storekeepers. You simply run an ad and then dash down to your bulging mailbox to pick up all the money nice people from all over the country have been kind enough to send to you. Sounds great, and sometimes it is. Unfortunately, it's not that easy. If it was everyone would be a mail-order millionaire. If you are interested, see the chapter on "Mail Order" in this book.

GOOD BOOKS ON THE SUBJECT

Selling What You Make, by Jane Wood.
A large format paperback, published by Penguin.

How to Start Your Own Craft Business, by Herb Genfan and Lyn Taelzsch. Watson-Guptill, Publishers.

A FEW BUSINESS IDEAS

THERE ARE a great many businesses in which you can become profitably involved that require a relatively small cash outlay. In many instances several hundred dollars will do the trick. In others a thousand, or a little more or less, will get you started. Few if any of them will make you rich if pursued in the usual fashion, but get into them imaginatively and aggressively, and who knows? The potential is there. Whether or not you realize that potential depends on how far you are prepared to go.

Following are some ideas I think may have potential. Before you read them, bear in mind that the worth of an idea is directly proportional to the imagination of the conceiver of that idea. To some people a little store selling cheap notions is just a little store selling cheap notions. To F.W. Woolworth it was a multimillion-dollar enterprise.

To most people a hamburger is just something to eat that costs around 75¢. To MacDonald it is a far flung empire that throws off millions in profits every year. It all depends on how you look at it.

On the outskirts of New York City there is a man named Tom Carvel who has franchised close to 700 soft ice cream stores. I am sure the annual income he derives is astronomical, to say the least. That man got started on an ice cream truck and a happy combination of imagination, hard work and an interesting stroke of fate made him the multimillionaire he is today.

As he relates it, he was driving his ice cream truck through a small town outside of the city when he had a blowout. While he was parked and in the process of fixing the flat, he did a surprisingly brisk ice cream business—so brisk, in fact, that it gave him an interesting idea. He gave up the truck, opened a store, on the very same spot, and parlayed his recipe for soft ice cream and his conception of how it should be sold into a fortune. Who would have dreamed it could all start with one ice cream truck? Who but a man with desire and imagination and the drive to make it happen?

A Few Business Ideas

Following are some thoughts about a few businesses you can get started in with very little cash. Look them over and see what you think, and envision them not in terms of a way to grind out a living, but as the substantial enterprises they could be if you promote them aggressively.

PAINTING CONTRACTOR

I think this has a great deal of potential, but it has to be handled properly. House and industrial painting is a fairly substantial business. There always seems to be enough work around to support a lot of painters, and so far as I can see none of them are particularly promotion-minded. Except for a rare post card from a local painter—I have received two in the last ten years and I live in a very affluent suburban community—and unimpressive ads in the yellow pages, their efforts are virtually nonexistent. I don't think it would be too difficult to garner a lot of the business in your area even if you don't know too much about painting, and then farm it out, retaining a fair share of the action for obtaining the work and assuming the responsibility for getting it done.

I think your main problem will be in the know-how department. Unless you happen to be an expert, making estimates and planning jobs may be pretty rough in the beginning, but you'll learn fast. You might start by paying an experienced hand to go on calls with you, or you might team up with an expert (your promotional expertise and his painting know-how). Or, if you prefer to go it alone, I have a feeling that paint companies could probably supply you with the basic method for estimating costs and there are probably books, like the Audel series (check your bookstore), that will give you enough information on estimating and every other aspect of the art to make you fairly expert.

In any case, I think that part of it is academic. You'll learn soon enough. If you know how much surface a man can paint in a given time and you know how much paint it takes to cover that surface, and you can do simple arithmetic, you are on your way. Like everything else, the first few times are always the hardest.

This may be just the deal for an ambitious, reasonably aggressive sales-type person with solid conception of how to put some of the advertising and promotional principles in this book to work for him. I can't see where it would cost more than a few hundred dollars to get started. All you need is a couple of good painters to do jobs for you, some stationery, a good, fair-sized ad in the yellow pages, and a couple of classified ads in your local paper.

There is really no limit to how far you can go in this field if you really know what you are doing and you do it well. Some years ago I met a man who was an enormously successful painting contractor. His specialty was large industrial jobs, and the size of some of them was staggering. One of his projects was the George Washington Bridge which spans the Hudson river between New Jersey and New York. His people painted that bridge constantly, month after month, year in and year out, and as soon as they finished, they crossed back and started all over. I was quite impressed and I still am.

Check out the details on this one. In this instance your investment will be more time and effort than money, and the potential is limitless.

GROWING HERBS AND MAKING MONEY FROM THEM

If you live in the country or in an area where you have access to about an acre of ground—or less—you can get involved in a business that could be reasonably profitable in its initial stages and could ultimately turn into a very substantial business if you handle it properly. And you can get started in your spare time, with a very small investment.

There is a steady, year-in, year-out market for herbs that is increasing by leaps and bounds. Every health-food store, grocery, supermarket, and food-specialty shop is an outlet for these herbs.

In essence, you grow herbs on your own piece of ground, harvest them, process them—basically a matter of drying—and then package and sell them. None of the processes are difficult, and most of them can be performed by or with the help of your kids or, for that matter, any unskilled labor available.

Most herbs sprout like the weeds, which they really are. Information

271

on propagating techniques is readily available, and a minimum amount of attention will assure you of a good crop. Just remember that the growing and drying and packaging are more or less academic. Anyone can do it, and a lot of people do! The real trick is to promote successfully, because that is what is going to make you rich!

The majority of herbs prefer a sunny location and well-drained soil that requires no special nutrients or enrichment. Some, however, will thrive in partial shade. Cultivate soil to a depth of eight inches or so, rake smooth, sift the surface a quarter inch, and place the seeds on the surface. Pat down gently, water, and keep moist until seeds germinate. Thin out rows when plants have at least four true leaves. Some recommended varieties to grow follow, in alphabetical order.

Anise. Annual, grows eighteen inches tall. Sow directly in garden when weather turns warm. Ripe seeds should be pulled off heads. Used for cakes, bread, soups, and stews.

Basil, lemon. Annual. Plant when weather is warm, keep soil moist, and thin to one foot apart. Used with salads and fresh vegetables.

Basil, sweet. Annual, twelve to eighteen inches tall. Rapid grower. Plant after last frost, thin to one foot apart, and pinch stems to promote bushier growth. Harvest leaves before small white flowers bloom. Used fresh or dried for salads, meat, fish, poultry, and sauces.

Borage. Annual, eighteen inches tall. Sow when weather is warm. Use flowers or sprigs of leaf to flavor summer drinks and salads.

Caraway. Biennial, two feet tall. Plant in the spring and harvest seeds the following June. Young leaves and shoots used to season salads and seeds used to flavor pastry, teas, sauces, and cakes.

Catnip. Perennial, two to three feet tall. Sow in spring or early fall. Use as seasoning and for catnip tea. And as a treat for cats, too, of course.

Chervil. Annual, eighteen inches tall. Plant in rich, moist soil in shade or under taller plants. Use in salads, with poultry or veal, in omelets, or as a garnish.

Chives. Perennial. Plant in early spring. Use in soups, salads, and vegetables.

Dill. Annual, two to three feet tall. Make successive plantings until early summer. Harvest seeds when ripe, flat, and brown. Used to flavor salads, soups, sauces, and lamb dishes.

Fennel. Perennial in mild climates, annual when winters are cold, thirty inches tall. Used in sausages and Italian dishes.

Horehound. Perennial, fourteen to eighteen inches tall. Set seeds in sandy soil in spring and thin to one foot apart. Leaves boiled to extract flavor for medicinal-type candies.

Lavender. Perennial, two feet tall. Dried leaves and flowers used in sachets and potpourris.

Marjoram, sweet. Perennial in mild climates, annual where winters are cold. Used in salads, vegetables, sauces and meat dishes.

Mint. Perennial, two feet tall. Fresh leaves used as garnishes or in salads and fruit desserts; dried for winter teas.

Oregano. Perennial, thirty inches tall. Sow seeds in sunny area and use moderate amounts of water. Used in Italian foods, meat and vegetable dishes, and sauces.

Parsley. Annual. Sow in sun or partial shade when weather is warm. Used in salads and on vegetables and sauces.

Rosemary. Perennial where winters are mild and annual in colder areas. Somewhat difficult to grow. Likes sunny location. Used with lamb, chicken, or veal.

Sage. Perennial, one to two feet tall. Thin to fifteen inches apart and water plentifully. Used with poultry, fish, sauces, and stuffing or in herb breads.

Summer savory. Annual, one foot tall. Sow when weather is warm. Thin to twelve inches apart. Used in salad dressings, gravies, and stews.

Tarragon. Perennial. May be difficult to grow from seeds. Used in salads, soups, baked fish.

Thyme. Perennial, one foot tall. Sow when weather gets warm and do not overwater. Used in soups, poultry, meat loaf, stews, and sauces.

Harvesting Your Crop

Generally, the best time to harvest herbs for drying is right before the flowers open, when the concentrations of aromatic oils are at their peak. Ideally, work on a warm, dry, sunny day when the plants are free from early dew. Snip stems at the base, leaving some stalks behind for next year's supply.

Drying Your Herbs

Dry your herbs in a cool, dry, well-ventilated area. Spread them out on a table made of very light wooden slats, on window screens, or on paper towels or tie them into loose bunches and hang them upside-down in a dry, sunny spot. If your weather remains dry, herbs should be ready in three to four days. If humidity prevents complete drying, herbs in small quantities may be set on a cookie sheet in an oven just warm enough to dry out remaining moisture.

Working with one variety at a time, spread a clean cloth on a flat surface, and holding stalks several inches above it, gently strip leaves from stems, discard bits of stem and woody pieces, and store in airtight jars or bottles. Date and label jars for easy reference and store in a cool, dry place. Dried herbs quickly lose their flavor when exposed to bright light or warmth.

Freezing Your Herbs

If drying your large crop is too arduous, herbs may be safely frozen.

How to Package Your Herbs

Probably the best way to package your herbs is in quarter-ounce quantities in small heat-sealed plastic envelopes. It might be a good idea to staple your envelopes to a nine-by-twelve-inch or, better still, an eleven-by-fourteen-inch card. If you staple them in three rows of twelve each, you'll have thirty-six packages to a card, and at $.50 a package, the retail value of each card will be $18.00. Deduct 40 percent, which is a typical dealer markup, and that's $18.00 less $7.20, or a gross profit of $10.80 per card. Roughly speaking, an acre of herbs should yield enough to make up at least a thousand cards, which means a gross profit of almost $11,000.00 per acre. Now if you deduct roughly $2,500.00 for expenses, the cost of your initial seeds, some labor, packaging materials, and so on, you still end up with a tidy $8,500.00 profit, which isn't too bad.

Of course, this is all hypothetical. These are ballpark figures. Will you really be able to grow an acre of herbs? Will you be able to dry them satisfactorily and package them as easily as it would seem possible? Can you really sell a thousand cards? You'll never really know until you try. But certainly there are interesting possibilities here. The success with which you exploit those possibilities is really up to you. All I've done is throw out the rough idea. You'll have to dig up the details yourself.

Write to the Department of Agriculture in Washington, D.C., and see what they can tell you about growing herbs. Consult your local county extension officer. He probably has a lot of information on growing techniques applicable to your area. There are books on the subject as well.

If you think this concept has merit, check it out. Find out what is really involved in actually growing herbs. See if there aren't some good professional techniques for drying them. Investigate the possibility of packaging apparatus. You probably won't want to invest in anything at first, but if the idea takes off, you will ultimately want to use more sophisticated packaging techniques.

Learn about the harvesting, too. Usually only certain parts of each plant are usable. Sometimes it's the leaves, sometimes it's the seeds, and in some instances it's the entire stem. These are the things you have to find out, and certainly they should present no particular problem.

Working out the merchandising techniques to make you successful is another story. That's where your ingenuity, intelligence, and creative ability come into play. Selling herbs, like selling anything else, is essentially a matter of promotion. The best herbs in the world are meaningless sitting in your backyard. They take on a little more significance when they're packaged and ready to sell. But not until some consumer pays hard cash do they become a real asset for you.

Think hard before you get involved. Make careful plans. Check out the potential. If there are outlets in your area or even in nearby communities—supermarkets, food-speciality stores, health-food stores, possibly even some hardware stores—that you think will handle your merchandise, then you may have a deal. If you do, you'll have to think in terms of making your product appealing. You'll need a good name and an attractive way to package.

Cards are probably the least expensive, but possibly you ought to consider another technique. If you put them up in thin glass vials with ordinary corks, would that give them an interesting, appealing, possibly special look? Are there plastic containers of some kind that would work well? Should you package them in larger quantities, possibly in plain manila coin-type envelopes in, say, one- or two-ounce quantities, stressing the idea that you are selling in bulk for much less? That might be a unique way to go, and as far as I know, you have no competition.

What kind of point-of-sale displays or advertising are you going to use? Obviously, on a low-cost item like herbs, which are going to be selling in relatively small quantities, advertising is impractical. Point-of-sale displays are another story, however. If your card is attractive and large enough to carry a sales message, it may make an impact. What should your card say? Concentrate on something meaningful to the consumer. Perhaps something to the effect that these are "locally grown herbs . . . far fresher than you buy anywhere else." That is true, and it is a sales point. Kick that concept around and see if you can come up with a good way of saying it.

If I were involved, I probably would try to get across the idea that my herbs were home grown and that they were in fact fresher than the store-bought variety that have probably been sitting around in warehouses for who knows how long. I'd stress that they were less expensive, and I'd be sure that they were.

Possibly I'd offer a bonus. That sounds like it might be a good idea. You might offer one package *free* with the purchase of two or three, or you might make sachets and offer them as premiums. If you don't know what a sachet is, ask your wife. Chances are she can tell you all about them and even make them for you.

It's simply a matter of taking little squares of organdy, silk, or any fancy material that you can get hold of and filling them with a pinch of lemon balm, lemon verbena, lemon thyme, mint, rosemary, tarragon, or lavender flowers. Mix them up in various combinations and tie them off in a little ball of cloth approximately an inch or an inch and a quarter in diameter. Sachets not only make good premiums, but they also make good items on their own merits.

That's about it on the herb story. I've given you the basics. The rest is up to you. There definitely is a market for fresh, home-grown herbs. If you're clever enough and ambitious enough, it's certainly within the realm of possibility that you can exploit the market and ultimately expand to the point where you are running a substantial, full-time herb empire.

GROWING GINSENG

All I know about ginseng is what I have read, and if what I have read is true, I can't understand why any farmer in the United States is growing anything but this incredible root. According to what I have been able to ascertain, ginseng is a root much sought after by the Chinese, who regard it as a potency drug. It is being sold in an increasing number of health-food stores as a medicine. It is easy to grow and is currently selling for twenty-five dollars a pound. I have also read that a single acre of ginseng can bring as much as twenty-five thousand dollars!

Apparently ginseng grows best in the New England states, New York, New Jersey, Pennsylvania, Delaware, Ohio, Virginia, West Virginia, Maryland, Kentucky, North and South Carolina, Tennessee, Georgia, Alabama, Illinois, Idaho, Michigan, Minnesota, Iowa, Missouri, Arkansas, Oregon, and possibly a few more states, although Florida is definitely not one of them. It is also said to grow well in almost any type of soil, to like the shade, and once the crop is in, to require little in the way of attention except for occasional weeding.

Sellers of ginseng roots and seeds to potential growers like yourself run classified ads in various publications. I haven't responded to any, so I don't know what they are selling, but I must confess that I am somewhat skeptical. If the crop is really that profitable, why sell seeds and roots to potential competition?

If you have access to land, this certainly seems worth following up. Just be careful, however. Don't invest in anything until you are absolutely certain there is a definite and confirmed market for ginseng, and even before that, check with your county extension agent and see what the Department of Agriculture has to say on the subject.

PRODUCING SIMPLE FORMULATIONS AT HOME

Here's a thought that might be worth considering. A great many simply formulated items such as glazier's putty, wallpaper paste, paintbrush cleaners, and so on, are available in supermarkets and hardware and specialty stores. Most of these items are very easy to make, and they throw off a very substantial profit. If someone produced items such as these, packaged them with relative simplicity, and sold them with an accompanying poster or point-of-sale display indicating that because no advertising or heavy commercialism was involved, consumers could buy them for considerably less than they could buy competitive products, I think the operation could be successful.

Think about it. You can make half a dozen jars of fingerpaint—a perennial favorite of kids all over the nation—simply by mixing a half cup of cornstarch, three cups of cold water, a quarter ounce of unflavored gelatin, a half cup of soap flakes, and a little coloring. The process is quick, simple, and sure-fire, and the overwhelming odds are that you can sell your product directly to toy stores, card shops, and other places where toys and art supplies are sold, for a lot less than a bigtime manufacturer can. The same with library paste, paint remover, tar remover, silver polish, copper cleaner, marble cleaner, and dozens of other products.

There are a number of good books on the subject that will give you enough formulas to keep you busy for the next hundred years. The *Up with Wholesome, Down with Store bought* book of recipes and household formulas, a Random House publication, contains great formulas and recipes for everything from catchup and chutney and root beer and

India relish to homemade soap and stain removers and natural cosmetics. I have seen several other books of formulas you will probably find helpful as well.

With the proper approach, perhaps the idea of buying more for less, you may have the makings of a very solid, very substantial business.

THE FOOD BUSINESS

Some time ago a little store in a small city in Pennsylvania made a vivid impression on me. It was a tiny white clapboard structure situated in a hard-to-reach section of town, but every night from about seven o'clock on, a long line used to form in front of that shop and stay formed for hours. Why? What was the magic that drew so many people? Would you believe just sandwiches? They made great submarines or wedges or whatever they called them, and the lure of those sandwiches attracted people from miles away.

What am I getting at? Simply this. Good food, well priced, always finds a ready market. What better proof than the fact that the fast-food business is growing more rapidly right now than probably any other. If it can be digested, somebody is making it and selling it, and maybe even getting rich in the process. Why not you?

The problem is simple enough. All you have to do is make food that people really like, sell it reasonably, and then let your audience know of its availability. That's really what it's all about, but how can you get involved with very little investment?

Obviously, not by buying a restaurant and not by building one. You have to operate right out of your own kitchen, where you have no extra rent to pay, no fancy fixtures to buy, no extra overhead except for the gas or electricity you need to run your stove.

What are you going to make in that kitchen? Not soufflés, not duck à l'orange, and not anything fancy or difficult or expensive. You want to be successful right at the start, so pioneering or experimenting is out. You have to function in an area in which an established market already exists, so to begin with, you are going to sell three things—sausage, meatballs, and barbecued beef sandwiches just like everyone else sells, except that yours are going to look better and taste better and be better! And your advertising is going to make their availability known to all your potential customers!

Okay. First things first. You need three great recipes for three great sandwiches. Check it out with your wife. Check it out with other great cooks you know. Look up sandwich recipes in cookbooks at your bookstore or your library. Check out restaurants and see how they do it. It shouldn't be that hard to copy and improve upon good hero sandwiches that are already being sold. Your sandwich should be big, attractive, and a little bit different from everyone else's. It should be packaged attractively too. Look around, experiment, use your ingenuity.

Okay, you have the place you're going to work from, and you have your sandwiches. Who are you going to sell them to? That really depends on where you are. If you live in a small house in a small community, you can sell right out of your kitchen.

Your market consists of people pretty much like you and your neighbors and their neighbors. To attract them, you're going to have to advertise—not in the local paper . . . not yet, anyway, because you have a fairly long story to tell and it would be too costly to buy enough newspaper space to tell it well. Since your market comprises a group of people within several miles of your house, the best and the least expensive way to reach them would be by means of a simple flyer. Suppose, for example, you decide that everyone within a radius of, say, two miles, is a possible prospect for your sandwiches. Step number 1 is to write your advertising copy. It might read something like this:

"Joe's sausage sandwich . . . the most incredible sandwich you've ever tasted in your life, anywhere! Two large, top-quality Italian sausages . . . the finest money can buy . . . simmered for hours with fresh herbs and spices—oregano, garlic, green peppers, etc.—and our own sweet tomato sauce, cut in half and laid between the slices of an individual loaf of superb Italian bread a full twelve inches long! Then sprinkled with oregano, thyme, and other fresh spices . . . not too much, not too little . . . and slathered in half a cup of tomato sauce and wrapped in aluminum foil while it's still steaming hot! . . . A fabulous meal in itself! . . . If you don't honestly agree this is far and away the best hero sandwich you have ever tasted, anywhere, just tell us and your money back, no questions asked!"

Use the same basic approach for your meatball and barbecue sandwiches. Don't be embarrassed about the superlatives you are using. Say great things about your sandwich and then make that sandwich good enough to live up to them.

When your copy is written, consult with your local photo-offset printer. Tell him what your problem is and get his advice. He can put your flyer or brochure together for you, or he can show you how to do it yourself so that you can save much of the production costs. In either event, once your flyer is produced, you have to get it into the hands of your potential customers, and this can probably be best accomplished by personally placing one in the mailbox of everyone in the area from which you feel your customers are going to come or, better still, by hiring some young person with transportation to do it for you.

Don't forget to include your name, your address, easy instructions for how to reach you, and the time period during which you will open. It seems to me that the most practical time to operate would be in the evenings, when people are most inclined to snack—probably between seven and eleven, or possibly even later when everyone else is closed and you have no competition.

Remember this, incidentally. In the initial stages of your operation all you have going for you is your advertising. Nothing else! You are not a restaurant. You have no reputation. Nobody has tasted one of your sandwiches. You may be making one of the most delicious, most incredible concoctions in the whole world, but until people try them, taste them, talk about them, there can be no word of mouth. You are coming on cold, so you have to do a great selling job to convince people to take a chance. Once you do, of course, and if your sandwiches are really good, you're in business and the sky is the limit!

Remember, too, that in the final analysis, the success you enjoy will be directly proportional to the excellence of the food you serve. Your advertising will get you off the ground, but it won't be able to keep you there, so don't stint. Don't look for shortcuts. If food costs keep soaring, it is better to raise your prices than to cut back on the quality of the food you serve.

If selling out of your kitchen isn't practical, and in many cases it won't be, you might consider the possibility of selling sandwiches in factories and such. Somewhere in your town, perhaps not far away, there may be a number of large and flourishing factories with lots and lots of hungry employees. Some of them eat out at lunchtime, and some of them bring their own lunches, but all of them eat.

This is a flourishing market if you can tap it. You would have to get permission from the managers of local shops and factories to post or to distribute your flyers. Then, for starters, you could take phone orders and deliver. Possibly you could work out of a truck or van. Ironing out the details takes a lot of time and a lot of thinking. You're bound to run into problems, because there are obviously many of them. One of them, for example, is that in many communities you will probably require some kind of a license for handling food. But the point is, there is a viable business here somewhere. It's up to you to ferret it out and make it work. Think about it. It could make you rich.

CATERING

If you are an expert cook, or better yet, a great organizer who knows an expert cook, consider catering. It is not a simple business, and it is certainly not for everyone, but it can be very profitable, and it can be started with a relatively small cash expenditure.

Whenever there are people of means—in large cities, and/or rich suburban communities—parties of various types are a fact of life, and to help the party givers cope, a small army of caterers have sprung up. These range anywhere from ladies who can make good canapes to Chinese chefs to very professional staffs that take over at party time and supply everything—bartenders, servers, food, drink, and sometimes even entertainers.

It's a business you can start on a small scale, it has substantial growth potential, it's a good family type pursuit, and if you are really good, word of mouth can be a potent factor in building your operation.

A Few Business Ideas

How do you get started? Try to go to as many affairs as you can. Observe carefully. Think about what you can do that's different. If you have a friend who is throwing a big bash—cocktail party, dinner party, wedding or whatever—offer your services on a for whatever-it-costs-you basis.

See how you like the work and see what kind of reaction you get from your guests. If it really went well and everyone was pleased and you would like to continue, start to think about it seriously. Put together a small brochure. Write to organizations that run affairs. Call up entertainment chairmen of various groups. Run a couple of classified ads in the local paper and see what happens. Work inexpensively at first and try to establish yourself. This could be an interesting and lucrative way to make it.

BAKING

Certain food items evoke a very strong response in certain areas. For example, in New York and its environs, and perhaps in most large cities, cheesecake has a huge and dedicated following. There are a lot of people who will go out of their way for a good piece of cheesecake, and they don't mind paying well for the pleasure.

There is a bake shop in a fairly remote corner of New York city that has been famous for its cheesecake for years. Afficianados travel from all over the city to sample it, and that shop is just one of many highly successful establishments that have made it on the basis of one or two very special desserts that have caught the public fancy.

This is an interesting area to ponder. Now obviously you are not going to blossom into a master baker overnight, but perhaps you don't have to. Suppose, for example, that you did a little bit of research and experimentation in the kitchen (or someone did it for you), and you came up with your own great cheesecake . . . not an ordinary cheesecake, but something really unusual, really different. It is possible. There are a lot of great recipes around and most of them are no further away than the nearest good bookstore.

O.K. What do you do with your fabulous concoction after you have

283

it? Simple enough. You sell it. There are a number of successful baking operations that started out by selling to one or two fine restaurants. There is nothing unique in that concept. If you live in or near a large city or a thriving suburban community where there are fine restaurants, chances are you have a market for your wares.

The requisites are simple enough. You have to have a really exceptional product, and you have to convince your potential customers that you are a rock of dependability who can be counted upon to deliver whenever called upon. The idea is to start with one item and then, if it appears that you are on your way to a successful operation, add other specialties as you develop them.

Instead of, or perhaps in addition to working through restaurants, you might try selling through local specialty shops. Fine suburban neighborhoods generally have an outlet or two which caters to fairly affluent customers who are interested in good food and don't mind paying for it.

There are definite possibilities here, and one of the nice features is the fact that you can operate right from your home and get started with a small cash outlay. Just beware of the fact that restaurants aren't always the most stable of businesses. Don't be too trusting. If the people involved are not long established, try to work on a C.O.D. basis, at least until you are sure you are on safe ground.

TATTOOING

Check out tattooing. The art is as old as time and there are always customers around. If you have any artistic ability (according to the equipment suppliers you really don't have to draw because designs come in stencil form and can be traced) and if you live in an area that has no restrictions (tattooing is against the law in a lot of places), you may be able to make a lot of spare time cash at home with a minimum investment.

Equipment isn't too expensive. Two electric needles, one for drawing outlines and one for shading, a few jars of ink, some designs to trace, a booklet that tells how, and a willing subject, and you are in business.

A Few Business Ideas

You'll find the names and addresses of tattoo supply houses in the classified ad sections of *Popular Mechanics* and similar magazines.

ANTIQUES AND NOSTALGIA ITEMS

Almost everything you can shake a stick at nowadays is worth money. When I was six or seven I had a little cast iron bank shaped like a dirigible. Nothing fancy. Just a simple shape, about six inches long, with a slot in the top. It must have cost all of a quarter, and perhaps even less. A few years ago I saw that identical bank in a fancy toy shop for $30! Incredible but true!

Almost everything you can think of that was made thirty or forty years ago is worth a small fortune today. Imagine a Micky Mouse watch selling for $300, a Shirley Temple doll going for $100, a back issue of *The Saturday Evening Post* for $7.50! Tractor seats, old Hoover buttons, early and not so early comic books, toys, beer cans, bits of barbed wire, baseball cards, bottle caps, candy boxes and calendars! You name it and somebody wants, it, collects it, and will pay good money to own it.

Old barns and attics are still yielding treasures. A lot of people, particularly in rural or country areas, are becoming part-time dealers. Some just find the material and sell it to or leave it with established shops to sell for them. Others are setting up their own small shops or deal out of their barns or homes or work the flea markets.

Check it out. You don't really have to be an expert to get involved. There are books which illustrate a huge array of items and list current prices. Antique and nostalgia magazines will give you a great deal of information as well. This could be a source of money and a good future business, so hang on to those old Orphan Annie mugs and secret decoder rings.

(Incidentally, the various trade and consumer magazines are one of the best sources of information on almost any subject. There are literally hundreds and hundreds of them and they cover an overwhelming range of subjects. If there is a particular topic you would like information on, consult your local librarian. She can probably tell you whether or not there is a trade or consumer magazine devoted to the subject and how and where you can get it.)

MAIL ORDER

If you have an item that is readily available, that has very wide appeal, that has a very substantial profit margin, that is not easily obtainable through normal channels of distribution, and that is unique and interesting and the type of object or thing or whatever that people are really intrigued by, you might try mail-order . . . careful, cautiously and judiciously.

As we have discussed earlier in this book, mail order is a difficult, risky and highly competitive business. When it pays out, it frequently does so handsomely, but the odds that it will are not very good. (The hottest mail order outfit around right now . . . a group of eminently successful super-pros, actually test around forty new items every single month—a prodigious, almost unbelievable feat—and they are quite satisfied to come up with two real winners each month.)

The key, as you should be well aware of by now, is copy. Put together a good ad based on the precepts presented in this book, and then test it in a good medium. Don't run your ad in any publication which does not run a great deal of mail-order advertising. Some publications pull mail order responses and some do not. Mail order operators flock to any media which works and they shun like the plague those that do not, so it is simple enough to tell if any particular medium is good. Just look.

Following are items (in random order) which have consistently done well down through the years:

Garden Items . . . strawberries, fast-growing shade trees, novelties like small palm trees, exotic plants with strange pecularities (Venus' Fly Trap), chemicals that promote quick growth, super-fertilizers, bargain fruit trees, rose bushes, etc.

Books . . . self-help, how-to, diet, financial advice, health, sex, weird, mysterious, occult.

Beauty and Health Aids . . . reducers, hair restorers, bust developers, skin and complexion creams, inexpensive exercise devices, body-building gadgets, products that grow "longer, thicker hair," longer, lovlier fingernails, etc.

Automotive Devices . . . spark plugs and other gadgets that save gas, increase power, make old cars run smoother, more economically, chrome restorers, etc.

Jewelry . . . Novelties like slave bracelets, rings made from shanks of fancy spoons, rings with stones that change color, simulated diamonds, synthetic stones, etc.

Unique items of apparel . . . sexy lingerie, caftans, embroidered shirts from India, etc., highly styled clothing, bargain shoes and slacks.

Leather goods . . . wallets and ladies purses, luggage at bargain prices.

The clue as to whether any item is being successfully sold via mail order is always whether or not the ad is repeated. Nobody repeats a loser. Incidentally, remember this axiom: "It's difficult—almost impossible—to sell a preventative, far easier to sell a cure." A product that will keep your hair from falling out someday may sell. A product that will grow it back surely will!

STRIPING

If you are neat, creative, and artistically inclined, here is an idea that could blossom into a good part-time source of extra income, and it will cost you all of a couple of dollars to get started. How? You paint decorative stripes on automobiles, trucks, and motorcycles! A striping brush will cost you under a buck and a can of automobile enamel will cost you not much more. From then on its a matter of practice.

Observe as many stripes as you can. Check out Art Noveau and Art Decco art books for ideas. Start to make sketches and dream up good designs. Get in as much practice as you can. It's not easy, but it's not anything that a steady hand can't achieve. When you can have it down well enough to proceed, do the best job you can on your own car, cruise around to garages and gas stations, exhibit your handiwork, and leave your card.

DOG BOARDING KENNELS

If you like dogs, live in the country where you have plenty of space—at least enough for a kennel and runs for twenty-five dogs (which you can probably put up yourself if you are a good man with tools), you may be able to put together a nice little enterprise. Twenty-five dogs at $2 per day times seven days equals $350, of which you ought to be able to net half. Of course that is purely theoretical. There is no guarantee that you are going to be able to keep your kennels filled. There may be an idea here, however. There are more dogs around today than ever before, and if you are located close to a fairly substantial city or affluent suburban community, you may be able to build this into something. Space for one hundred dogs starts to sound a bit more respectable, and that's not an impossible notion. There are kennels that do very well.

If you want to carry the idea to its ultimate conclusion, start your own kennel. Then work out the details, package the whole set-up . . . advice, information, plans for the equipment and structures, and everything else that anyone will need to run a successful kennel in their area, and sell the plans outright, on a percentage, or as a franchise deal.

Perhaps you would be better off opening your own chain of kennels. In any case, don't scoff. This is just the germ of an idea, but it could work if properly promoted. You have to have a really good ad in the yellow pages of the area in which you anticipate your customers will come from, and make it different. Perhaps it should be an all-copy ad in small type. That's what I would do. I would run an ad in straight 8-point type and I would say something to the effect that we were more than just a good kennel: "Of course our premises are spotless, our facilities are the very best available, we feed the dogs plentifully and well, but most important of all, we love dogs, and they love us . . ." I'd build that concept up, and if my premises were clean and good, then I'd feel fairly confident.

Check it out carefully. It might be worth considering but, don't make a move without investigating it thoroughly. See other kennels.

Board your dog around and learn as much as you can. Read books on dog care. If you know a vet, get his advice. And check out the arithmetic. How many dogs do you have to board and how many baths do you have to give or how much grooming do you have to do to make out? Get the answers before you make your move.

KEY-MAKING

There is no doubt about key-making. It's a staple business. For years there have been men who have made a living from single key machines and little else, but what if it were done on a really promotional basis?

Suppose you had a small, distinctively painted stand . . . perhaps some outlandish design . . . a round stand that looked like a giant padlock or a house key? Perhaps if in addition to key-making you had a constant sale on padlocks, which are in greater demand today than ever before, or sold them at a discount, or you made one free key for every two ordered?

Suppose you had a big sign that said, *"Our keys must work or double your money back"*? How many keys don't actually work, and besides, how many customers would ever bother to come back anyway? And even if they do, isn't it worth it to have some kind of a gimmick to build an operation around?

And most important, suppose your stand was located in a high traffic area, which is really what this business is all about? It's conceivable that for a thousand dollars or so for a good key-making machine and the necessary blanks and other assorted gadgetry you need to set up shop, you might be on your way.

If your stand threw off enough money to pay for a full-time employee and about fifty dollars a week besides, you could be looking into the possibility of setting up in other locations as well. At twenty five dollars a week it would take about forty weeks to pay off your entire investment, and if you can manage enough credit you might be in business.

Of course it takes a lot of thinking and thorough investigation before you take the plunge, but if the arithmetic is right, it might be worth thinking about. Check the key-making ads in *Popular Mechanics* and see what they are offering.

MINIATURE GOLF

Miniature golf courses have been coming and going with monotonous regularity for the last forty years or so. Some of them flourish, some of them provide a bare subsistence for their owners, and a great many take a brief crack at it and then go under.

The requisite for success is essentially location. The course has to be interesting, attractive and fun to play, and it must be located in an area or locale which is heavily frequented by teenagers, who are the main participants. This may be a way to make a pretty fair living, and possibly, a very good one, particularly if you are operating more than one course, but it is a seasonal deal at best unless you happen to be located in Southern climes.

SKATE BOARDS

Skate boards are no doubt the fastest growing craze in America today. They were quite popular a few years ago. Then they faded from the scene, but in the last year or so they have come zooming back with a vengeance. How can you get involved? Can you manufacture them? Probably not to any significant degree, unless you happen to have the set-up for it, in which case that might be a way to make some extra cash. You can buy the trucks and wheels separately and if you can produce a good board, perhaps of fiberglass, you might be in business. It shouldn't be too difficult to induce your local stores to handle your product or perhaps you can get a good salesman type to load up a car and try to sell them direct in front of high schools or other places where skate board aficionados are to be found.

What about some type of practical skate board arena you could build that kids would pay to use? . . . Perhaps an area with slight hills, inclines, slalom-type arrangements and such that skate boarders would find interesting, ideally, it should be surfaced with some kind of material that would have less disastrous consequences on tender skin than concrete.

Would you be legally absolved from responsibility if the kids signed a waiver of some type upon entering? Your lawyer could answer that one for you. This may be a totally impractical idea, but it seems to me that if motorcycle parks are successful, and apparently some of them are, a skate board arena would be better yet. It occupies less space, could be run day and night, and would probably be better indoors than out thus eliminating the uncertainties of inclement weather.

I can see a whole string of skate board palaces across the country right now, and they all have your name emblazoned across the front in big neon letters. Think about it. If the craze continues, some smart operator is going to do it one of these days, and he might just start out by refurbishing one of the many unoccupied skating rinks one sees.

BATTING CAGES

I always thought that good baseball batting cages would really make it, and perhaps in some areas they have, but not with the degree of success I once envisioned. I still think they have a potential, despite the fact that they, too, are seasonal (unless you are properly located climate-wise).

Perhaps indoor baseball batting cages are the answer, and perhaps the pitching machines should be adjustable. Some of the present models throw so hard that they discourage all but experts from trying. I'm not recommending batting cages, but they might be worth checking out.

GOLF RANGE

What with the tremendous increase in golfing enthusiasm in recent years, one would think that indoor golf ranges that would give fans an opportunity to keep their hand in would be naturals. I am not a golfer and don't really know too much about the game, but it seems to me that it would not be too difficult to devise a driving cage which would somehow indicate the distance and accuracy of the drive. For all I know, there may be one already, and if there is, and it is properly located and promoted, I don't see how it could do anything but make it.

TENNIS RANGE

I seriously doubt if anyone has come up with a tennis range yet, but this seems to have a great deal of interesting potential. Suppose a tennis buff could go to an indoor tennis court, and have balls machine served to him to his specification? That would be an ideal situation, but obviously highly impractical because of the amount of space involved. But suppose the same thing could be done in considerably less space? It would still be costly for the player, but once they are hooked on the game, they seem perfectly willing and able to pay for the privilege.

Again, this is just an amorphous idea, but I think it does have potential. I am sure there are enough players who would pay well for the opportunity to practice to make an endeavor like this pay out. Come up with an ingenious idea and you may be on your way to that fortune.

TYPING SERVICE

This might be a good way to supplement your income and possibly build a good full-time business if you like. The need for good typing is almost endless. At the same time, there are a lot of highly skilled typists, mostly homemakers, who, while well occupied with domestic chores, have enough free time and a desire to earn extra money. The trick is to make the twain meet, and that shouldn't be too difficult. Your problem would be to locate willing typists and then run ads soliciting business. You would then arrange to get the work to your typists, see that the job was done satisfactorily, and pocket the difference between what your customers and what you pay your typists. The whole operation could be run from your home and your initial expenditure would be minimal—a few classified ads, perhaps a letter to business establishments that use typing, and an answering service or someone at home who could answer for you.

A *Few Business Ideas*

USED CARS

A good many of the classified ads offering the family car for sale are actually placed by individuals who buy, repair and sell cars professionally. For the most part, these people operate on a part-time basis but there are some who do it for a living and make out quite well. For all practical purposes they operate just like a used car lot, but on a much smaller scale, and since they have no lot to contend with, they have that much less overhead to worry about as well. If you know anything about cars, particularly if you can repair them, or know someone who can, you might have a business here, and not a bad one at that.

A lot of people would rather buy a car from an individual than out of a used car lot. They have a general mistrust of car lots and salesmen, or they feel they can get a better deal from a private individual.

Aware of these foibles, a lot of pros have discovered that this is a good way to unload used cars at a more substantial profit then they normally could. Some time ago a group of professionals in New York operated in precisely this fashion, but with a few twists of their own. Women members of their ring advertised cars for sale. Dressed in widow's weeds, they presented their vehicles as the property of their recently departed husbands who, long ailing as they were, had little opportunity to drive the "almost new" vehicles. To reinforce the story, the gang took the precaution to set the odometers back considerably —a violation of the law, as you are probably aware.

The group has recently been indicted and face stiff sentences.

CARMELIZED POP CORN

You can buy a good machine for around $300 or less and the manufacturer will supply all the details, recipes, information concerning sources of supply, and so on. There are several directions you can take. If you live in a fair-sized city—population half a million or so— you might consider a small retail store, with the ultimate goal a chain. You need very little space, but you do need a choice location. Traffic is the name of the game. You should be located where people can see—and smell—your wares. That's about 7/8ths of the battle. People like Carmel Corn. They don't have to be sold, but they do have to be made aware of its availability.

One possibility might be to locate in a shopping center. Another possibility is the premises of a large, generally crowded store. Another approach is to work at home and deliver the finished product, neatly packaged, to stores, theatres, ball parks and wherever else you can induce people to handle your product.

Pushcarts might work. If you had enough of them, perhaps manned by high school boys in sparkling white uniforms, or better still, cute high school girls in flashy outfits, you might have the beginning of something. Baskets might be substituted for pushcarts. Don't sell this type of merchandising short. Hot dogs, Italian ices, pretzels, hot chestnuts, assorted craft products like belts, jewelry, and almost everything else you can think of have and are being sold successfully out of pushcarts and valises and baskets and boxes.

SELLING IDEAS

I suppose it is possible to sell a simple, unadorned, undeveloped idea. I have heard, vaguely, that people do it, but I have never met anyone who has, and although I consider myself a prolific idea man and I have always been involved in businesses in which ideas were important, I have never sold a single raw idea myself.

It would be nice work if you could get it. Just sit back, dream up a new idea and peddle it to someone. He backs it, he develops it, he turns it into a viable, workable, money-making activity, and he pays you for the privilege. Not likely! It's fairly obvious that if he is capable of bringing your idea to fruition, he is capable of dreaming up his own ideas in the first place, and is probably so busy with them that he doesn't have the time to develop yours. Or he might find it more convenient, and cheaper, to steal your idea than pay for it. There is no way to protect an idea that I know of.

A Few Business Ideas

That is not to say that you can't make money with ideas, but you have to carry them forward. That's what it's all about. Some years ago an overweight lady and some of her fat friends met in her cellar to try to talk each other into getting slim. Out of those meetings grew an idea. If she had tried to sell that idea or give it to someone else to develop, chances are she would still be a fat lady with an idea. Instead she did it herself and today she is the slim, attractive, famous zillionaire head of Weight Watchers.

If you have an idea you have to do it yourself or with someone you can trust who will work with you. People who can afford to pay for your idea don't want to do the leg work themselves. Recently, for example, a good friend of mine had an idea for a book. He had a good title, a good concept, but the book required a lot of art work and a lot of development. He casually roughed out his concept and sent it to a top publisher who happened to be a good friend of his. The publisher agreed that it was a good idea, but he certainly didn't have the time to develop it or to get involved in plans for its development with his staff, so the concept, good though it was, was rejected. Sometime later my friend met an illustrator, told him the idea and they agreed to set up a partnership and take a crack at it.

The illustrator spent a great deal of time and money putting together a presentation. He dummied up the book, drew a beautiful cover for it, illustrated a number of key pages for the book and so on. My friend, meanwhile, concretized his loose idea and wrote several good chapters for the book. When they re-submitted the new material for the same old idea, the publisher flipped out. They received a fantastic advance and everyone concerned is confident they have a potential best seller on their hands.

Better to develop one idea than dream up a hundred! Nobody has any imagination. You have to show them what you have in mind in very specific terms, and you have to assure whoever is going to back the idea that you are going to be around to handle all of the details. That's the only way that it works!

295

A Few Business Ideas

BOOKS

An idea for a book is not enough. Unless you are Norman Mailer, you have to present a complete outline plus a couple of finished chapters or a finished manuscript to a publisher or an agent who will charge you 10% and make the submission for you if he or she likes your work well enough. Chances of this happening are extremely remote, however. Literary agents are constantly being bombarded with unsolicited manuscripts. As usual, your best bet is to know someone at a publishing house to whom you can speak before you submit your material.

Don't get snowed by those ads by publishers who offer to print your book or story or whatever and then promise you all kinds of advertising and publicity if you foot the bill. In my estimation those outfits, known as vanity publishers, are not in a position to do you any good. They profit from their services to you, and chances of anything good happening with your material are remote, to say the least.

TV SHOWS

Perhaps ideas for TV shows can be sold, but again, unless you are well known and have terrific contacts, chances of that happening are probably one in a million. If you do have an idea, write to the networks and ask them how to submit it. If they will look at it at all, they will probably want you to sign a release form first which absolves them from all responsibility if they have already thought of your idea, if someone has or does submit a similar idea at a later date, if one of their employees steals your idea, or whatever.

MOVIES

Theoretically it is possible to sell a movie idea. You write a "treatment" which is a couple-of-pages version of your idea, and then you submit it to producers or better still, to an agent who, if he or she likes it, will submit it for you.

SONGS

Songwriting is another area fraught with get-rich-quick potential.

Don't succumb to those "WANTED: POEMS FOR SONGS" ads. They will put your poem to music—for a fee—but chances of anything happening with it are pretty remote. If they were such great musicians they would be rich and famous and wouldn't be running little ads in magazines. If song writing is your thing, make the rounds of publishers if you live in or near a big city, or submit some material by mail and see what reaction you get. Better yet, invest in a phone call. Call up a publisher cold, tell the girl at the switchboard you want to speak to someone who can fill you in on how to submit some tunes, and tell the person she connects you with that you are calling long distance, you need some advice, and ask him to do you a personal favor and oblige. You can learn an awful lot that way in a very brief span of time, and besides, you may have made a helpful friend.

GADGETS

If you have an idea for a mechanical gadget it's probably best to check it out with a patent attorney, but beware! That can be an expensive proposition. You can have a preliminary meeting without disclosing your idea. Tell him the area in which you are working and explain that you are just there to get some idea of the kind of fees involved, the procedure to be followed, etc. If you like the man, and you think you can get along with him, then proceed further. Chances are the first thing he will suggest is a patent search to see if you really have anything. Don't be too shocked if you discover that other people have thought of your idea years ago.

I think it might be best to have your own lawyer, if you have one, find a patent attorney for you and set up the meeting. Incidentally, I've always been suspicious of those IDEAS WANTED ads or other solicitations to inventors that appear in magazines and newspaper ads. I don't know what their pitch is, but I've seen too much as an old mail order man not to be skeptical. Beware.

CARTOONS

It is possible to sell gags for the one-panel cartoons you see in so many magazines, and if you are any good at it, you can make out quite well by so doing. It works something like this. You get a funny idea for a cartoon and, based on the cartoons you see, you think you know which cartoonist can best do justice to it. You write up your gag and you indicate the kind of picture you think should go with it, on a 3 x 5 file card, put your name and address on the card, and mail it to the cartoonist. Since you don't know his address, you can send it to the magazine where you have seen his work and they will forward it to him, or you can write him a letter in care of the magazine, tell him you have a great idea for him, ask if he buys gags (most cartoonists do), and if he does, request that he send you his address.

Most cartoonists regularly get their material in this fashion. Writers send them gags. They do a rough of those that they like and they return those that leave them cold. They then submit their rough to the magazine they regularly work with, and if the idea is accepted, they do a finish. When they get paid, you get paid . . . usually one third of their fee, which may be anywhere from $15 on up to several hundred depending on the magazine they sell to.

Sometimes gag writers sell directly to magazines who, if they like the material, submit it to the cartoonist whose style it best fits.

This is a good way to make extra money, provided you can dream up a sufficient number of gags. After a while you will get to know a great many cartoonists and cartoon editors, have a good idea of the type of material they use, how much they pay, and so on.

COMIC STRIPS

Selling a successful comic strip is another matter. One of the top people at King Features Syndicate, which is probably the largest syndicator of newspaper features, once told me that each year they receive around two thousand new cartoon strips and of those they *may* select one which they will attempt to sell to newspapers. Those are not very good odds. It doesn't mean that it can't be done. You may have the next "Peanuts" floating around in your head right now, but don't bank on it, at least for a while.

HOW to JUDGE PEOPLE

THE SUCCESS with which you conduct your business dealings, whether setting up an important deal or merely selling a retail customer a small item, is often directly proportional to the degree with which you size up that person and understand what motivates him.

Is he a genuine prospect or just a browser? Is he listening to your sales story carefully, or is he a million miles away? Can he really afford what you are selling? Is he sincere or just conning you along to be agreeable?

For these and dozens of other good reasons, the ability to understand a person and what makes him tick is a decided asset. In recent years, psychologists, who are primarily interested in human behavior, have become increasingly aware that what a person says and what he means are often miles apart and that more accurate indications of what people really mean are to be found in the signals they make with their bodies. They call this area of study *kinesics* or, more commonly, body language or body signals.

Body signals are a method we humans, and for that matter, many living creatures use to communicate inner feelings. Occasionally we use them consciously, but for the most part they are an unconscious manifestation. You see and use body signals every day. When you are surprised, for example, you raise your eyebrows. If you are very surprised, you may open your mouth as well. Without saying anything—indeed, without even thinking about it—you communicate that you are surprised, and anyone watching undoubtedly gets the message.

If they are properly interpreted, body signals can give you a true insight into what an individual is really like, because most body signals are unconscious and therefore uncensored. Most people are not even aware that they are constantly transmitting their true feelings, and for that very reason, body signals are often a far more accurate key to what a person is really all about than the spoken words he uses.

301

How to Judge People

Often, for example, a person will say no when all his actions clearly indicate that he really wants to say yes. We have all seen examples of that. We offer a guest another helping of dessert and he says, "No, thank you," but all his body signals indicate that he would really like another piece, and if we persist, he generally gives in.

That individual said with his face and his body what he was afraid or embarrassed to say in words, a trait common to most of us.

Of course, body signals are only an indication of what a person is really like or really thinking about—they are not absolute or sure-fire. But in general, we can safely conclude that body signals almost always reveal a person's true feelings more accurately than his words do, and once you become aware of this and sensitive to it, you will be in a better position to make judgments about people.

Following are descriptions of various body signals and their meanings. Bear in mind that although they are good indications of what people are thinking, they are not infallible. The success with which you interpret body signals depends upon the keenness with which you make your observations and the skill with which you evaluate all the factors and draw conclusions from them.

SITTING OR STANDING WITH LEGS CROSSED, ARMS FOLDED ACROSS CHEST

Guarded, uptight, difficult to get through to, not particularly receptive to you.

SITTING OR STANDING IN A LOOSE, RELAXED, CASUAL MANNER

Friendly, probably outgoing, easy to deal with, and probably in a good mood.

STANDING TALL AND STRAIGHT

Confident, self-assured, possibly domineering and opinionated.

SLUMPING, DIMINISHING OWN HEIGHT

Has feelings of inferiority, doesn't want to be noticed or to take the initiative, and is probably easily dominated.

LOOKING AWAY FROM YOU WHILE SPEAKING TO YOU

Frequently a sign that he or she wants to finish statement without interruption or possible confrontation.

RETURNING YOUR GAZE WHILE YOU ARE SPEAKING

Generally, but not invariably, a sign that he or she is listening to you.

CHAIN SMOKING

Person is nervous, restless, possibly upset or worried.

PIPE SMOKING

Generally calm, fairly reserved, and possibly, though not necessarily, scholarly.

SLOW, MONOTONOUS TONE OF VOICE

Person may feel dejected and defeated by life.

RAPID SPEECH

Person is generally agitated, excited, anxious to get moving (and/or, in this drug-oriented era, may be on "uppers").

LOUD, BRASH BRAGGING

Although it is certainly unscientific to generalize, in many instances persons who exhibit these characteristics are unfulfilled and very possibly suffering from an inferiority complex.

CARELESS DRESS

Although in this day and age men and women are frequently casual about their appearance, it is fairly safe to conclude that very sloppily dressed persons are often equally sloppy and casual about other aspects of their lives as well. A frequent symptom of psychotic behavior is utter indifference to one's appearance.

QUALITY OF CLOTHING

Possible indication of a person's financial status, but less so now than formerly. Still, good tailoring and proper fit certainly indicate that clothes must be reasonably expensive.

QUALITY OF JEWELRY

If you can tell the real thing from the costume variety, you can tell a great deal about a person's financial status.

UNCERTAINTY AND SLOWNESS ABOUT MAKING A CHOICE
WHEN CONFRONTED WITH A TRAY OF CANAPES OR A MENU

Chances are he or she is equally hesitant and uncertain about making most decisions and would probably prefer you to make the decisions, provided you do so with confidence and assurance.

SPEAKER FAILING TO MAKE EYE CONTACT WITH ONE MEMBER
OF THE GROUP HE IS CONVERSING WITH

He or she is, in effect, excluding that person from the conversation.

TAPPING FINGERS AGAINST DESK, ARM OF CHAIR, ETC.

A sign of impatience. Person would rather be involved in some activity, but for one reason or another is being frustrated in that desire.

GIRL SITTING ON EDGE OF CHAIR, HANDS ON LAP,
FEET FLAT ON FLOOR, LEGS CLOSE TOGETHER

She is conscious of being observed; she is prim and perhaps uptight, or at least trying to convey the impression of being very proper and ladylike.

SHIFTING EYES ABOUT RAPIDLY, PARTICULARLY AFTER HAVING SPOKEN

Insecure, anxious to ascertain reactions of others to what he has just said.

LOOKING AT YOU WITH STEADY, OPEN, UNWAVERING GAZE

May be completely honest and candid or may simply be aware that a steady gaze is generally accepted as being a sign of honesty and is calculating—and strong—enough to hold a steady gaze.

BITING KNUCKLES

A sign of deep anxiety and stress.

SITTING WITH HANDS OPEN, PALMS UP

Open and receptive to what you are saying.

ONE EYEBROW RAISED

A sign of puzzlement or disbelief.

HANDS HELD FLAT ON DESK OR ARMS OF CHAIR OR ON THIGHS

Not receptive to ideas being presented and probably has mind already made up.

NODDING HEAD IN AGREEMENT AS YOU SPEAK

Person is encouraging you by paying, or appearing to pay, close attention and is agreeing or apparently agreeing with you. This is a deceptive signal, and its real meaning must be determined by other signals the person is sending.

SLAPPING HAND TO FOREHEAD

A signal of self-reproach and chagrin because he or she has forgotten something or committed a blunder of some type.

It is interesting to note, incidentally, that kinesics was practiced for long years before the psychologists ever got around to it. The early practicioners of the art were—and are—the so-called readers, fortune-tellers, psychics, and other mystics who allegedly communicate with the great beyond.

Their specialty, reading your future, is based, not on the psychic powers they claim to possess, but rather on simple, observable clues.

Through practice, experience, and a great deal of intuition and perception, a good cold reader is capable of telling a great deal about an individual, with a surprising degree of accuracy.

Some of the clues they depend on are as basic as the wedding ring that tells them their client is married. Other clues are more subtle—the way a person sits, the way he stands, the quality of his clothing, and so on. Individually those clues don't mean too much, but together with others, and especially when combined with anything the client may let slip about himself, they add up to a fairly conclusive picture.

Cold reading, so-called because it is done cold, without prior preparation, is a rather fascinating skill. Try it yourself and see. Look over the next stranger you come into contact with. Observe his clothing, his stance, the way he walks, and the way he talks.

Note how one observation leads to another and how, with a little practice, you are soon capable of learning a great deal from cold reading.

Another interesting and possibly effective way to determine an individual's characteristics is through what is known as *face reading*. Whether this method really works, however, is something I am not really prepared to say. The ancient Chinese made a very careful study of faces and recorded a great number of so-called facts in respect to various facial characteristics. They claimed, for example, that such traits as honesty, sincerity, contentment, promiscuity, criminal tendencies, gullibility, the state of one's mental health—in fact, almost every conceivable human characteristic—are clearly indicated by the size, shape, and location of the eyes, mouth, nose, facial hair, wrinkles, and so on.

To give you a more specific idea, they claim that short, thick, heavy eyebrows indicate an evil personality; that long, delicate eyebrows indicate a superior intellect; that an extremely narrow nose means a life of toil; that square nostrils indicate an inflexible and stubborn character, but round nostrils signify resourcefulness and creativity; that a mouth that tilts to one side means a nervous and dissatisfied person; that a line between the lips that curves upward means alertness; and on and on.

Of course, other factors enter into the situation. The shape of a nostril or the bump on a nose is hardly enough evidence from which to draw conclusions. All the elements must be considered in relation to each other. The general shape of the head and the size, shape, and balance of the various features must be carefully weighed before decisions about a person's character can be reached.

I must confess that I am somewhat skeptical, but if you are interested in pursuing the matter further, an interesting book on the subject is *Face Reading*, by Timothy T. Mar, published in paperback by Signet.

Another interesting book on the same topic, one that makes more sense to me, is *Face Language*, by Robert L. Whiteside, published by Pocket Books. Many of the author's observations appear quite logical. He points out that certain facial characteristics are indicative of certain personality traits and that an awareness of those traits enables one to deal more successfully with an individual. He says, for example, that persons who have up-and-down lines between their eyes, called worry lines, are difficult to deal with. They are fussy and worrisome, and they require that you deal with them promptly and precisely.

If a person has large eyes, the author claims, he or she is emotional and must be dealt with in a calm, friendly, genuine, and personal way. If a person has thin lips he expresses himself in few words and would prefer you to do likewise. Contrarily, if he has thicker lips and a looser, softer mouth, he requires more talk and is more easy going.

HOW to CONVERT the INFORMATION in THIS BOOK into DOLLARS

O.K. YOU HAVE read the book. The title says this is the book that can make you rich. Can it really? In my estimation, the answer is a resounding "Yes."

If you are reasonably alert, reasonably aware, reasonably on the ball, I don't see how you can help but use the information in this book to great advantage in almost everything you do.

Why? Because it is all valid, all meaningful, all based on sound, solid, proven principles that really work!

They have made fortunes for me, they have made fortunes for people I know, they can make fortunes for you if you use them well.

IF YOU ARE IN BUSINESS

If you are in business of any kind—retail, wholesale, manufacturing, or service—you can apply the principles in this book to great advantage. Why? Because no business is an isolated entity. Because big or small, dormant or flourishing, every business needs customers. Whatever you make, whatever you sell, you have to influence people to buy, and the principles in this book will help you to do that efficiently and well!

DO YOU USE ADVERTISING?

Reevaluate your ads. Look at them critically. Examine them in the light of the sound selling principles delineated in this book. The information here could be worth a fortune to you! It is all carefully explained and ready to use. Take advantage of it and see!

DO YOU USE SALES LETTERS?

The chapter entitled "How to Write Impelling Letters" is based on long years of successful experience. The principles outlined work! Use them in the next sales letter you send, and they can't help but increase your results, as they have for the many successful men who use them.

DO YOU SELL OR EMPLOY MEN TO SELL FOR YOU?

The chapter "The Principles of Great Advertising" is just as applicable to an orally delivered sales pitch as to a written one, which, after all, is all that advertising is. Study it carefully in light of your own selling problems. Even if you are a great natural salesman, incorporating these well-thought-out principles can't help but improve your results.

ARE YOU WORKING FOR SOMEONE ELSE?

Read this book carefully. Study the principles it presents and utilize them! Learn to think promotionally. Make suggestions to your employer. Show him how to use these principles to make money. The more valuable you are to your employer, the more money he has to give you in order to keep you!

If there is too little potential where you now work, think about moving on, and soon! There are only twenty-four hours in a day. As long as you are expending time and effort, do it in an area where the potential financial rewards are the greatest. And remember, the *greatest* financial rewards will come when you are in business for yourself!